INTERCULTURAL COMPETENCE

 A catalogue record for this book is available from the National Library of Australia

INTERCULTURAL COMPETENCE

Cultural Intelligence,
Pastoral Leadership
and the Chinese Church

Michael K. Chu

INTERCULTURAL COMPETENCE
Cultural Intelligence, Pastoral Leadership and the Chinese Church
© Michael K. Chu
First published in Australia in 2019

Morling Press
122 Herring Rd
Macquarie Park NSW 2113 Australia
Phone: +61 2 9878 0201
Email: enquiries@morling.edu.au
www.morlingcollege.com/morlingpress

The publication is copyright. Other than for the purposes of study and subject to the conditions of the Copyright Act, no part of this book in any form or by any means (electronic, mechanical, micro-copying, photocopying or otherwise) may be reproduced, stored in a retrieval system, communicated or transmitted without prior written permission.

All Scripture quotations, unless otherwise indicated, are taken from the Holy Bible, New International Version® Anglicised (NIVUK), NIV®. Copyright ©1979, 1984, 2011 by Biblica, Inc.™ Used by permission. All rights reserved worldwide.

ISBN: 978-0-9945726-4-6 (paperback)
ISBN: 978-0-9945726-5-3 (e-book)

Designed by Brugel Creative www.brugel.com.au
Cover image by freepik.com

❝This ground-breaking study of the plight of the minority ethnic churches, who are facing a new generation of believers who may or may not feel comfortable in the churches of their parents and grandparents, is both penetrating and welcomed. Dr Michael Chu has researched the project from a deeply personal angle, as a pastor in a Chinese church in Sydney and as one who is concerned with pastoral care for a younger generation. This is a universal issue facing the ethnic churches throughout the Western world, and Michael approaches it from a pastoral leadership perspective with the latest advancement in the study of Cultural Intelligence. His meticulous attention to detail and his deep perception of the issue at hand is to be congratulated. The result is very useful and can apply to almost all ethnic churches, so has universal relevance.

Justin Tan

Vice Principal (Academic), Senior Lecturer
Research Fellow and Director of the Research Centre for Chinese Christianity
Melbourne School of Theology, Australia

❝First-generation Asian leaders, despite their faith commitments, often lack intercultural competencies when dealing with younger generation church members in the West. Michael Chu's well-researched application of the theory of Cultural Intelligence (CQ) offers a penetrating analysis of intergenerational identities and highlights practical insights for increasing cultural intelligence, managing conflicts and building multicultural teams. Although the study focuses on Chinese churches in Australia, this book is highly recommended for leaders of churches and organisations interested in diverse Asian and Western contexts.

Kang-San Tan

General Director of BMS World Mission

"Raising a vibrant and authentic next-generation faith community has been a challenge that has confounded the Chinese churches in diaspora for decades. Michael Chu's research provides us with a sound framework in investigating such conflicts from the perspective of Cultural Intelligence, with its four dimensions. His work offers us insights into how Chinese church leaders in diaspora can problematise the conflicts and how practical solutions can be implemented through the lens of Cultural Intelligence. As someone who engages in research into the faith journeys of local-born Chinese Christians in Canada, I highly recommend Dr Chu's study to all who are concerned about the future of the Chinese churches in diaspora.

Enoch Wong

Assistant Professor of Practical Theology and Director of Centre for Leadership Studies
Canadian Chinese School of Theology, Toronto, Canada

"Intergenerational conflict among pastors of Chinese churches in the West is a widespread problem that is in desperate need of ongoing research and reflection. With the author having served for many years in such contexts, Michael Chu's book arises out of a deep concern to reduce such conflicts for the good of the church and the world. His research applies the framework of Cultural Intelligence (CQ) to this issue, and in so doing not only helps us better understand the Australian Chinese church context but also offers valuable practical suggestions for equipping pastors with intercultural competence.

David H. F. Ng

Lecturer in Intercultural Studies, Melbourne School of Theology, Australia

---

"The concept of Cultural Intelligence has become increasingly significant in developing healthy intercultural teams in the corporate world and in NGOs. This research conducted by Dr Michael Chu highlights how Cultural Intelligence could be applied to pastoral leadership, in particular to the Chinese church. It is especially relevant in the context of multigenerational and multilingual Chinese churches located in a non-Chinese environment. Dr Chu has integrated theory and practice with scholarly analysis and a pastoral heart. The final chapter, *Practical implications for churches, mission agencies and theological education*, is extremely insightful and helpful and should not be missed.

Patrick Fung

General Director, OMF International

MICHAEL K. CHU

"Within this study, one finds a rigorous examination of the cross-cultural competence of intergenerational leaders of the Chinese churches in Sydney. Beyond being a detailed empirical study that leads to concrete recommendations for pastors, churches, theological colleges and mission agencies, this study also provides an illuminating history of Chinese immigrants and their churches, a helpful introduction to the relevance of Cultural Intelligence in the study of intergenerational group dynamics, a theological reflection on the value of multicultural ministries, a pastoral analysis on the role of personal relationships within ministerial settings and a testimonial that gives voice to an immigrant community that has played an important part in the history and culture of modern Australian society. Privileging neither the first- nor the second/third-generation leaders, Dr Chu's work provides a framework within which a fruitful dialogue between the two groups is made possible. As such, it should find itself in the hands of both practitioners and theoreticians involved in this area of ministry and research.

David W. Pao

Professor of New Testament and Chair of the New Testament Department
Trinity Evangelical Divinity School, USA

"The pursuit of a knowledge of Cultural Intelligence is important and relevant for pastors and church leaders of Chinese churches in Sydney. Many Chinese churches now have second generations whose culture is different from the Chinese subcultures of their parents. Some bigger Chinese churches also engage Caucasian pastors to minister alongside pastors of traditional Chinese cultural background. In this situation, intercultural competence is essential. Michael Chu, possessing thirty years of pastoral experience in a big Sydney church and having contacts with a large number of Chinese churches in Sydney, writes as an insider. In this well-researched work on the subject, Michael points the way forward in acquiring greater intercultural competence for pastors and pastoral teams as well as strengthening its place in theological education and mission organisations. I heartily recommend this timely book (with its many practical recommendations) for all who are involved in the bilingual or multilingual ministry of a local church in Sydney.

Charles Cheung

Consultant Chaplain, Chinese Theological College Australia

❝A key component of Michael Chu's study is his examination of the history of Chinese churches established in the Western cultural context of Australia. His study reviews their periods of growth and stagnation and explores solutions to help these churches revive and move towards future growth. Michael uncovers the complexities of Australia's Chinese churches and gives helpful insights into the causes of stagnation in these congregations. Michael's work has the potential to generate further studies in this area. I hope and pray that this research will encourage the formation of a new generation of *servant* pastors and believers and assist our churches in moving forward, empowered by God to continue our gospel ministries.

Joseph Fung

Cross-Cultural Chaplain, Moore College, Australia

MICHAEL K. CHU

"With a pastoral heart for the strengthening of the working relationship among pastors from different cultural backgrounds in the Chinese churches, Rev. Michael Chu has set out through his research to find a better way of understanding the cultural differences between OBC and ARC/ABC pastors. Through his historical survey of the Chinese churches in Sydney and their cultural backgrounds, coupled with a quantitative and qualitative survey on the cultural intelligence of a large group of pastors, Rev. Michael Chu has shed light on the key issues involved. His findings and applications will have a significant impact on building healthy pastoral teams, training culturally competent pastors and raising up more effective workers for cross-cultural ministries.

Calvin Ma

Deputy General Director and International Director for East Asia North, OMF International

---

"Michael's many years of experience and thoughtful reflection have come together in this study, which is ultimately about demonstrating the needs for and means to increase in one's cultural intelligence. The experiences described and reflected upon in this book are crucial for understanding how to get the most out of multiethnic, intercultural teams in a multicultural context. My experience working with Michael in a team comprised of multiple backgrounds (at one point we had staff born in Australia, South Africa, Vietnam, Hong Kong and China) was one where I was entrusted and freed up to do ministry in a culturally appropriate way for my congregation, but I was also constantly challenged and pushed in how to work well and communicate effectively with people from vastly different backgrounds and experiences.

Michael's thoughtful reflections and bold recommendations should be attended to by all who are seeking to best serve and understand others in Christian ministry.

Doug Fyfe

English Pastor, Northern District Chinese Christian Church, Sydney, Australia

---

❝Extensive research, coupled with years of experience in applying the gospel of reconciliation to the complexities of cross-cultural and cross-generational ministry, makes Michael Chu's *Intercultural Competence* a rich and valuable contribution to all engaged in God's ongoing mission, 'Salvation to the ends of the earth'. Michael presents deep insights applicable to a much broader ministry context, whether pastoral ministry or theological and ministry training, equipping workers for a world in which the need for gospel-shaped cultural intelligence is hopefully becoming increasingly obvious. Having benefitted greatly through serving as Michael's 'fellow-worker' in pastoral ministry, and being life-long 'cross-cultural' brothers and friends, it gives me great pleasure to recommend this work to all who are passionate for gospel growth and the greater praise of God's glory in and through his church.

John Dickson

Co-Chairman of Pioneers International Foundation, Thailand

❝Australian Chinese pastors, especially those in Sydney, have wrestled for many years with how two generations of Overseas-born Chinese (OBC) and Australian-born Chinese (ABC) can serve together in unity. OBC pastors have a desire to promote harmony and enable the two generations to serve under one roof, but often these attempts fail. ABC pastors struggle to help OBC pastors understand the unique ministry and role they have. I am delighted that Dr Michael Chu has undertaken the task of exploring these issues and proposed a possible solution. By applying the theory of Cultural Intelligence (CQ) to these challenges of cultural conflict, both generations can work together for the growth of the church and the glory of God. I highly recommend this book to both OBC and ABC pastors, whether in Sydney or beyond.

Dennis Law

Principal, Chinese Theological College Australia

"The wave of Chinese migration to the USA dates back to over a century ago. The same wave to Australia was more recent. For decades, Chinese churches in Australia have learned from our counterparts in America. Despite many similarities in these two phases and destinations of the Chinese diaspora, there are certainly vast differences in the contexts and times in which the people movements occurred. Michael's research and dissertation fill this important gap for the Australian Chinese churches.

On a wider scale, as we prepare to enter the third decade of the twenty-first century, it is evident that the Chinese diaspora will become a permanent component of the global migration movement. As a consequence, ministry to the Chinese is anticipated to become more and more global. Michael's contribution to this conversation will be a blessing to 'Next Gen' ministries.

Rev. Dr David Tse

Senior minister, Evangelical Free Church of Australia

CONTENTS

FOREWORD xvii

PREFACE xx

INTRODUCTION 1

CHAPTER ONE
RESEARCH QUESTIONS AND HYPOTHESES. 14

CHAPTER TWO
LITERATURE SURVEY AND ASSESSMENT 25

CHAPTER THREE
HISTORICAL OVERVIEW 94

CHAPTER FOUR
SOCIOLOGICAL INQUIRY 139

CHAPTER FIVE
RESEARCH ANALYSIS 205

CHAPTER SIX
PRACTICAL IMPLICATIONS 237

CONCLUSION 271

APPENDICES

APPENDIX A:
RESEARCH TOOLS: QUESTIONS OF QUESTIONNAIRE 286

APPENDIX B
RESEARCH TOOLS: DEMOGRAPHIC QUESTIONS 289

APPENDIX C
INTERVIEW QUESTIONS 290

APPENDIX D
BOOKLIST ON INTERCULTURAL LEADERSHIP FOR PASTORS . 294

APPENDIX E
SUGGESTED REFLECTION QUESTIONS 297

APPENDIX F
SUGGESTED OUTLINE FOR POST-TRIP DEBRIEFING 302

APPENDIX G
BIBLE STUDY SCHEDULE 305

APPENDIX H
ONE-DAY WORKSHOP DESIGN 307

BIBLIOGRAPHY 319

FOREWORD

It seems to me that effective pastoral ministry has always involved a peculiar mix of professional and personal competencies. I'm also quite sure that none of us ever manages to do it perfectly. In many ways, Michael Chu's pastoral ministry among the Chinese congregations of Sydney has been exemplary. Although I'm quite sure that Dr Chu would readily admit that he is far from perfect, he has shown a genuine desire to understand the changes taking place within the Chinese churches in cities such as Sydney and has to tried to respond to the changes with sensitivity and care. This book, his first, contains the patient and careful investigation he undertook as the necessary steps in understanding the precise nature of the changes occurring within the Chinese churches of Sydney in the opening decades of the twenty-first century.

As a pastor for many years, Dr Chu became increasingly perplexed by tensions he observed within the leadership teams of the various Chinese churches in Sydney, among which he was a respected senior figure. Whereas some leaders might too readily have concluded that the tensions and conflicts were primarily doctrinal or even interpersonal, Dr Chu began to understand them as primarily focused around cultural differences.

This conclusion was surprising to some, for the leadership teams within the Chinese churches were, and remain, largely composed of ethnic Chinese pastors, elders and deacons. Some of Dr Chu's friends wondered how such teams could experience conflict because of cultural differences. After all, even if speaking Mandarin or Cantonese was an obvious difference, they were all the same culturally, weren't they?

While serving as a pastor, however, Dr Chu realised that there were some subtle differences on display between younger, second- and third-generation migrant pastors, born and educated in Australia, and the older, first-generation migrant pastors who were born and educated elsewhere, many of them in China. Searching for a way to make sense of these differences, Dr Chu turned to the emerging discipline of Cultural Intelligence (CQ) and used this to great effect. In highlighting some of the main areas of cultural difference, Dr Chu has provided an extremely detailed case study of the Chinese Christian community here in Sydney. He has also outlined some steps that can be taken to address some of the tensions and misunderstandings that he believes will continue to emerge within the vibrant and growing Chinese churches of the city.

The story of any migrant community of believers is always likely to prove fascinating and challenge traditional patterns of ministry and mission. This study, in its telling of some of the story, will engage readers with an interest in the history of the Chinese churches in Sydney. The need for a detailed reference work of this history remains, but Dr Chu gathers and presents important historical data that provides valuable resource material for future historians of Chinese Christianity in Sydney. For the present, his chief concern is to trace the story of how individuals, families and communities have settled in Sydney over the last century and a half and to show how their experiences and history have shaped them in ways that are barely noticeable on a cursory view.

FOREWORD

It has been a personal pleasure for me to have come to know Michael Chu over recent years and to see him add new competencies to the gifts and graces that God's Spirit has given him. As he has grown in his own understanding and practice of Cultural Intelligence (CQ), he has integrated this very effectively with his intellectual abilities (or IQ) and his emotional maturity (EQ). It's all the more thrilling, therefore, that he is now able to equip others through his teaching ministry at one of Hong Kong's theological seminaries.

By way of commending the value of this book, I believe that Dr Chu's work has been thorough, careful, pastoral and sensitive. He has probed, listened to and dialogued with pastors over the years of his study and describes here what others might have sensed but were never quite able to articulate in the way that he has done.

This is a book that will repay careful reading, and my prayer is that it will help to reduce the number of Chinese congregations that experience the sad, and ultimately unnecessary, legacy of cultural misunderstanding within their leadership teams. May the peace of Christ dwell ever more richly in the churches that Dr Chu describes here. Amen.

Associate Professor Rev. Darrell Jackson,
Morling College and the University of Divinity
17 December 2018

PREFACE

This book is a revised version of my dissertation, 'Drawn Together for His Glory: The relevance and application of Cultural Intelligence (CQ) to the pastoral leadership of the congregational Chinese Churches of Sydney with culturally diverse leadership teams and members'.

My love for intercultural leadership has come from my pastoral ministry at a Chinese church in Sydney where, since 1992, I have performed pastoral leadership and interacted with various church leaders. Throughout this ministry, unexpected disputes and setbacks have been a frequent source of frustration for me. The experience has left me pondering the issue of intercultural and intergenerational leadership in Chinese churches. Finding clarity in this subject became my inner yearning, leading me to engage in research.

In September 2015, I met Dr Darrell Jackson in his office. After I shared with him my research question, Darrell proposed that I take on Cultural Intelligence as a tool towards the study of intergenerational conflict. Since that day, the course of my life has irrevocably changed.

My deep gratitude goes to my supervisor, Dr Darrell Jackson, who ushered me into the world of research and opened a new chapter of life-long learning. His patient guidance, inspiring

PREFACE

insight and scholarly advice have brought pleasure and joy to my study. Over the course of the research, Dr Jackson in effect demonstrated to me what intercultural communication truly is. I am greatly indebted to him.

My sincere thanks go also to my second supervisor, Dr Justin Tan. Dr Tan is so knowledgeable in theological research and experienced in Asian pastoral ministry. It was Dr Tan who encouraged me to write the chapter on the history of the Chinese churches of Sydney. His inspiring comments and guidance have been invaluable.

A research project like this could not have been accomplished without the help of many people. At the risk of offending by omission, I would like to mention a few.

I am grateful to Dr Stephen Lee, the president of China Graduate School of Theology at Hong Kong. It is Dr Lee who encouraged me to put this dissertation into print. My gratitude also goes to editor Gina Denholm and the team at Morling Press. Their painstaking patience has been a great encouragement to me.

My thanks go to Rev. Dennis Law, Rev. Charles Cheung, Rev. Joseph Fung, Dr Nancy Fung and Rev. Ming Leung. Without their ongoing trust and support, I would not have served in pastoral ministry with such longevity. It was because of their earnest encouragement that I dared to take up such a research project.

My wholehearted thanks go to the members, deacons and pastors of the Northern District Chinese Christian Church, Sydney. The last two and a half decades in NDCCC have been the best part of my life. I feel overwhelmed by their confidence in me, allowing me to minister among them with the word of God every week. I feel undeserving of their trust in me, that they would even share with me their inner struggles and joy all these years. In particular, I thank them for their unceasing prayer and generous support over the two-year research period, enabling me to fully devote my time to reading and reflecting upon pastoral leadership. Walking alongside such a community is beautiful!

Thanks also go to Hannah Chu, my beloved daughter. She is always a joy and a gift to me. I thank her for her prayerful encouragement and for taking the time to proofread my proposal within a day. What an excellent support.

Thanks to my dearest wife, Ruth Chu, with loving gratitude. Ruth is the anchor of my life, a truly supportive friend, a self-giving companion and a prayerful partner over the last thirty-six years. After all these years, she is still my one and only. Without her tireless support, delightful patience, warm encouragement and kind-heartedness, this research project would not have become a reality.

No words can fully express my thanks to my gracious Saviour and Lord. Without his steadfast love and abundant grace, I could never have imagined a wretched sinner like me would inherit new life in Christ. It is even more surprising that he entrusts me with such a noble task as preaching and pastoral ministry. God is so good! *Soli Deo gloria.*

INTRODUCTION

A personal introduction

As a pastor in Sydney for more than twenty-five years, I have been told many stories by other pastors of Chinese churches in Sydney. For example, one newly graduated pastor shared that, after two years in pastoral ministry, he wanted to quit, indicating that pastoral ministry was too tough for him to continue in. His senior pastor expected unrealistic levels of performance from him. This young pastor just could not meet his senior pastor's unspoken expectations. He knew he needed to persevere and endure the first few years in pastoral ministry, but he came to his wits' end. He just needed a break. A long break.

Another young pastor shared with me her discouragement and distress in feeling that pastoral ministry was too demanding and draining. It was not the tasks that drained her energy. It was the relationships. Although she had been working in a highly competitive profession before she entered ministry, she could not endure the complicated and enmeshed relationships. She just could not please everybody at church. She even hinted that she might leave pastoral ministry altogether.

A pastor in his sixties expressed anger with his fellow pastors. 'They just don't do what a pastor is supposed to do.' He was referring to his young pastors' capacity for being lazy, calculative and disobedient. His younger colleagues were not devoted to pastoral ministry and not faithful to God's calling. Obviously, his expectations were not being met. He simply took back all the pastoral responsibilities from the young pastors and did all the tasks by himself. His pastoral team was virtually over.

When asked about the main reasons for their anguish and frustration, these people's answers commonly revolved around relationship difficulties between pastors. Relational struggles generated endless disappointments and discouragements that consumed the emotional energy of the younger pastors and subsequently wore them down. Senior pastors felt that their fellow pastors were not submissive, nor were they following instructions. The younger pastors felt that their senior pastors were overly demanding and not supportive.

Over the years, I have observed and reflected on the phenomenon of the relational struggles among pastors in Chinese churches in Sydney. I began to notice a common thread, in that many senior pastors (or lead pastors) failed at two major tasks. Firstly, they did not develop their younger fellow pastors with any appreciation for their cultural backgrounds or stages of development. As a result, younger pastors could not feel a sense of achievement and fulfilment in their pastoral ministry. They perceived that their potential and gifts were underutilised. Secondly, senior pastors did not facilitate open and genuine communication among their fellow pastors. Some churches did not have pastoral team meetings at all. Without frequent and genuine communication, teamwork and collaboration could not be established.

INTRODUCTION

Apparently, there were many reasons for younger pastors feeling they were not being fully developed and utilised. These included personality clashes, unmet expectations, diverse ministry styles and even doctrinal emphases. However, I considered the primary factor underlying these phenomena to be the huge cultural differences between the younger and senior pastors. Because of the generational and cultural gap, the senior pastors did not understand the inner longings and wishes of younger fellow pastors. This situation was aggravated by their non-communication or miscommunication. Thus, further investigation seemed warranted to understand the nature and characteristics of the generational differences, the complicated dynamics contributing to the avoidance of communication and the factors shaping interaction (or non-interaction). These were the observations and questions that led me to my research proposal.

At this stage, it is worth posing some preliminary questions. Is the conflict I have observed grounded in a lack of intercultural[1] competence, so that these pastors are unable to cross the generation gap and the cultural barrier? Secondly, if the answer to the first question is yes, does this lack of intercultural competence mean that they are unable to communicate and interact with other pastors from different cultural backgrounds? If their level of cross-cultural competence is low, it is worthwhile understanding the underlying factors.

The context for the study

By June 2016, according to the database of Chinese Christian Mission Australia (2016), ninety-eight Chinese churches had been

---

[1] In this book, the terms 'intercultural', 'cross-cultural' and 'transcultural' are used interchangeably.

established in Sydney. Most of these Chinese churches consist of two groups of members (or two congregations). One group comprises Chinese-speaking migrants,[2] while the other group comprises the younger, English-speaking second generation of those migrants.

The cultural identities of these two groups are quite different. The first-generation migrants, who are mostly overseas-born Chinese (hereafter abbreviated as OBC) when they arrive in Australia, are largely culturally traditional Chinese. As time goes by, and as they acquire more English language and local culture, their cultural identity becomes less traditionally Chinese, but still far from culturally Australian.

The cultural identity of the second generation, which includes both Australian-raised Chinese (hereafter abbreviated as ARC) and Australian-born Chinese (hereafter abbreviated as ABC), is very different. The cultural identity of the ARC, at the moment when they arrive, is not yet culturally Australian; their cultural identity is a mix of Chinese and Australian components. But the rate of their cultural learning and development towards their feeling that they are Australian is much faster than that of their parents' generation. Similarly, the cultural identity of the ABC is also a mixture. In the first few years after birth, ABCs are greatly influenced and shaped by their families and parents, who are predominantly culturally Chinese. As they grow, receive an Australian education and are exposed to Australian society, the cultural identity of the ABC shifts gradually towards becoming culturally Australian.

---

2   The Chinese-speaking members of some Chinese churches may be further subdivided into two language groups, the Cantonese-speaking and the Mandarin-speaking.

INTRODUCTION

Thus, the cultural identity of ABC and ARC can be understood in terms of cultural hybridity, or a mixture of culture.[3] This cultural identity is a mixture of home culture (the culture of their parents), the host culture (the Australian culture), the peer culture and various subcultures. One of the characteristics of cultural hybridity is fluidity, in which it is difficult to ascertain one's cultural identity. This is because hybrid culture is determined by many factors, such as the number of years in Australia, language proficiency, parental influence, personality traits and the degree of social assimilation. Thus, it is difficult for both the second generation and their parents to locate their cultural identities.

As the two generations speak different languages, naturally, the Chinese churches organise two different services, a Chinese service (Cantonese and/or Mandarin) and an English service. The two services are conducted in different styles in terms of language, music, sermon style, flow of service and even seating plan. Beyond these visible differences lie other invisible and subtle, yet discernible, differences; for example, ministry philosophy and doctrinal emphasis. All these behaviours and patterns reflect their cultural identity.

Normally, these two groups in Chinese churches experience no problem within their individual ministries. However, when it comes to joint ministries such as church anniversaries and festivals, leaders from the two congregations may disagree and clash. It can be a matter of differing interpretations. For example, the traditional Chinese members see Chinese New Year as a time for family reunion and, therefore, the highlight of the church calendar. But the younger generation may see the same purpose achieved through Christmas, birthday parties or even wedding

---

3   Fuligni et al., 'Attitudes', 1031–40; Phinney et al., 'Cultural Values', 528–30; George, *Understanding the Coconut Generation*, 65–89; Lalonde and Giguère, 'Two Cultural Worlds', 58–60; Pollock and Van Reken, *Third Culture Kids*, 19–35.

ceremonies.[4] Different cultural symbols or forms can carry the same meaning. In the same way, the same cultural symbols can convey different meanings.

Another subtle difficulty is the boundary between the notions of the church as a family and church members' own families. In traditional Chinese families, children show respect and total submission to parents. Accordingly, older leaders and senior pastors at church expect younger church members to show respect and total submission to them, even if they are not their blood parents. The pastors fail to maintain 'self-differentiation' or draw boundaries in leadership.[5] Such an expectation certainly causes strong reactions from the younger generation.

These conflicts and disagreements originate from the cultural differences between the two generations. These differences might arise from different worldviews,[6] diverse cultural identities,[7] separate cultural interpretations[8] or different cultural values.[9]

In order to address such conflicts and disagreements within this particular cultural and ecclesial context, it is necessary to conduct a thorough inquiry into the cultural differences between the two generations within Chinese churches in Sydney and the underlying factors behind these cultural differences. I believe studying the application of Cultural Intelligence (hereafter also known as CQ) can provide the necessary mutual understanding between senior pastors and younger pastors and will create a strong incentive to reduce the distance and resolve conflicts.

---

4   Tan, *Contextualization*, 118–19.
5   Friedman, *Generation to Generation*, 220–49.
6   Ling and Cheuk, *'Chinese' Way*, 89–106.
7   Liu, 'Searching', 33–34; Stroink and Lalonde, 'Bicultural Identity Conflict', 44–45; Pollock and Van Reken, *Third Culture Kids*, 19–35, 121–29.
8   Tan, *Contextualization*, 115–32.
9   Hofstede et al., *Cultures and Organizations*, 28–29, 180–91, 230–31, 244–46.

INTRODUCTION

The relevance and application of Cultural Intelligence in this study

Cultural Intelligence is adopted as the theoretical model in this study. A basic question is whether CQ offers sufficient analytical rigour to allow problems to be adequately described and solutions outlined.

Cultural Intelligence is defined as 'an individual's capability to function and manage effectively in culturally diverse settings'.[10] It is one of the major tools that has been developed to measure a person's intercultural competence.

Over the last thirty years, five major intercultural models have been developed.[11] Among them are the Global Leadership Competency Inventory, Global Mindset Model, Multicultural Personality Model, Developmental Model of Intercultural Sensitivity and Cultural Intelligence Scale. Among these five models, the Global Leadership Competency Inventory is relatively comprehensive but quite new.[12] The Global Mindset Model, Multicultural Personality Model and Developmental Model of Intercultural Sensitivity assess a more limited number of dimensions of intercultural competence.

The Cultural Intelligence Scale comprehensively measures four factors of one's intercultural competence.[13] Moreover, the validity of the conceptualisation of Cultural Intelligence has been

---

10 Ang et al., 'Cultural Intelligence', 337.
11 Leung et al., 'Intercultural Competence', 491–93.
12 Global Leadership Competency Inventory was developed in 2010 (Bird et al., *Defining the Content Domain*).
13 The four factors of Cultural Intelligence are CQ knowledge, CQ strategy, CQ drive and CQ action. The four factors of CQ are sometimes known as four dimensions. The terms 'four factors' and 'four dimensions' will therefore be used interchangeably.

academically assessed and tested.[14] So far, Cultural Intelligence has been primarily applied in global business sectors, international leadership development and entrepreneurial personnel training.

In this study, I have investigated the extent of the relevance of Cultural Intelligence for the pastors of Chinese churches in Sydney. This research may shed light on the application of Cultural Intelligence among pastoral leadership teams as an effective way to increase intercultural competence and intercultural awareness.

Anticipated outcomes of the study

This project is more than just a theoretical study. Instead, this research is performed with the purpose of practical theological interpretation.[15] According to Osmer, practical theological interpretation includes four tasks: a descriptive-empirical task, an interpretive task, a normative task and a pragmatic task.[16] In other words, this study is an interdisciplinary inquiry, which includes a sociological survey, a literature review of various relevant fields and ministry implications.

Thus, my research is undertaken with an explanatory objective (articulating and explaining the previously outlined phenomena of the Chinese church), an exegetical aim (interpreting and critically evaluating the root issues and elements of the phenomena) and a practical goal (prompting remedial and preventive practices).

The first outcome is an in-depth understanding of the phenomena of intergenerational and cultural conflict in Chinese churches in Sydney. Through questionnaires and interviews, I

---

14 Matsumoto and Hwang, 'Assessing Cross-Cultural Competence', 863–69; Leung et al., 'Intercultural Competence', 495.
15 Osmer, *Practical Theology*, 6–8.
16 Ibid., 11.

INTRODUCTION

have gathered information on, and the inner voices of, a sample of Chinese pastors, with the aim of facilitating pastors to share knowledge of relational dynamics among their teams. This information and understanding will help pastors understand the nature and characteristics of relational struggles and conflicts. The inquiry is thus beneficial for self-knowledge and mutual understanding.

Secondly, this study does more than just introduce the concept of Cultural Intelligence into Sydney's Chinese churches. I have also interpreted the cultural behaviours in light of existing cultural theories and through the theoretical framework of the four factors of Cultural Intelligence. Thus, the study also contributes to the Chinese churches by widening the scope of their task of practical theology, so that church matters can be interpreted in terms of cultural, generational and relational perspectives.

Thirdly, since the practice and process of inquiry is transferable, the experience of this inquiry may be shared with and demonstrated to other pastors at churches and researchers at colleges and seminaries. This would be beneficial to those who perform similar studies in the field of practical theology in the future. The notion of Cultural Intelligence could be made relevant in training pastors, preparing missionaries and building missionary teams of various cultural backgrounds and generations.

In summary, I have high expectations in regard to this inquiry. It has benefit to me, to other pastors, to the Chinese church at large and to other Christian institutions. My intention is that this study of Cultural Intelligence will inject a new element into the Chinese churches and advance the proclamation of the gospel.

Overview and structure of this study

- Chapter 1 outlines the research questions and hypotheses. It includes the focus and scope of the research and the value and significance of the research. The limitations of the research are also articulated.

- Chapter 2 reviews the relevant literature in the field. First of all, works on migration and migrant theories, and experiences of Chinese migrants in Australia, are examined. This is followed by a review of the literature on cultural identity and cultural hybridity. Writings about intergenerational conflicts within the church are then reviewed. Literature on leadership and church ministry are also evaluated. Lastly, books and articles on theories of Cultural Intelligence are surveyed.

- Chapter 3 provides an overview of Chinese churches in Sydney, beginning with a brief history of Chinese migrants in Australia. This is followed by a summary of the development of Chinese churches in Sydney, particularly in the last thirty years. The cultural context of Chinese churches and pastoral leadership is then described and analysed. Lastly, I survey the occurrence of conflict in Sydney's Chinese churches.

- Chapter 4 outlines and defends the use of interpretative phenomenology as a research methodology. I also justify the adoption of mixed research methods. The chapter also outlines the research sample, the research process, the data collection, and the preliminary findings of the research.

- Chapter 5 outlines the research analysis. The findings of the semi-structured interviews are analysed and discussed in detail, with special reference to the four factors of Cultural

INTRODUCTION

Intelligence. I discuss ministry implications for Chinese pastors in Sydney. The challenges to intergenerational pastoral leadership are also evaluated.

- Chapter 6 draws some practical and pastoral implications for churches, mission agencies and theological education.

The Conclusion closes the study by providing post-research reflection, as well as suggesting directions for future research.

Definition of key terms

For the purposes of this research, the following definitions are applied.

Cultural competency. This is defined as 'a set of behaviours, attitudes, and policies that enable a system, agency, or professional to work effectively in cross-cultural situations'.[17]

Cultural Intelligence (CQ). According to the conceptualisation of the first CQ researchers, Cultural Intelligence is defined as 'an individual's capability to function and manage effectively in culturally diverse settings'.[18] Ang and Van Dyne further explain that the focus of Cultural Intelligence is on an 'individual's ability to grasp and reason correctly in situations characterised by cultural diversity'.[19] They argue that Cultural Intelligence is a multidimensional concept or an aggregate construct, which specifically refers to metacognitive, cognitive, motivational and behavioural dimensions.[20]

---

17 Isaacs and Benjamin, *Towards a Culturally Competent System*, 16.
18 Ang and Van Dyne, 'Conceptualization', 3.
19 Ibid., 4.
20 Ibid., 4, 7.

Leadership teams and pastoral leadership. In this study, the terms 'leadership teams' and 'pastoral leadership' refer to the group of people who have received the calling of God, have trained in a theological or Bible college and are currently employed by a church. They exercise pastoral leadership and spiritual guidance for the church. The term specifies the target group of this study, which excludes the lay leaders, deacons and elders and general members of the church. The term also excludes student pastors, part-time pastors, itinerant evangelists, interim pastors and retired pastors.

Hermeneutic phenomenology. Hermeneutic phenomenology is a qualitative research methodology. 'Phenomenology is an approach which attempts to understand the hidden meanings and the essence of experience together with how participants make sense of these.'[21] The approach attempts to describe certain aspects of the lived experience of a person as it appears, and to examine the meaning of the experience in its sociocultural context. Hermeneutic phenomenology assumes a constructivist epistemology, which means that the observed reality being described is best understood through interpretation by the researchers.[22] The assumption underlying hermeneutic phenomenology is that all human awareness has to be engaged through interpretation.[23]

---

21 Grbich, *Qualitative Data Analysis*, 84.
22 Heidegger, *Being and Time*, 62.
23 Van Manen and Adams, 'Phenomenology', 451.

CHAPTER ONE
RESEARCH QUESTIONS AND HYPOTHESES

Target group, subject matter, focus and scope of the research

This book is titled 'Intercultural Competence: Cultural Intelligence, Pastoral Leadership and the Chinese Church'. This title can be understood from four perspectives: the target group, the subject matter, the focus and the scope.

The *target group* of this study is pastoral leadership. A church is a community of complicated human networks. Behaviours are the results of interactions between all members and parties in the church. In order to keep this inquiry focused and at a manageable scale, this research targets pastoral leaders, which include pastors with various roles, pastors of different language congregations, and pastors of different ages and genders. In other words, lay leaders, such as deacons and elders, are not included in this study. Similarly, general members of the church are not included. It is estimated there are about 150 full-

RESEARCH QUESTIONS AND HYPOTHESES

time pastors working in various Chinese churches in the greater Sydney area.

The pastors of the Chinese churches in Sydney are of different generations. Specifically, the pastors can be divided into two main groups. The first group of pastors are above fifty years of age (and can be up to seventy-five), the age group usually classified as 'baby boomers'. The second group of pastors are from thirty to fifty years old, and thus mostly fall into the category of 'Generation X', with some in 'Generation Y.'

Nowadays, there are a wide range of 'pastors': student pastors, part-time pastors, pastors serving for a short period of time (before moving on to other ministries, such as mission agencies or parachurch organisations), children's pastors, women's pastors, itinerant evangelists, mission pastors, executive pastors, interim pastors, mentor-pastors, ministers-at-large and church planting pastors, to name some. There are also those pastors who have served for a period of time but are then perceived as incompetent or unsuitable and are forced to move on or even drop out of ministry. In this study, the pastors surveyed are a group of people who have received the calling of God, have trained in theological or Bible colleges and are currently employed by a church.

The *subject matter* of this study is Cultural Intelligence. This study examines the cultural dimensions of pastors through the four-factor framework of Cultural Intelligence. The approach of this study does not include research on other perspectives of pastoral leadership, such as leadership styles, church management skills, life cycles of churches, pastors' theological training, pastors' doctrinal positions or the interaction of pastors according to relational dynamics or system theory.

In examining the cultural dimensions of pastors, this study also intentionally does not focus on cultural issues such as cultural assimilation or integration, comparison of various cultures, conflict resolution styles, racism or discrimination. Instead, this study will emphasise the subject matter of cross-cultural competence,[1] with special reference to the Cultural Intelligence (CQ) of the sample pastors.

The *focus* of this study is the relevance and application of Cultural Intelligence. This research attempts to achieve three objectives. Firstly, it attempts to assess the cross-cultural competence of the pastors. Secondly, it examines the fundamental factors shaping their cross-cultural competence level. Thirdly, it explores various ways of improving the cross-cultural competence of the pastors of Chinese churches in Sydney.

The *scope* of the study has been narrowed to congregational Chinese Churches of Sydney with culturally diverse leadership teams and members. In the context of Sydney, apart from some Chinese congregations that are established as Episcopal or Presbyterian churches, the majority of Chinese churches operate according to congregational governance. Congregational governance is adopted by most independent churches and by many Chinese churches in denominations such as the Alliance Church, the Baptist Church and the Evangelical Free Church. As Episcopal and Presbyterian governance are different from congregational, the scope of this research is limited to a study of those congregational Chinese churches where most decisions are made in lay-leadership-driven boards.[2] In other words, the board

---

[1] Strictly speaking, the term 'cross-cultural' means a movement from one culture to another. The term 'intercultural' refers to mutual interchange, dialogue and debate between cultures. Thus, 'intercultural', in a sense, includes 'cross-cultural' (Cosgrove et al., *Cross-Cultural Paul*, 4). In this study, the terms 'intercultural' and 'cross-cultural' are used interchangeably in a generic sense.

[2] Primarily, congregational governance refers to governance by lay leaders, whereas Episcopal and Presbyterian governance is by bishops and presbyters.

is the decision making and ruling body for major agenda issues, such as finance, employment and personnel.

Research hypotheses and research questions

This study is founded upon two research hypotheses. Firstly, as the pastors are Bible-believing, God-fearing and gospel-driven men and women, their commonality in godly character and purpose is strong and obvious. However, their relational disagreements and conflicts seem unusual and uncharacteristic. Thus, here I assume that there are some deep-seated cultural factors. Through the theoretical framework of Cultural Intelligence, these factors can be perceived as relating to the four dimensions of Cultural Intelligence. For example, intuitive discomfort or dislike derived from differences in core values or beliefs is characteristically identified by Cultural Intelligence authors as a factor of CQ drive. Language deficiency is categorised as a component of CQ knowledge.[3] The Cultural Intelligence researchers classify ethnocentric bias as a constituent of CQ metacognition. They also identify inflexibility as an element of CQ behaviour.[4] All these factors contribute to shaping the low level of cultural competence of pastors.

Secondly, pastors involved in pastoral ministry usually embrace the core message of the gospel and adopt the ministry of reconciliation in this broken and alienated world.[5] In general, reconciliation (between God and humans as well as among human beings) is the pastor's primary task. Therefore, no Chinese pastor intentionally disregards their normal cultural values or sets out to create conflict and disagreement. Tragically, however, there

---

3   Ang and Van Dyne, 'Conceptualization', 5–6.
4   Earley et al., *CQ*, 26–27; Livermore, *Cultural Intelligence*, 232–41; Ang and Van Dyne, *Handbook*, 163–68.
5   Rom 5:1–2, 2 Cor 5:17–21, Eph 2:11–22, etc.

are some dysfunctional leaders and relationships, which lead on to rivalry, miscommunication, misunderstanding, tension, conflicts and disputes. Chinese pastors instinctively want to seek to bring forth peace and restore relationships.[6] Hence, it is assumed that pastoral leadership that understands and has effective strategies to respond to cultural change and diversity in Sydney will be most likely to avoid unintended hostility and conflict arising from cultural differences, whether ethnic or generational.

Accordingly, I pose three research questions for this study to answer. Firstly, what is the level of intercultural competence of the pastors of Chinese churches in Sydney? Secondly, what are the root issues shaping the level of their intercultural competence? And finally, what resources and creative options are available to improve their intercultural competence?

Value and significance of the research

Value to the Chinese churches in Sydney

The value and significance of this research is anticipated to be multifaceted. First of all, this study will make an immediate impact on pastoral ministry in the Chinese churches of Sydney. By answering the preceding research questions, I aim to uncover the hidden factors behind the constant conflicts among the pastors of Chinese churches. The pastors (and, subsequently, the lay leaders and church members) will also become aware of the cultural dimensions of the conflicts. As an outcome of this study, I aim

---

6   Certainly, the fact that pastors do not intentionally intend to create conflict doesn't mean that conflict and disagreement can be totally avoided among pastors. Many other factors can, and do, bring forth conflicts and disagreement, such as different perspectives, varying aspirations, different ways of doing things and cultural diversity.

RESEARCH QUESTIONS AND HYPOTHESES

to develop a number of effective approaches to help the pastors of the Chinese churches cope with their intercultural context. I also aim to equip the pastors with intercultural competence.[7] Hopefully, this initiative will reduce cross-cultural conflicts among pastors so that they can direct their energy and time towards the tasks of gospel proclamation, disciple-making and church development. This will allow pastoral ministry to become a joyful and pleasant vocation.

Value to other Chinese churches in Australia and other countries

Although this study is limited to Chinese churches in Sydney, the value and impact could be extended to other areas and regions. Similar inquiries could be performed in the Chinese churches of other cities and states in Australia. Some relational strategies could be borrowed and adapted by pastors of other Australian Chinese churches.

Moreover, it is noted that a similar phenomenon of conflict occurs in many Chinese churches in various Western nations,

---

[7] Preferably, pastors should receive cross-cultural training at college. However, it is noted that many pastors are inadequately trained in cross-cultural leadership and cultural competence at colleges. Some colleges in Sydney are implementing various ways to help students acquire some cross-cultural understanding. For example, one college in Sydney recruited experienced Chinese pastors to give a once-a-year one-day seminar for those students who intended to work in Chinese churches. The content covered Chinese church history, ministry strategies in Chinese churches and harmonious working relationships with senior pastors and senior members. However, this scheme transferred head knowledge with limited practical advice. Some colleges organise overseas or cross-cultural short-term trips for students. These experiences are helpful only if thoughtful debriefing is used after the trips. In the debriefing, students should be prompted by a well-trained facilitator, with perceptive and reflective questions for further investigation. However, it is noted that most of the post-trip debriefing is not fully utilised. I address these issues later in the book.

such as America, Canada, the United Kingdom and Europe. As Chinese diaspora are prominent in Western countries, it is certain that the Chinese churches there face similar situations and issues. Thus, the process and results of this study may be beneficial in those contexts also.

Value to other Asian churches in Sydney and Australia

The significance of this research may be even more extensive—beyond Chinese churches. As international and trans-regional migrants become prominent, it is anticipated that churches of various cultural backgrounds will increase in the coming decades. It is noted that there are many other Asian or language-based churches in Sydney and other parts of Australia, for example, Korean churches, Thai churches and Vietnamese churches. Between these Asian churches and the Chinese churches, there are likely to be similarities in cultural landscapes and cultural conflicts. Hence, the process and results of this research may provide certain insights and prompt similar inquiries in other Asian churches in Australia.[8]

Value to mission agencies

Outside the Chinese and Asian churches themselves, this research may have specific practical implications for overseas missions undertaken by Australian Chinese Christians and churches.

There are two branches of overseas mission: the mission field and the sending base. Before entering the mission field,

---

8   I am aware 'Asian churches' is a generic term referring to a variety of Asian regions, such as East Asia (Japan and Korea), South Asia (India and Sri Lanka), Southeast Asia (Singapore, Malaysia, the Philippines and Indonesia) and North Asia (China) (Yong, 'Review Essay').

most missionaries receive pre-mission cross-cultural training and orientation, preparing them to cope with and relate to the people of the country in question. However, the Chinese missionaries also have to relate to and work with fellow missionaries and team members from various generations and from diverse cultural backgrounds. A functional missionary team requires effective leadership, harmonious relationships, trustful communication and team development. Unfortunately, many Chinese missionaries direct their attention to the native people in mission fields and are inadequately prepared to adjust to fellow missionaries from different generations and unfamiliar cultural backgrounds. And they seldom acquire intercultural skills or the capacity to cope with and adjust to fellow missionaries. For example, they do not have the required level of English, which is essential in communicating with team members from other parts of the world. Thus, conflicts arise.

At the sending base, the home office in Australia generally sets up mission policies and guidelines for various aspects of mission: for organising the personnel who provide supervision and pastoral care, for organising orientation and training, and for the arrangement of 'home assignments' and retirement. Since mission agencies set up these policies and guidelines, they must consult with many missionaries from different generations and cultural backgrounds.[9] The policies and guidelines will be implemented on mission fields of various cultures. All these involve much cross-cultural communication, cross-cultural leadership, cultural sensitivity and language capability in order to avoid disagreements and arguments.

As mentioned, the need for assessing the intercultural competence of missionaries is tremendous. There is also a great

---

[9] For example, Chinese missionaries sent out from Australia might be of Chinese culture. They might also develop reverse cultural shock after many years overseas (Palmer, 'Issues', 1–4; Hawley, 'Research').

need for examining the factors behind conflicts and developing collaborative solutions. Hence, mission agencies could perform similar studies on intercultural competence among their missionaries and among their leaders at the mission base. It is believed that the results of this research would benefit the relevant parties in these mission agencies.

Value to theological education

Furthermore, seminaries and theological colleges may also benefit from this study. As the migrant population is increasing, the demand for ministry training of Chinese pastors also grows. Therefore, the intake of students in theological colleges becomes more and more multicultural and multinational. This research can benefit faculty members in such colleges. By doing self-assessment using Cultural Intelligence, faculty members may evaluate whether they are 'Asian literate' or 'Chinese literate'. In this regard, faculty members may need to adjust their way of relating to students who are in their twenties and thirties and have different cultural assumptions and expectations. The faculty might also conduct brainstorming sessions to uncover the factors shaping their CQ and to find ways of understanding the 'thought patterns' of the Chinese students. The faculty may become more aware that, because they are predominantly Westerners, the modes of lecturing and educating a significant number of Asian students may need to change. This might entail things like giving out more handouts and written materials or giving extra time to Chinese and other Asian students in order to provide them with individual guidance. Should seminaries and colleges perform Cultural Intelligence studies, their faculties' self-knowledge of Cultural Intelligence will improve, which in turn will develop the quality of their theological education.

RESEARCH QUESTIONS AND HYPOTHESES

In summary, my study of Cultural Intelligence in relation to pastors of Chinese churches in Sydney is likely to be valuable to the Chinese churches and other Asian churches in Sydney and in wider Australia. The study should also be beneficial to mission agencies and other ministry-related organisations such as theological institutions.

Limitations of the research

This study has profound value and significance. Nevertheless, there are a number of inevitable limitations. The first limitation relates to the sampling of this study. Due to the constraints of time and resources, this research could only study the pastors of Chinese churches in Sydney. Only eighty-five pastors (out of an estimated 150 pastors in Sydney) participated in the questionnaire survey, and twelve pastors participated in the interview component of the research. Geographically, the research did not extend to other major Australian cities or rural areas. As there is enormous research potential in other regions of Australia, this research could be regarded as a microcosmic paradigm, which may be later developed and extended into macrocosmic research in other cities in Australia.

The second limitation concerns the approach to data collection. The questionnaires and interviews in this study were based on self-reporting of the perspectives and assessments of the pastors. Although self-reported data may be regarded as subjective information, the data collected using such an approach allowed pastors to share their personal 'insider' voice.

The third limitation relates to the unique perspective of the researcher. The intention of this research is to enhance the Cultural Intelligence of the older pastors (baby boomers) and pastors of the younger generation (Generation X and Generation

Y).¹⁰ I am fully aware that I am a Chinese-speaking senior pastor from the baby boomer generation, with my personal doctrinal stance, worldview and ministry philosophy. My observational perspective and the thought patterns of my inquiry come from a senior pastor's stance. This can create certain biases and can impact the accuracy of the research. Therefore, I am always alert to my 'positionality', which involves 'insider/outsider predisposition',¹¹ and which might affect the data collection. Therefore, developing a trustful rapport with the pastors in the interviews was of primary importance.

The final limitation relates to the literature used in my research. Although this research was about the Chinese church, the works consulted in this study were largely published in English, not Chinese. Nevertheless, the literature about Chinese churches in Australia referred to in this study are of high quality and easily accessible, both online and in the libraries of local educational institutions.

---

10   I include only the Generation X and Generation Y but purposefully leave out Generation Z (or Centennials). This is because Generation Z is around twenty years old, which is regarded as too young to become a pastor. However, if a similar study is conducted in a few years' time, Generation Z pastors would have to be included.

11   Mohammad, "'Insiders'"; Vargas-Silva, *Handbook*, 118.

CHAPTER TWO
LITERATURE SURVEY AND ASSESSMENT

The purpose of this literature review is to inform my present research by identifying relevant issues in the proposed study and examining the research gaps. As the focus of this research is to understand the cultural competence of pastoral leaders in Chinese churches in Sydney, and as most of the pastors and leaders are primarily Chinese migrants and their succeeding generations, this literature review will set out by reviewing the works on migrants and migration.

The migrant experience

This section reviews the writings on the background of migrants, such as migrant history, migrant theories and migrant experiences.
  The world is undergoing a 'people on the move' phenomenon. Populations are moving from one country to another and moving from rural to urban areas. Migration has become a phenomenon too big to be neglected or ignored. A myriad of authors, representing multiple academic disciplines and interdisciplinary research, have provided an ocean of literature in the study of

international migration. In the last two decades, writers have noted the phenomenon of global transnational migration from various perspectives.

Research methodology and interdisciplinary approaches to migration studies

I begin with the research methodology of migration studies. Vargas-Silva introduces the major methodologies and research methods used in the area of international migration.[1] However, I note that the writers in this multi-author volume are mostly from North America and Europe, with very few Asian and African perspectives and no specific examples of Chinese migrants in the Australian context.

More and more researchers see migration as a multifaceted topic, and interdisciplinary approaches should be recognised as a trend in migration study.[2] Although many interdisciplinary researchers are within the spheres of political science, sociology and social science, they gradually expand to education, human science, psychology and history.[3]

Brettell and Hollifield have developed a theoretical ground for interdisciplinary dialogue on migration theories.[4] Their book outlines basic branches of research into migrant experience, such as history, demographics, economics, sociology, anthropology, geography, politics and law. The specific disciplines cover the major topic of migration with awareness of other disciplines, which results in a comprehensive theoretical orientation and overarching research questions for each discipline.

---

1   Vargas-Silva, *Handbook*.
2   Boswell and Mueser,'Introduction', 519–21; Messer et al., *Migrations*, 3–14; Schiavon, 'Migration Studies', 455–57.
3   Apitzsch and Siouti, 'Biographical Analysis, 6.
4   Brettell and Hollifield, *Migration Theory*, 2014.

LITERATURE SURVEY AND ASSESSMENT

Two initial observations are made here. Firstly, although many of the preceding authors claim that their studies are interdisciplinary, it is noted that the analytical focus tends to be predominantly economic. This orientation frequently shifts the discussion of migration towards the sovereign rights of countries to open or restrict border crossings, often revealing a movement into the disciplinary field of political science.

Secondly, the same books and articles mostly neglect the theoretical perspectives of certain disciplines, such as theology and religion. Theology and religion are the primary disciplines that frame my own research. Groody rightly points out that

> A theology of migration not only dialogues with other disciplines but integrates their findings into the overall task of faith seeking understanding in the modern world . . . Social science without theology does not give us a perspective wide enough to account for the deeper relational and spiritual dimensions of human life that shape, define, and sustain human existence—a fact that becomes more evident especially amid crisis and trial.[5]

Groody's works fill the theoretical gap from a theological perspective, laying a theological foundation for the discussion of migration.[6] Such theological perspectives provide the present discussion on migration with its primary orientation and framework.

---

5   Groody, 'Crossing the Divide', 664.
6   Groody and Campese, *Promised Land*, 3–86; Groody, 'Crossing the Divide', 642–64; Groody, 'Theology of Migration'. More literature on theological and religious frameworks are seen at section 3.1.7

Demographic investigation in migrant studies

Demographic and statistical evidence of migration provide data of age, gender, fertility and mortality within international and trans-regional people movements. Studies by the OECD (Organisation for Economic Co-operation and Development) and UN (United Nations) reveal the rising trend of migration in the United States, Australia and Europe. Studies also show trends in transnational migration, with focuses on impacts upon national economics, international refugees and asylum.[7] The International Migration Wall Chart 2015 provides an overview of migrant distribution, as well as age and gender.[8] A UN Web Services report also highlights the trends of intra-regional migration.[9] The data show preliminary explanatory factors and effects of migration, help in analysing the phenomenon and identify the issues arising from migration.[10]

The preceding discussion demonstrates, firstly, the fact that migration is no longer an exception but is a normal part of the modern world. Immigration is an unavoidable matter that every government, community and academic must attempt to address or respond to in some way.

Secondly, the statistics of Chinese migrants and Australian immigration are valuable to my research. These figures illustrate the significant social and cultural backgrounds, trends of migrant movements and varieties of origins of birth of Chinese migrants. The figures also show the complexity of human relationships and the multifaceted dimensions of intergenerational conflict.

---

7 UN-Department of Economic and Social Affairs 2013; UN Web Services Section 2016.
8 United Nations Population Division 2015.
9 UN Web Services Section 2016.
10 Bean and Stevens, *America's Newcomers*, 1–11.

Thirdly, it is noted that some Chinese migrants do not travel to Australia directly from China, Taiwan or Hong Kong. They may travel to Australia via intermediate countries; for example, some Chinese migrants travel to Vietnam, Indonesia, Malaysia and then to Australia. Many demographic studies appear to struggle in measuring such dimensions. These observations demonstrate that migration is more than just a movement from one point to another point (for example, China to Australia). The complicated, even miserable, stories behind the routes of migrants may affect the migrants' cultural identity and cultural adjustment or integration. This is certainly not easily revealed by statistical data.

Historical discussion in migrant studies

The historical study of migration helps to locate the discussion of migration in a chronological context.[11] From a historical-sociological perspective, Harzig and Hoerder depict the historical development of migration with reference to its economic, social and cultural impacts.[12] They particularly examine various theories and concepts that interpret the human transnational and trans-regional movements, such as gendered and racialised labour, refugee migration and migrants' social identities. These theories are helpful in understanding Chinese migration, migration in Australia and religious dimensions of migration.

Casiño provides a historical sketch of migration theories and models from the late nineteenth century onward, with emphasis on economic and labour-market theory.[13] Casiño's proactive and reactive migration model distinguishes between people who 'move-because-reasons' (cause or drive) and those who 'move-

---

11	Cohen, *Cambridge Survey*; Goldin et al., *Exceptional People*; Manning and Trimmer, *Migration*.
12	Harzig and Hoerder, *What is Migration History?*
13	Casiño, 'Why People Move'.

for-reasons' (motive or attraction). Although the discussion is not directly about Chinese migrants, the work provides a theoretical framework for understanding the process, dynamics and motives of Chinese migrants moving to Australia.

As a provisional remark, historical discussions on migration tend to take a more macroscopic perspective. These discussions assume a global view, focus on the world economy and discuss global migration policies. Such an approach only provides a generic overview of migrants and migration trends. A microscopic, historical discussion of individual migration is also necessary for any historical study of migration. For instance, biographical approaches as focused on individual migrants or specific people groups (such as younger, female, Vietnamese migrants at a certain period of time) are better able to describe the process of relocating cultural identity and struggles through a process of cultural integration.

Sociological perspectives on migrant studies

Sociological perspectives on migrant studies focus on two main areas: the causes (or determinants) of migration and the lived experiences of migrants. Both areas are expected to benefit and inform the background theories of this study.

Traditionally, researchers have noted that economy-related factors (livelihood, poverty, unemployment, welfare concerns and the labour market) are the main causes of migration.[14] Even the seminal work of Massey et al., which reviews a comprehensive range of models of factors influencing migration, locates the

---

14   Harris and Todaro, 'Migration, Unemployment'; McDowell and De Haan, *Sustainable Livelihoods*, 10–11; De Haan et al., 'Migration, Livelihoods' 54–56; Dustmann and Preston, 'Racial and Economic Factors', 26–27; Hagen-Zanker, 'Why Do People Migrate', 6–16.

economy (or market economic relations) as the main focus of conceptualisation.[15]

However, as humans are holistic beings, human activities are not just shaped by the economy. Research on causes of migration extends beyond economic-related factors, including such dimensions as racism,[16] social networks and social capital.[17]

Studies of social network and social capital are helpful to this research. It is noted that some Chinese migrants in Sydney use Chinese churches as platforms for social networking or as a social haven.[18] In this regard, Chinese churches are more than just a place of worship and spiritual growth, but also provide a significant relational network or a web of friends of similar culture and language. Such a social network enhances social capital (such as job opportunities and survival skills), especially in the early stages of migration.

Apart from identifying causes of migration, sociological studies also inform perspectives on the lived experience of migrants, in particular, the factors shaping their assimilation and integration. Two groups of theories are distinguished by researchers. The first group relates to external factors, such as government policy,[19] citizenship status, political acceptance (or disadvantage) by the host country and cultural distance.[20] The second group relates to internal factors, such as the motivations of migrants and their incentive to integrate into the host society.[21]

---

15   Massey et al., 'Theories', 463.
16   Dustmann and Preston, 'Racial and Economic Factors', 20–23.
17   Haug, 'Migration Networks', 585–87.
18   This could be related to one of the characteristics of Chinese traditional culture, namely, *guanxi*, which means connection or relation (Matthews, 'Chinese Value Survey', 118).
19   Fargues, 'Imigration without Inclusion', 275–80.
20   Adida, 'Too Close', 1389–90; Bean et al., 'Unauthorized', 28–30.
21   Adida, 'Too Close', 1374–75.

However, I note that external factors and internal factors are in fact interrelated. For example, illegal status often induces high levels of anxiety and avoidance, which result in slower rates of socio-economic integration.[22]

Research shows that Asian and Chinese migrants focus on the education and professions of their second generation and see these as efficient ways of climbing up the social ladder. These accelerate the rate of social assimilation.[23] Moreover, the cultural distance 'gap' reported in the two-generation migrant families creates difficult family dynamics and cultural tensions within the community.[24] This leads to the confusion of cultural identity and difficulty in cross-cultural integration.[25]

Mohammad opens a new perspective in the study of lived experiences of migrants by suggesting the researcher's positioning: as either insider or outsider.[26] She suggests a notion of 'between-ness' to describe the researcher's flexible status as both insider and outsider. For example, she describes herself as 'a British, Pakistani Muslim (by birth), but non-practising and non-believing, a little Marxist, somewhat feminist, of middle working-class origins'.[27] Such a background could make her an insider to some, while an outsider to others. This prompts every researcher to be highly alert to their status and relationship with the subjects of their research, as the status of being 'insider/outsider' will impact the quality and the depth of study. The social proximity or cultural distance of relationship between the researcher and the research subjects may affect whether the research subjects

---

22 Bean et al., 'Unauthorized', 2–3.
23 Zhou, 'Segmented Assimilation', 977–78; Zinzius, *Chinese America*, 153–201.
24 The term 'two-generation families' denotes the two generations of family members, namely the migrant generation and the descendent generation.
25 Tung, *Chinese Americans*, 23–59.
26 Mohammad, '"Insiders"'.
27 Ibid., 107.

trust the researcher, especially in qualitative research exploring sensitive issues. This relational distance affects the quantity and quality of information collected by the researchers. This is particularly relevant to the manner and design of my later interview research.

Thus, researchers employ different trajectories for self-reporting in social studies, and the advantages of the self-reporting method are noted.[28] For instance, Paulhus and Vazire suggest that self-reporting methods bring forth certain advantages in research, such as 'easy interpretability, richness of information, motivation to report, causal force, and sheer practicality'.[29] This is helpful in understanding the insider perspective of the migrants' lived experiences.

Another study by Austin et al. indicates 'a positive association between self-assessment and reflection-in-action', concluding that there are direct 'associations between self-assessment, reflection, and critical thinking'.[30] In other words, it is logical for me to employ an approach of self-assessment in my study, an approach that may possibly improve the research subjects' reflection of their cultural identity, cultural integration and intercultural interaction.[31]

This group of sociological studies provides perspectives on the lived experience and social integration of migrants. The studies reveal the upward and downward assimilation of migrants, which is shaped by both internal factors (incentive and family structure) and external factors (racial stratification

---

28 Paulhus and Vazire, 'Self-Report Method'; Austin et al., 'Use of Reflection'.
29 Paulhus and Vazire, 'Self-Report Method', 227.
30 Austin et al., 'Use of Reflection', 48.
31 This is a helpful insight for my later discussion about insufficient reflection of the pastors in Chinese churches, derived from research findings. See chapter 5.

and economic opportunities). These are helpful in understanding migrants' lived experiences and their degree of assimilation.

Anthropological approaches to migrant studies

Anthropological studies contribute to the migrant discussion from an ethnographical perspective. Both Jackson and Horton give attention to migrant subjectivities and cultural identity.[32] Jackson examines the struggles and perplexity of African migrants residing in south-east London. The study shows the subjects' confusion of cultural identity and their profound sense of disconnectedness with their homeland. Horton conducts a phenomenological study on the perplexity of transnational, undocumented migrant mothers: 'I work here but my heart lies there' precisely unveils the 'torn-between' cultural identity and isolated social role of these transnational mothers.[33] These articles identify factors shaping migrants' cultural identity. In both articles, the migrants' basic longings for security and stability have been unmet and their survival is being jeopardised. Their experience of vulnerability and anguish are of tremendous impact on their cultural identity and cultural integration.

Geographical investigation in migrant studies

From a geographic perspective, Nowicka investigates the issue of return migration with special attention paid to the notion of 'home' for highly mobile professionals. His finding is that mobile professionals understand home not as a fixed location but as a heterogeneous network of relationships.[34]

---

[32] Jackson, 'Shock of the New'; Horton, 'Mother's Heart'.
[33] Horton, 'Mother's Heart', 21–22.
[34] Nowicka, 'Mobile Locations', 5–7.

As an interim reflection, highly mobile professionals might consider a 'network of relationship' to be a replacement for a fixed location or home. However, adopting a 'network of relationship' as home requires long-term, stable relationships. If migrants have high mobility across a short period of time, relationships cannot be established, maintained and developed. The sense of home cannot be easily achieved.

Moreover, in relation to this study, most of the professional Chinese migrants to Sydney are in their thirties or forties. Employment and professional development, rather than relationship building, remain the prior developmental tasks of middle-aged people. To this extent, the attainability of 'network of relationship' remains uncertain. Equally, high levels of mobility mean moving from one location to another, leaving the negotiation of cultural identity in a new community as a low priority. They are unlikely to achieve satisfactory levels of cultural integration.

Theological/ecclesiological perspectives on migration

Jackson and Passarelli add an ecclesiological and theological angle to the discussion of migration.[35] They depict and explore the phenomenon of European migration, with a special focus on the degree of the migrants' social inclusion, integration and belonging. They also provide a sociological and theological analysis of migration. With such a foundation, Jackson and Passarelli investigate the response of churches to migration and assess the effect on migrants.[36] Their work establishes a paradigm of engagement with, and dialogue between, migration and

---

35 Jackson and Passarelli, *Mapping Migration*.
36 Ibid., 31–46.

ecclesiology. Their work also shows that the church may serve as a community fostering social inclusion and building a sense of belonging, which leads to new migrants negotiating individual cultural identity.

From a Christian perspective, Conde-Frazier and Lee study the notion of the 'pain of lament' in Hispanic and Asian migrants.[37] The pain 'leads to a life of double marginalisation, being accepted neither in America nor in their own homeland'.[38] In view of this, Groody draws attention to the mission of the church. 'Reducing people to their legal or political status not only denies dignity to those in need but also dehumanises those who have the opportunity to help'.[39]

The role of the church is to walk alongside the migrants as they struggle with identity confusion and the lack of language expressing for their internal emotions.

Christian churches typically search for a theological framework and for biblical guidance in their engagement with vulnerable migrants. Writers from an Asian church background provide a range of biblical and theological reflections, focusing on themes such as hope and church unity.[40] The collection of essays edited by Padilla reviews various contemporary issues of migration from a theological perspective.[41] Key to the discussion are notions of justice and fairness, and the discussion takes place against a backdrop of socio-economic abuse of migrants. Although the book is clearly written from an American background and perspective, the discussion's framework and conclusion shed light on Australian ecclesiology.

37　Conde-Frazier and Lee, 'Intergenerational and Intercultural Issues', 69.
38　Ibid., 67.
39　Groody, 'Crossing the Divide', 666.
40　Cha et al., *Ministry Insights*, 145–63, 183–200; Cha, 'Building', 28–29.
41　Padilla and Phan, *Contemporary Issues*, 157–77, 211–31.

LITERATURE SURVEY AND ASSESSMENT

My review of literature constantly reveals a common thread, namely the significant contribution of interdisciplinary study. Migration is an issue related to demography, history, sociology, anthropology, economy and theology. The exploration of migration reveals the complexity and multifaceted nature of the issue. It requires a collaborative effort by academics from all the disciplines mentioned. These writings provide a theoretical foundation for this study. However, the bulk of studies are from a North American or European perspective. Comparatively, Asian and Chinese contributions are far fewer. Even though some researchers write from an Asian church background, not many of them give attention to the migration of Chinese Christians and to Chinese churches. My work modestly attempts to address this omission.

The literature provides wide knowledge and valuable analysis of the migration phenomenon and the migrant narrative. However, most of the works lack the migrants' self-disclosure and self-articulation. Migrants are objects of study rather than subjects forming part of the exploration. Yet, the 'insider' voice and personal perspective are indispensable in the course of study. The work of Jackson and Passarelli and Conde-Frazier and Lee are two exceptions that offer migrants' 'insider' voices.[42] Nevertheless, the voice is not the voice of Chinese Christian migrants in Australia.

Furthermore, if the church has a role in helping migrants in cultural assimilation and integration, two prerequisites for church leaders are implied. Firstly, language proficiency is essential in communicating and engaging with migrants. Pastors of Chinese churches may be encouraged to learn English and pastors of local churches encouraged to acquire some Chinese.

---

42 Jackson and Passarelli, *Mapping Migration*, 115–22; Conde-Frazier and Lee, 'Intergenerational and Intercultural Issues', 16, 98.

Secondly, the Chinese pastors, as church leaders, should practise and demonstrate cultural assimilation before they can give guidance and advice to migrants.

The historical and social experience of Chinese migration in Australia

This section of the literature review focuses on Chinese migration in Australia, with special reference to their historical and social experiences.

Host cultural context of migration

The phenomenon of Australian migration is greatly determined by government multicultural policy. From the perspective of a political scientist, Jupp critically compares the immigration policies (variously incorporating multicultural policy, economic rationalism and the intake of refugees and asylum seekers) of governments over three decades since 1972.[43]

Kasper contends that the sustainability of immigration cannot be disconnected from the notion of cultural integration, whereas multiculturalism assumes non-integration. Therefore, he argues, the policy of multiculturalism should be abandoned.[44] He further argues that the intake of migrants, particularly Asian migrants, must be regulated, without segregated communities.

Apart from migration policy, myriad works discuss the social context of migrants. Guerra and White investigate the social contexts of ethnic minority youth in Australia.[45] They discuss the notions of social justice, ethnicity, equity, sports and

---

43 Jupp, *White Australia*, 61–122.
44 Kasper, *Sustainable Immigration*, 23–34.
45 Guerra and White, *Ethnic Minority*, 13–67.

LITERATURE SURVEY AND ASSESSMENT

human rights, through examining ethnic youth as a group within the institutions, welfare systems, processes and structures of Australian society. Cox outlines the vulnerability of migrants by providing an extensive account of welfare policy formulation and service provision.[46] From an interdisciplinary approach, Burnley's collection examines the social life (education, health and the mass media) of non-Anglo ethnic migrants in Australia.[47]

The preceding authors adopt the perspective of politics, policies and social systems. Their works outline and analyse the historical and social experience of Chinese migrants in Australia and Sydney. They provide an overall picture of the process of social adjustment and obstacles to the cultural integration of Chinese migrants in general and Chinese youth in particular. These writings provide a helpful background context for my study.

White and White provide a phenomenological discussion of the mass media, particularly the printed press, in the years between 1935 and 1977.[48] Their study reveals how migrants were 'stereotyped' in the mass circulation press in Australia. It also examines the tendency towards the use of negative connotative language and labelling by the press. This discussion explains the public's general disapproving perception of migrants, particularly of non-Anglo-Saxon groups. Mass media usually reflects and shapes popular opinion in society. It negatively portrays non-European migrants and reinforces the status quo of majority social groups. It also implicitly and indirectly reflects the difficulties and hindrances to the survival and cultural adjustment of Asian and Chinese migrants. Although White and White's work presents what was happening several decades ago, similar trends exist, to some extent, in today's Australian society.

---

46   Cox, *Migration and Welfare*, 103–78.
47   Burnley, *Impact*, 258–97.
48   White and White, *Immigrants and the Media*.

In other words, Asian and Chinese migrants continue to live in an unfavourable social and cultural context.

The implications for my study are tremendous. If the pastors in Chinese churches have to disciple church members in such a context of complexity, it is obvious that one must consider the degree to which hostile attitudes impact the negotiation of cultural identity and the cultural integration of Chinese pastors. The unfavourable environment might also lower pastors' levels of incentive, willingness and determination to integrate culturally.

Lived experiences of migrants in Australia

Lived experiences as recounted by the migrants themselves always provide insider perspectives on the migrants. A number of studies portray and explore various dimensions of lived experiences of Chinese migrants in Australia, such as language, religion, education, family and employment.[49] Hammerton and Richards collect oral history and personal stories spoken by Australian migrants.[50] The book explores 'sensitive' or painful subject matter within the experience of Australian migration, such as gender issues and memories of the Holocaust.

The ethnological study of Travaglia et al. explores the migrant experience of the second generation of non-Anglo-Saxon immigrant women.[51] The work demonstrates the struggles and agony of living between two cultures, the host culture and the homeland culture—an aspect of lived experiences seldom fully comprehended by non-migrants.

Some books focus on specific ethnic groups. Cresciani traces the historical development and cultural uniqueness of the

---

49 Coughlan and McNamara, *Asians in Australia*, 120–70; Pung, *Growing up Asian*, 7–9, 15–21, 133–40, 159–66.
50 Hammerton and Richards, *Speaking to Immigrants*.
51 Travaglia et al., *Who Do You Think You Are?*

LITERATURE SURVEY AND ASSESSMENT

Italian migrant community in Australia, with special emphasis on Italian family relationships.[52] Viviani extensively maps the resilience and perseverance of Vietnamese migrants and refugees in Australia.[53]

This body of work, focussed on the stories of migrants in Australia, provides an extensive and profound description of the Chinese migrants' determination and struggle to adjust and adapt to the new country. Many of these internal thoughts, unspoken yearnings and deep-seated aspirations are not easy to disclose to Caucasians, who are of different appearance, language and culture. In other words, the Chinese migrants' insider voices and agony are seldom heard and detected by people from the mainline society. That is why this current study, which largely investigates the self-disclosure of Chinese migrants' living experiences, has the potential to make a valuable, though modest, contribution to the literature.

Lived experiences of Chinese migrants in Australia

A few studies focus on the first Chinese settlement in Australia in the mid-nineteenth century. Quaife provides a historical account of the social situation of the first Chinese miners at Ballarat, Victoria, at the time of the gold rush.[54] Choi provides a detailed and comprehensive historical account of Chinese migrants and settlement in Australia.[55] McGowan's work focuses on the difficult lives of Chinese miners/migrants in the Riverina region of New South Wales from 1860 to 1960.[56] Hon and Coughlan identify the socio-demographic and economic characteristics

---

52   Cresciani, *Italians*, 97–179.
53   Viviani, *Long Journey*, 157–275.
54   Quaife, *Gold*.
55   Choi, 'Chinese Migration and Settlement', 48–78.
56   McGowan, 'Transnational Lives', 47–62.

of early Chinese immigrants.[57] The collection of studies reveals how the disadvantaged early Chinese settlers (most of the time under the White Australia policy) exercised resilience in the face of immigration restrictions and how the public animosity continued.

A study by Burnley explores the impact of immigration by examining economic and socio-demographic factors, encompassing both metropolitan and rural Australia.[58] In particular, Burnley explores the cultural differences between Chinese and Australians by extensively detailing aspects of Chinese business services, local Chinese newspapers, areas of settlement, language variations and even Chinese churches. It gives an on-the-spot depiction of the lived experience of pre-1960s Chinese migrants.[59]

Kamp reveals an alternative account of the lived experiences of Chinese women from the White Australia period to the multicultural era and unveils the struggles of Chinese women migrants.[60]

Chinese migrants do not struggle only in the first years of migration. They have to search and negotiate their identity as well. Shen gives a historical account of Chinese-Australian migrants by examining archived documents and reconstructing the cultural identity of both the first-generation Chinese migrants and the second-generation Australian-born Chinese, tracing their painful search for cultural identity.[61]

Newspaper records are a valuable source for unearthing the Chinese migrants' lived experience. In an article titled 'We're All Aussies Now', Stubbings reports the mixed experiences of

---

57   Ho and Coughlan, 'Chinese in Australia', 120–70.
58   Burnley, *Impact*.
59   Ibid., 272–82.
60   Kamp, 'Chinese Australian Women', 78–97.
61   Shen, *Dragon Seed*, 108–50.

LITERATURE SURVEY AND ASSESSMENT

migrants, a mixture of negative feelings (loneliness, hostility, isolation and bewilderment) and positive feelings (excitement, challenges and opportunities).[62]

Stone observes the change of cultural identity in the second generation of Chinese migrants.[63] It is a longitudinal report, covering the different stages of life, beginning with the subjects' desire to dump their parents' history and ending with a treasuring of their parents' past and homeland. As the second generation are bilingual and accept their parents' cultural values, they are more advantaged in helping Australia move towards multiculturalism. This is particularly valuable in understanding the inner world of second-generation migrants and their subsequent descendants.

Finally, Tan adopts a form of graphic novel to display the uncertainty and anxiety of new migrants.[64] Tan narrates the inner world of a newly arrived and lonely migrant on foreign, unknown soil. In an artistic form, Tan provides a complementary contribution to the vast array of works on migration.

As an interim conclusion of the preceding review demonstrates, the literature surveyed contributes considerable richness and depth from historical and sociological perspectives. The literature also supplements our understanding of the factors underlying cultural assimilation, cultural adjustment and cultural integration. Furthermore, the works show the variety and the range of genres in migrant studies.

However, it is noted that Chinese Christians and Chinese churches are largely absent from the literature. Chinese Christians are also unrepresented as authors of studies. Furthermore, Chinese churches are rarely the focus of inquiry. The paucity of theoretical/empirical research and theological study in this

---

62 Stubbings, 'We're All Aussies Now'.
63 Stone, 'Second Generation'.
64 Tan, *Arrival*.

area constitutes a gap in academic studies, especially from the perspective of Chinese pastors. This deficiency is further reflected in the fact that the study of Chinese Christians and Chinese churches is seldom found in the 'suggestions for future research' section of journal articles. In other words, the study of Chinese Christians and Chinese churches is absent from the agenda of academic research. Because of the absence of candid accounts of Chinese Christian church experiences and the shortage of theoretical analyses of the complex situations, the real problems underlying Chinese Christians and Chinese churches are yet to be fathomed.

Specifically, certain aspects of migrant studies are deficient or missing. Firstly, most of the studies explore and examine the *inter*relationships between the host culture and the migrants' home culture. However, studies on *intra*relationships among migrants, specifically the intergenerational relational dynamics of migrants, hardly appear. With the number of migrants reaching a critical mass, the need to address this gap is urgent. If the migrants do not see the need for cultural assimilation to the host country, they might retreat back to their cultural ghettos, such as community groups or Chinese churches.

The second aspect is closely related to the first. There are some studies on second-generation migrants, specifically their lived experiences and cultural assimilation. However, we are in great need of studies that examine intergenerational relationships among migrants and their interrelational dynamics with respect to cultural differences.

Thirdly, there are studies on cultural assimilation of migrants, and English language learning (reading, writing, listening and speaking) is a significant part of cultural assimilation. However, studies on the elements and process of language learning among various generational groups of Chinese migrants are largely missing.

Lastly, we usually assume migrants (naturally) undergo cultural assimilation once they touch down on Australian soil. Although studies reveal various factors and determinants of cultural assimilation, the literature unconsciously neglects the extent to which the intercultural competence of migrants may impact the process of their cultural assimilation. It may be because many writings subtly assume that all migrants have the same intercultural competence, disregarding the cultural distance between the host culture and the migrants' home culture.

Cultural identity and cultural hybridity

Multiculturalism

Multiculturalism became official policy in Australia in the mid-1970s as Australia abandoned its White Australia policy. Multiculturalism has shaped social policy and informed the political debate in Australia over the intervening decades.

It is important to note, however, that there are many forms of multiculturalism. McLaren distinguishes three basic forms of multiculturalism: conservative multiculturalism, liberal multiculturalism and left-liberal multiculturalism.[65] Following an alternative line of analysis, Ivison, an Australian scholar, proposes three logics of multiculturalism: protective or communitarian multiculturalism, liberal multiculturalism and imperial multiculturalism.[66] Crowder, who is also an Australian writer, outlines a liberal and value pluralist approach to cultural

---

65 McLaren, 'White Terror', 47–52.
66 Ivison, *Multiculturalism*, 2–5.

diversity, approaches underlined by a strong emphasis on personal autonomy.[67]

Primarily, multiculturalism is a study within the sphere of political science. Zubrzycki traces the historical development of multiculturalism in Australia as government policy.[68] Jupp also outlines the stages of the implementation of multiculturalism policies in Australia, highlighting the political and social implications of the term 'multiculturalism' in different periods.[69] In general, the term emphasises and informs the equality of political and social opportunities for ethnic and cultural minorities. Hence, the policy implies the retention of settlers' ethnic identity, the rejection of cultural assimilation and the denial of cultural conformity to Anglo-Saxon superiority and cultural patterns.[70]

In a multicultural community, certain cultural changes can be expected. Lewins distinguishes two approaches to cultural change: cultural assimilation and cultural integration. Cultural assimilation stresses cultural accommodation toward the dominant group, while cultural integration emphasises mutual change.[71] Lewins points out that within academic circles and political circles in Australia, integration is preferred to assimilation. However, inconsistency occurs in social circles (such as education systems, trade unions and churches) where migrants are excluded from positions of influence.[72]

It is noted that multiculturalism has become a contested notion. It is controversial not only at a theoretical discussion in the academic arena but also because multiculturalism is usually

---

67   Crowder, *Theories*, 191–208.
68   Zubrzycki, 'Multicultural Australia', 128–30.
69   Jupp, 'Politics'.
70   Zubrzycki, 'Multicultural Australia', 129.
71   Lewins, 'Assimilation and Integration'. 857–58.
72   Ibid., 858–60.

appreciated by minority groups and criticised by the people from the host community, especially in view of increasing fears concerning terrorism and Muslim migration.[73] Various critiques have been raised against multiculturalism. For example, some criticise multiculturalism policies on the grounds that they have been created by political elites rather than by general public demand.[74] Other cited criticisms are that it undermines national cohesion, diminishes collective identity,[75] betrays Western civilisation,[76] and results in a movement towards ethical and cognitive relativism.[77]

Multiculturalism is, by and large, framed by academic dialogue surrounding political theory and by discussion in the arena of politics (in terms of policy making and funding). This dialogue contributes little to mutual cultural integration and cultural dialogue, which sit primarily within the discipline of cultural theory. Also, multiculturalism does not necessarily promote a spirit of collaboration towards relating to people who are of different cultural backgrounds and worldviews.[78]

In the discussion of multiculturalism, language education remains an important dimension.[79] In a multicultural society, notes Kymlicka, 'a common language has often been seen as essential if all citizens are to have equal opportunity to work in this modern economy . . . a common language has been seen as essential to democracy—how can 'the people' govern

---

73 Ivison, *Multiculturalism*, 14–15.
74 Crowder, *Theories*, 4.
75 Ibid.
76 Huntington, *Clash of Civilizations*.
77 Bloom, *American Mind*.
78 The discussion by Zubrzycki and Lewins demonstrates the relative inability of the concept of multiculturalism to aid our understanding of cultural identity and of the cultural integration of individual migrants. That is why cultural hybridity is required as an essential notion in the related discussion.
79 Clyne, 'Language Policy'; Smolicz, 'Cultural Diversity'.

together if they cannot understand one another?'[80] Having a common language does not exclude bilingual education. In fact, bilingual education is frequently affirmed as a basic element of multiculturalism.[81] According to Smolicz, bilingualism with English as the mainstream language and another language as community language has helped to maintain the stability of implementing multiculturalism in Australia.[82] In other words, practising multiculturalism does not rule out the learning of English. On the contrary, the acquisition of English provides a common communication tool and is, therefore, essential in maintaining societal cohesiveness and national unity.[83]

In a multicultural society, it is important to understand the identity of the individual, especially the individuals of minority groups. Research shows that multiculturalism provides 'a vehicle to define migrants' national identity' and is 'a response to majority nation-building'.[84] According to Kymlicka, multicultural nation-building usually 'promotes a sense of common national identity and membership'.[85] However, although multiculturalism may contribute to an individual's political identity, 'one's political identity does not yet strongly engage the dominant social and ideological cleavages in American politics'.[86]

Another related dimension concerns the further development of views concerning cultural diversity in a multicultural society. As noted by Smolicz, some have maintained a separatist view that 'ethnic groups should remain as a self-

---

80   Kymlicka, 'Liberal Theories', 240.
81   Crowder, *Theories*, 3.
82   Smolicz, 'Cultural Diversity', 870–71.
83   According to the later research findings, deficiency of English is one of three main factors that causes intergenerational conflicts in Chinese churches of Sydney.
84   Ivison, *Multiculturalism*, 203, 228.
85   Kymlicka, 'Liberal Theories', 240.
86   Citrin et al., 'Multiculturalism', 272.

LITERATURE SURVEY AND ASSESSMENT

contained enclave encrusted within its own value system'.[87] Such a separatist view is incompatible with multiculturalism, as minority cultures cannot merely be conserved; they will experience cultural development and change. In other words, practising multiculturalism or cultural diversity does not mean culture (whether mainstream nor minority) is static or unchanged. Rather cultures (both mainstream and minority) are transitional, developing and evolving.[88]

In summary, non-English speaking migrants have broadly welcomed the inception and implementation of multiculturalism policies in Australia, because those policies help to ensure justice and civil rights in all walks of life. Multicultural policies promote diversity, mutual respect, freedom, tolerance and the co-existence of minority ethnic groups. They also acknowledge and appreciate, to a certain extent, the cultural and economic contribution made by ethnic and cultural minority groups to the Australian society at large.

However, as mentioned earlier, multiculturalism is basically a discipline of political science. Although multiculturalism nurtures national and political identity, it does not ensure cultural identity. In terms of policy, the implementation of multiculturalism in Australia shows signs of non-engagement, social fragmentation and even separatism, where people of different cultural backgrounds do not interact and cooperate. It is, therefore, necessary to move on to review literature dealing with cultural identity and cultural hybridity.

---

87   Smolicz, 'Cultural Diversity', 872.
88   This evolving or transitional dimension of culture is congruent with the concept of cultural hybridity. This explains why the discussion of cultural hybridity complements multiculturalism to a great extent.

Cultural identity

As the primary focus of this study is the cultural dimensions of two-generation conflict within the Chinese church, this section of the literature review will examine studies of cultural identity and cultural hybridity among Chinese migrants.

Schwartz et al. state that, at some stage of life, every individual will ask a question: 'Who am I?' The answer to this question should define the scope of identity. Through the self-search journey, a self-view or identity is formulated. This notion of identity refers to both the individual persona and collective distinctiveness.[89] Moreover, instead of one single identity, many individuals have multiple identities, such as a developmental, a relational and social, a self-perceived, a moral, a spiritual, a gender, an occupational, an ethnic, a cultural and a national identity.[90]

Methodology may determine the quality and accuracy of cultural identity studies. It is noted that disadvantages of self-reporting emerge (such as overlooking important variability that exists within groups). Identity studies have moved towards multifaceted models informed by one's orientation and attachment towards one's ethnic heritage.[91] Nevertheless, the self-reporting approach is still used by some researchers,[92] as the insider voice is valuable in understanding deeper meanings. Thus, some researchers may see the benefits of both approaches, and employ both *self*-assessment approaches and *other*-assessment approaches in their research.[93]

---

89 Schwartz et al., *Handbook*, 2–4.
90 Ibid.
91 Phinney, 'When We Talk', 920; Umaña-Taylor, 'Ethnic Identity', 792.
92 Atkinson and Gim, 'Asian-American Cultural Identity', 209–10; Schwartz et al. 'Structure of Cultural Identity', 159–61; Morris et al., 'Cultural Identity Threat', 763.
93 Ibrahim and Heuer, *Cultural and Social*.

LITERATURE SURVEY AND ASSESSMENT

Two groups of literature on cultural identity are noted. The first group of works conceptualises the formation of cultural identity. The second group of writings identifies cultural values or cultural dimensions.

Conceptual formation of cultural identity

Identifying components and elements shaping cultural identity is a chief focus in studies that conceptualise cultural identity. Ibrahim and Heuer highlight ethnicity, age, gender, cultural background, language, spirituality, social class and family as the main components of cultural identity.[94] Alternatively, Jones divides components of cultural identity into two main groups, namely core components (for example, race, sexual orientation and religion) and contextual components (for example, family background and life experiences).[95] Schwartz et al. take a different trajectory and seek to formulate a structure of factors in three dimensions (American-culture identity, heritage-culture identity and biculturalism) in the United States.[96]

These attempts are helpful in understanding the multifaceted cultural identity of migrants. However, research on migrants of specific ethnicities in North America (such as Asian, Hispanic, etc.) might implicitly or unconsciously assume that cultural identity of various ethnic migrants is stable and permanent.[97] Hall questions if such a unified, fixed and permanent identity exists in the postmodern world at all.[98] He argues that cultural identity is a 'moveable feast' and is 'becoming fragmented and

---

94 Ibid., chapter 2.
95 Jones and McEwen, 'Conceptual Model', 408–10.
96 Schwartz et al. 'Structure of Cultural Identity', 162.
97 Atkinson and Gim, 'Asian-American Cultural Identity', 210–11; Hong et al., 'Cultural Identity'.
98 Hall, 'Cultural Identity and Diaspora', 1992, 275–77.

composed of several contradictory identities'.[99] Elsewhere, Hall suggests that cultural identity is a matter of 'becoming' as well as of 'being'.[100] This notion of 'becoming', or the fluidity of identity, is particularly relevant to the issue of cultural hybridity and the discussion that follows about the cultural identity of first-generation Chinese migrant pastors and, even more significantly, second-generation, Australian-born Chinese pastors. They could not be labelled as a distinct, homogenous cultural group. Instead, there are many factors contributing to their search for cultural identity, and different pastors develop diverse identities—a core idea of the concept of cultural hybridity.

Some researchers also recognise the changeable and transitory nature of cultural identity and attempt to conceptualise factors in the transitional process of cultural identity.[101] These findings are particularly helpful in locating the cultural identity of second-generation migrants in my own research.

Some researchers have investigated cultural transition within both the migrant group and the host culture group. Morris et al. investigate the cultural transition of the host culture group by studying the degree of their receptiveness (or rejection) of the migrant group.[102] Sussman explores migrant groups (or cultural minority groups) with special attention to the self-concept, cultural identity and cultural transition of the migrants.[103] Jensen et al. direct their attention to adolescents and emerging adults within the migrant community.[104] They particularly highlight adolescents' cultural identity confusion as well as the cultural

---

99 Hall, 'Question of Cultural Identity', 1996, 598.
100 Hall, 'Cultural Identity and Diaspora', 225.
101 Sussman, 'Dynamic Nature', 362–69; Morris et al., 'Cultural Identity Threat', 766–69; Jensen et al., 'Globalization', 285–301.
102 Morris et al., 'Cultural Identity Threat'.
103 Sussman, 'Dynamic Nature', 362–69.
104 Jensen et al., 'Globalization', 296–97.

gap between immigrant adolescents (autonomy) and parents (authority) and the derived emotions such as resentment and conflict.

The preceding writings outline the components of self-identity, the changeability of identity and the factors of identity formation. Bottomley focuses on the relation between the migrant group and the host society by discussing the interconnection and interaction between the two groups.[105] She highlights gender, family, age, language, class, ethnicity and habitus as factors in the formation of cultural identity.

Kim also discusses the inter-dynamics between hosts and migrants, specifically the theories of the process and dynamics of cultural assimilation and cross-cultural adaption.[106] The listed axioms and theorems of the inter-dynamics of the host and ethnic groups highlight the importance of and modes of communication.[107]

Tan and Ang add to the discussion from an Asian perspective and give special attention to the notion of race.[108] Ang notes the process of locating cultural identity as a process of interrogation and negotiation within the tension of experience and the salience of race.[109] Tan's research shows that the Chinese race and face are dominating factors in cultural identity formation for Chinese in Australia, even up to the third and fourth generations.[110]

Such a perspective offers the migrant certain insights into the shaping and locating of their cultural identity. These studies point to factors of cultural identity within the host culture group and the migrants, and their connectedness. Tan and Ang's

---

[105] Bottomley, *From Another Place*, 1992.
[106] Kim, *Becoming Intercultural*, 45–95.
[107] Ibid., 88–92.
[108] Ang, 'Can One Say No to Chineseness?'; Tan, '"Tyranny of Appearance"'.
[109] Ang, 'Can One Say No to Chineseness?'
[110] Tan, '"Tyranny of Appearance"'.

writings highlight the extent of the impact of two major factors for negotiating identity, namely 'Asian families' and 'Asian faces'. 'Asian family' relates to the impact of traditional Asian or Chinese culture. 'Asian face' relates to appearance and colour. These two factors might increase the difficulties faced by the younger generation of migrants in their search for a new cultural identity. In turn, the younger generation may feel inferior and lack confidence during their developmental years. In my research, I consider the interactive dynamics of the pastors with the local population. I also give special attention to the dynamics between the first and second generations of the pastors in Chinese churches.

Cultural values

Studying cultural values is a prominent research approach in locating cultural identity. The work of Trompenaars and Hampden-Turner is primarily for the business world.[111] They identify five dimensions of cultural values: universalism versus particularism, individualism versus communitarianism, neutral versus affective, diffuse versus specific and achievement versus ascription.[112] In Trompenaars' work, only implications in international business and global leadership are discussed; implications for ethnicity and inter-generations are not covered. Although Trompenaars' five dimensions are not based on empirical research, the categorisation of cultural values is valuable.

Also focused on global business, and based on research of national culture in more than seventy countries and regions, is the work of Hofstede et al., which summarises six pairs of

---

111   Trompenaars and Hampden-Turner, *Riding the Waves*.
112   Ibid., 39.

cultural values.[113] In view of Hofstede's all-inclusive research of many countries, a group of researchers from the Chinese Culture Connection were concerned that the dimensions of cultural values in Hofstede's study were (Western) culture-bound.[114] They conducted another study to complement Hofstede's research, and the results have subsequently been included in Hofstede's revised edition.[115]

The cultural values identified in the preceding works are relatively specific to the business executives of various countries and regions. Matthews identifies Confucianism as the foundation of cultural values of the ethnically Chinese-background students in Australian universities, such as *guanxi* (meaning the sense of connection, network or relation);[116] 'Confucian values remain intact today in spite of, or despite, attempts to discredit his teachings'.[117] His careful study provides helpful information on the cultural values of Chinese in Australia for my own research. These cultural values among traditional Chinese are echoed by a number of researchers, who regard Confucianism as the orthodox, authentic Chinese culture.[118]

Kim and his team note the positive role of Asian values in the provision of culturally relevant and sensitive psychological services to clients of an Asian ethnic background. They identified six cultural Asian values: conformity to norms, family recognition through achievement, emotional self-control, collectivism,

---

[113] Hofstede, *Cultures and Organizations*. The six pairs of cultural values are power distance, individualism versus collectivism, masculinity-femininity, uncertainty avoidance, long-term orientation versus short-term orientation, indulgence versus restraint.
[114] Chinese Culture Connection, 1987.
[115] Hofstede et al., *Cultures and Organizations*, 236–64.
[116] Matthews, 'Chinese Value Survey', 118.
[117] Ibid., 121.
[118] Chan, 'On Translating', xxii; Yang, *Chinese Christians*, 44; Cha et al., *Ministry Insights*, 61–62.

humility and filial piety.[119] This observation echoes Tan's research that race and face are dominant factors of Asian cultural identity, even for the third and fourth generations.[120] Moreover, many writings agree that filial piety is one of the major cultural values.[121] Filial piety (also known as *xiao* or *hsiao*) is regarded as a primary traditional Chinese cultural value. The strong sense of familial cohesion has a significant impact on the mutual expectation of senior pastors and younger pastors. It also provides helpful practical insights for my study of the interaction between Chinese migrants and successive generations of ethnic Chinese.

Equally important, 'shame' is described as another major element of traditional Chinese culture. Cha et al. highlight 'toxic shame' as one of the cultural values of Asian Christians.[122] Shame is always an important cultural value among Chinese.[123] The experience of shame and the saving of face, discussed later, are basic factors deterring pastors from acquiring better English.

Cultural hybridity: Writings on bicultural identity

Asian migration has changed the cultural landscape of Australia society, propelling it from a predominantly European culture to a multicultural community. In a typical Chinese family, new migrants and their children, the second-generation migrants, encounter two cultures, namely traditional Chinese culture and younger generation culture.[124]

Chinese churches in Australia also have a similar cultural landscape. The cultural identity of second-generation migrants

---

119 Kim et al., 'Asian Values Scale', 351.
120 Tan, '"Tyranny of Appearance"'.
121 Weber, *Religion of China*, 157; Smith, *Confucius*, 62; Wang, 'Power, Rights and Duties', 169; Lewis, *When Teams Collide*, 267–70.
122 Cha et al., *Ministry Insights*, 19–38.
123 Ngan and Kwok-Bun, *Chinese Face*, 161; Pattison, *Saving Face*.
124 Law, 'Cultural Change', 10–11.

(and their subsequent descendants) are known as bicultural (or double-cultural) or even multiple-cultural. The younger generations have to interact with their parents' traditional Chinese culture, the postmodern Australian culture, the culture of their peers and the technological, global culture of the internet.[125] Their hybrid cultural identity, hence, is bicultural or multicultural.

Second-generation migrants have Chinese appearance and Chinese parents, and elderly Chinese may regard them as Chinese. However, they speak English rather than Chinese, and they feel more at ease with Australian culture. In this sense, they are not perceived as Chinese at all. Identity confusion is common.[126]

Sun outlines the positive and negative characteristics of the second generation of overseas Chinese with special reference to the Australian context.[127] He concludes his article by encouraging the next generation to mix well with people from other ethnic backgrounds.[128] More interaction with other ethnic and cultural background is probably good for cultural integration.

It is quite common that both generations attend the same church. According to Chung, 'family is the core value in Chinese traditional culture'; the parents want to 'keep their children along with them at the same church'.[129] However, Engebretson's empirical study of junior high students in Australia shows that 'church affiliation and practice does not necessary nurture young peoples' spirituality'.[130] The parents may 'coerce' their children to attend Chinese church, with an unspoken intention to impose and reinforce traditional Chinese culture on their children. In other

---

125 Chan, 'Challenge of the Global Age', 18–20.
126 Zhang, 'Reflection'.
127 Sun, 'Next Generation'.
128 Ibid., 9.
129 Chung, 'Chinese Young People', 63.
130 Engebretson, 'Expressions of Religiosity', 57–72.

words, the second generation of Chinese migrants has to search for its cultural identity and struggle with its cultural integration, both in society and in the church.

Chung's study verifies this phenomenon. She categorises the self-assessment of cultural identity among Chinese young people with four different sub-groups: more Australian than Chinese (A>C), more Chinese than Australian (C>A), torn between (A←→C), and Australian-born Chinese (ABC).[131] This categorisation improves the over-simplified dichotomy of the ABC-OBC model, which categorises all of the second generation of migrants as ABC. However, the cultural identity of Chinese young people in Australia remains in need of ongoing definitional and practical clarification.

People in bicultural societies encounter two cultures and gradually form a bicultural identity. Bicultural identity and bicultural identity integration are major themes in recent cultural studies.[132] Stroink and Lalonde's study predicts that bicultural people display lower levels of simultaneous identification with both their cultures.[133] This concurs with social identity theory that 'individuals define their own identities with regard to social groups . . . to protect and bolster self-identity'.[134]

If the process of cultural integration and transition of migrants and their descendants is difficult, it creates identity

---

131 Chung, 'Chinese Young People, 174–84.
132 Benet-Martínez and Haritatos, 'Bicultural Identity Integration', 1015–50; Chen, 'Two Languages, Two Personalities?' 1514–28; Stroink and Lalonde, 'Bicultural Identity Conflict', 44–65; Huynh et al., 'Bicultural Identity Integration', 827–42.
133 Stroink and Lalonde, 'Bicultural Identity Conflict', 59–62.
134 Islam, 'Social Identity Theory', 1781.

uncertainty and identity confusion, and writers label this 'identity crisis'.[135]

Huynh et al. highlight factors shaping the degree of bicultural integration, though the construct is not specifically directed towards Chinese or Asian people.[136] Benet-Martinez and Haritatos conclude that cultural distance (in contrast to blendedness) and cultural conflict (in contrast to harmony) are two main independent constructs shaping one's cultural identity and cultural transition.[137] Among bicultural migrant groups, cultural identification and self-perception are major variables of personalities and behaviours.[138] Besides, bicultural assimilation affects decision making.[139]

The identity of a multicultural individual is always in the process of formation. Adler portrays the cultural identity of a multicultural individual as 'more fluid and mobile, more susceptible to change, more open to variation. It is an identity-based . . . on a style of self-consciousness that is capable of negotiating ever new formations of reality'.[140]

Among these works, all concepts of 'blendedness', 'integration' and 'formation' point to one common point, namely, the cultural identity of people in a multicultural circumstance undergoes a cultural reshaping. This leads to the concept of cultural hybridity.

---

[135] This notion of identity crisis is different from the concept originated by Erikson, whose theory refers to the identity crisis (or role confusion) derived from the adolescent stage of development (Erikson, *Identity*). Such notion is differentiated by Baumeister, et al. as 'identity deficit' (Baumeister et al., 'Two Kinds of Identity Crisis', 407–8).

[136] Huynh et al., 'Bicultural Identity Integration'.

[137] Benet-Martínez and Haritatos, 'Bicultural Identity Integration'.

[138] Chen, 'Two Languages, Two Personalities?', 1518–19.

[139] Briley et al., 'Cultural Chameleons'; Mok, 'Cultural Identity Integration'.

[140] Adler, 'Beyond Cultural Identity', 364.

Cultural hybridity: Writings on hybridity

Cultural hybridity is a relatively new concept that has attracted academic attention over the last two decades. Kraidy suggests that hybridity is 'a conceptual inevitability'.[141] Ang et al. conceptualise hybridity by contrasting 'hybridity' with the notion of 'multiculturalism', pointing out 'that hybridity is a contested term that stresses mixture, cultural interchange and mutual cross-fertilisation'.[142] Elsewhere, Ang states that 'hybridity always implies an unsettling of identities' and 'the very condition of in-betweenness'.[143] Pieterse suggests that cultural hybridisation is a sign of an age of boundary crossing.[144] Yazdiha attempts to conceptualise hybridity in terms of race, language and national culture.[145]

The prototype of the concept of hybridity can be found in such notions as 'continuum' and 'spectrum', used as a way to describe the complexity of cultural identity. As early as 1984, Law, as reported by Ling and Cheu,[146] developed the dynamics of two generations of (Chinese) migrants in terms of a 'Dynamic Bi-cultural Continuum Model', a concept characterising the constant transitional nature of the cultural identity of migrants. Geertz describes our globalised world as 'a gradual spectrum of mixed-up differences'.[147] The terms spectrum and continuum later develop into the concept of cultural hybridity.

Instead of discussing hybridity in abstract terms, the hybrid culture of the children of migrants has attracted a satisfying

---

141 Kraidy, 'Hybridity', 329.
142 Ang et al. *Alter/Asians*, xix.
143 Ang, 'Together-in-Difference', 8.
144 Pieterse, 'Globalization as Hybridization'.
145 Yazdiha, 'Conceptualizing Hybridity', 31.
146 Ling and Cheuk, *'Chinese' Way*, 124.
147 Geertz, *Works and Lives*, 148.

number of studies. Migrant children behave differently in public and private spheres, as they receive different sets of cultural values from both families and from their schools or workplaces.[148] Children in migrant families adopt two sets of cultural norms and values because 'environmental cues activate only those beliefs relevant to the particular cultural settings'.[149]

The younger Chinese migrants in Australia are the target group of this study. They are exposed to various cultures: the home culture of their parents, the host culture of Australia, the peer culture of their multicultural friends or colleagues, the subculture and the online culture. Therefore, the resultant culture of their integration is not a biculture or multiculture but a hybrid culture, sometimes also known as the third culture or 'interstitial' culture.[150]

That group of people who spend a significant part of their developmental years outside of their parents' culture are frequently described as Third Culture Kids (TCK) or Global nomads.[151] TCKs develop relationships in various cultures; however, they do not easily develop a sense of belonging or full ownership in any of those cultures. Their developmental years are exposed to, immersed in and moulded by two or more cultures and/or subcultures. In other words, a TCK's cultural identity is a hybrid cultural identity, a mixed culture. Sometimes, it is hard to distinguish the components of their hybrid culture. Pollock and Van Reken discuss the 'who' and 'why' of the cultural identity

---

148 Fuligni et al., 'Attitudes'; Phinney et al., 'Cultural Values'; Lalonde and Giguère, 'Two Cultural Worlds'.
149 Hynie et al., 'Parent-Child Value Transmission', 231.
150 Useem and Downie, 'Third-Culture Kids'. Hereafter, the terms 'hybrid culture' and the 'third culture' will be used interchangeably.
151 Tanu, 'Global Nomads, 2; Gibbons, *Monkey and the Fish*; Pollock and Van Reken, *Third Culture Kids*, 19; Pascoe, *Raising Global Nomads*.

of their subjects by categorising and sub-categorising the third culture kids.[152]

As a third culture kid, George portrays the American Asian Indian as a coconut generation. He articulates the evolving identity and blended reality of their hybrid culture by providing an assimilation matrix.[153]

The work of Pollock and Van Reken and that of George are valuable references in discussing cultural hybridity, though unfortunately the parent generation is not included in the discussion and hence not much elaborated on.[154] As the cultural construct of the parents of third culture kids may impact their children to a great extent, a discussion of the parents' generation is needed to make the concept more complete.

Some writers recognise the increasing trend of cultural diversity among family members, dealing with practical aspects of raising children who are culturally hybrid. For example, Alperson stresses the importance of distinguishing the birth culture and the adoptive culture of adopted children, but at the same time recognises a third culture; a hybrid culture that will emerge.[155] Pascoe offers practical wisdom for parenting third culture kids, 'global nomads', with limited discussion on hybridity.[156]

Hermans and Kempen explore the dynamics of the process of cultural hybridisation. They dismiss the dichotomies of 'the west and the rest',[157] and suggest a better model, viewing 'culture

---

152 Pollock and Van Reken, *Third Culture Kids*, 19–73).
153 George, *Understanding the Coconut Generation*.
154 It is noted that the parent's generation also undergoes certain cultural hybridisation, although their process of hybridisation is much slower than that of the younger generation.
155 Alperson, *Dim Sum*.
156 Pascoe, *Raising Global Nomads*.
157 Hermans and Kempen, 'Moving Cultures', 1111–16.

as moving and mixing', out of which emerges a new form of cultural identity, a state of 'hybridization', or 'cultural mixture'.[158]

This cultural hybridisation occurs not only among the migrants but also among Asian students studying overseas or in Western countries. The study conducted by Oyserman and Sakamoto suggests that Asian American university students 'view their ethnic group as self-defining and themselves as good members of their ethnic group while also focusing on individualistic goals of self-definition'.[159] In other words, the young Asian Americans are undergoing a form of cultural hybridisation that combines elements of their ethnic culture with American culture.

Although theories of cultural hybridity or hybridisation are not fully developed, the notion is an important one for discussing the cultural interaction and cultural identity of people in multicultural settings. This concept is of particular significance to my study. It is a valuable prompt to migrant parents at home, and to the senior pastors at Chinese churches, implying that they should allow, and affirm, other cultures in addition to traditional Chinese culture.

The preceding literature distinguishes various methodological approaches and target groups in cultural identity studies. The revealed components and elements in the formation of cultural identity are helpful for gaining cultural knowledge and guiding appropriate intercultural behaviours. Identifying the factors affecting the degree of cultural transition is also valuable for understanding how to minimise cultural distance and how to blend various cultural groups. It is noted that Chinese pastors are not well informed about cultural identity and its determinants. Studies on cultural values are vital for Chinese pastors for the

---

158 Ibid., 1113, 1117.
159 Oyserman and Sakamoto, 'Being Asian American', 449.

mutual understanding of both the host culture group and the migrants.

However, some areas of study on cultural identity are only sparsely represented in the literature, such as longitudinal studies (study over various life stages) and religious studies (relationships between religion and ethnic/cultural identity). Studies of those areas can be beneficial, and may even be essential, for the understanding of cultural assimilation.

The concept of hybridity, especially the categorisation of third culture kids, is helpful for understanding certain cultural behaviours of second-generation migrants. However, most of the writings on the second generation are largely about adolescents. The discussion of the cultural identity and cultural values of young and middle-aged adults has so far been very limited. Moreover, the practical advice mainly relates to the family setting, with virtually no discussion on church ministry or the pastoral team setting. Furthermore, conceptual discussion on improving intercultural competence is hardly found. Second generation pastors—mainly young adults and middle aged-adults—are thus one of the key target groups of my own research.

In reviewing the various works on cultural hybridity and multiculturalism, I have demonstrated a preference for the notion of cultural hybridity over that of multiculturalism. I do so because the concept of multiculturalism *describes* social and political realities, whereas the concept of cultural hybridity *prescribes* the direction and orientation of cultural integration. Cultural hybridity promotes mutual cultural learning and transformation instead of one-way cultural assimilation, which has the possibility to produce a non-egalitarian, privileged group. For this reason, I do not intend the adoption of multiculturalism to exclude cultural hybridity. In fact, multiculturalism has to be complemented by theories of cultural hybridity in order to help the migrants to settle in a multicultural society. These two theories should go hand-in-hand.

Generational issues within the Asian and Chinese churches

Various writers and church practitioners note the generational cohorts at church, and there are numerous works on related topics, such as intergenerational relationships, leadership and spiritual formation.[160] Some writings specifically cover the Australian context.[161]

Generational characteristics

Every generation has its specific characteristics which give rise to different criteria for setting priorities, preferences and value systems. Various writers outline specific features of the different generations (the boomers, the busters/Generation X, and the bridgers/Generation Y) from a social research perspective.[162]

Those specific culture-shaped characteristics derive from different ways of perceiving the world.[163] Certain root factors influence different generational characteristics. Carroll and Roof pinpoint identity, life experience and religion as the three major cultural factors for understanding church congregations.[164]

---

160 Rendle, *Multigenerational Congregation*; Hilborn and Bird, *God and the Generations*; McIntosh, *One Church, Four Generations*; Allen and Ross, *Intergenerational Christian Formation*.
161 Powell, 'Australian Church Health'; Powell and Jacka, 'Generations'.
162 Beaudoin, *Virtual Faith*; McIntosh, *One Church, Four Generations*; Carroll and Roof, *Bridging Divided Worlds*; Rainer, *Bridger Generation*; McCrindle, 'Generations Defined'; Collins-Mayo et al., *Faith of Generation Y*; Allen and Ross, *Intergenerational Christian Formation*, 121–74.
163 Vanderwell, *Church of All Ages*, 55–69.
164 Carroll and Roof, *Bridging Divided Worlds*, 61–86.

Pattison highlights the fundamental characteristics of the older generations within Chinese churches, namely saving face, losing face and shamefulness.[165] Pattison provides extensive theological reflection on the issue of face, which is of special relevance to older Chinese. All these are attempts to highlight the different values and characteristics of various generations.

Generational issues and conflicts at church

Generational issues occur in church relationships. The phenomenon of Generation Xers dropping out of church has been noted.[166] Rendle also notes this phenomenon and identifies cultural values as the primary factor.[167] Ford and Denney call for pastors to introduce Jesus to this drop-out generation by speaking languages intelligible to that generation.[168]

Apart from dropping out, disagreements and conflicts occur in churches. In the case of Chinese churches, as analysed by Ling and Cheuk, two generations clash and fight.[169] Ling and Cheuk explore the 'Chinese way of doing things' and identify the cultural factors underlying the conflicts. Disagreements and fights occur in other Asian churches as well.[170]

Disagreements and diversity impact various aspects of the church.[171] From a Reformed tradition, Vanderwell concludes that generational diversity impacts worship services, Christian education and preaching.[172] In addition, Allen and Ross suggest

---

165 Pattison, *Saving Face*.
166 Merritt, *Tribal Church*.
167 Rendle, *Multigenerational Congregation*.
168 Ford and Denney, *Jesus for a New Generation*.
169 Ling and Cheuk, *'Chinese' Way*.
170 Cha et al., *Ministry Insights*, 66–67, 86–90; Yep et al., *Following Jesus*; Park et al., *Honoring the Generations*; Foster, *From Generation to Generation*.
171 Foster, *From Generation to Generation*.
172 Vanderwell, *Church of All Ages*.

LITERATURE SURVEY AND ASSESSMENT

that generational diversity impacts the church model, the ways of doing mission and group ministry.[173]

Pastoral implications of intergenerational conflicts

Generational differences become a challenge for the church and its leaders. Rendle suggests that intergenerational conflicts at church are a war right here.[174] Although Rendle's expression may be a bit too strong, the term 'war', to a certain extent, reveals the intensity and seriousness of intergenerational conflicts at churches. However, a church with various generations should not be seen as a problem, as Allen and Ross emphasise; intergenerationality in church should be seen as a benefit.[175]

Various writers endeavour to restore the rough and broken relationships of the two generations. McIntosh suggests that understanding one another is primary.[176] Elmer focuses on cross-cultural conflict resolution.[177] Yep and her team from various North American campuses are concerned with the difficult relationships and cultural misunderstandings of Asian Christian students and their parents, and recommend ways of 'following Jesus without dishonouring parents'.[178] Amidei et al. suggest a 'back-to-basics' approach, and advocate caring, praying, learning, celebrating and serving faithfully as ways to bring generations together.[179] Lawrence directs attention to the leaders, and stresses the importance of engaging Generation Y young people.[180] Goplin et al. suggest resources and ideas for building an effective cross-

---

173 Allen and Ross, *Intergenerational Christian Formation*.
174 Rendle, *Multigenerational Congregation*, 13.
175 Allen and Ross, *Intergenerational Christian Formation*, 47–63.
176 McIntosh, *One Church, Four Generations*; 197–233.
177 Elmer, *Cross-Cultural Conflict*.
178 Yep et al., *Following Jesus*.
179 Amidei et al., *Generations Together*.
180 Lawrence, *Engaging Gen Y*.

generational ministry.[181] All these attempts are more about skills and methods aimed at bringing all generations together.

Instead of methods, Roxburgh points to the strategy of shifting worldviews.[182] Instead of putting youth at the receiving end, Norheim calls for involving youth at the forefront of ministry.[183] Norheim identifies authenticity as the core value of youth; church could involve youth as an agent of global mission.[184] Rendle perceptively suggests leaders adopt four ministry approaches, namely moving to a reflective mode, working descriptively, seeking common space or community and installing civility by practising sacrifice, generosity and trust.[185]

Some Asian church theologians try to formulate a theological and biblical justification of intergenerational church. Park and his team provide theological and biblical reflection on various generational issues in Asian churches from the perspective of the church as a whole.[186] Cha and his team reflect biblically on issues in Asian churches from the perspective of developing healthy leadership.[187] Kim proposes 'bridge-makers' and 'cross-bearers' as two roles to reduce the generational distance at church.[188] From a practical theological perspective, Pattison provides theological reflection on the face of God as an alternative way to deal with losing face and shamefulness.[189]

In summary, the literature reviewed in this section provides comprehensive information and insight into intergenerational issues and conflicts. Certain traits are to be noted, however.

---

181   Goplin et al., *Across the Generations*.
182   Roxburgh, *Reaching a New Generation:* 31–62.
183   Norheim, 'Global Youth Culture'.
184   Ibid., 171–74.
185   Rendle, *Multigenerational Congregation*, 115–34.
186   Park et al., *Honoring the Generations*.
187   Cha et al., *Ministry Insights*, 58–99.
188   Kim, *Bridge-Makers*.
189   Pattison, *Saving Face*.

LITERATURE SURVEY AND ASSESSMENT

Firstly, I note that studies are more about the needs of the younger generation than the older generation. Such a trend may imply the younger generation is both more challenging and less resourceful. Hence, older intergenerational leaders may need to take up the responsibility of addressing intergenerational issues and conflicts. Secondly, the majority of writers are from North America or are Asian and Chinese writers from North America. Such a trait suggests this present research about Australia can contribute to the studies on generations by further examining factors of intergenerational conflicts and by providing further approaches in resolving, or reducing, the generational tension.

Intercultural leadership

Practices of intercultural leadership

In order to perform well in intercultural contexts, leaders require a whole range of capabilities and practices. Much research on high-level executives in foreign countries has been conducted, and this research reveals certain characteristic practices of intercultural managerial leadership. For example, one study indicates that performance is higher when management practice is congruent with the host culture,[190] and such a finding is congruent with the implicit assumption of the extensive research of Hofstede.[191] Another study notes that informal management control is stronger in cross-cultural contexts than in monocultural contexts.[192] According to Tusi et al., 'articulating vision, monitoring operations, risk-taking, communicating, showing benevolence and being authoritative' are the major factors shaping leadership

---

190   Newman and Nollen, 'Culture and Congruence', 753–54.
191   Hofstede et al., *Cultures and Organizations*.
192   Calori et al., 'Control Mechanisms'.

styles and decision making among CEOs in China.[193] In other words, stronger management skills are involved in intercultural contexts.

However, the tasks of intercultural leaders involve more than management. For example, the capability to develop teams is a major concern. Building trust, collaboration and empowerment are essential factors connected to performance in intercultural team building.[194]

In intercultural team development, disagreements and conflicts frequently occur.[195] Conventionally, conflict is perceived with negative connotations. However, recent research reveals a more optimistic view towards conflict. Conflict should be regarded as normal because it is a way to express differences in priorities and viewpoints among the team members.[196] Conflicts bring to the surface subtle organisational issues, so that team members learn to take on different perspectives.[197] Research also shows that, at times, individuals exposed to a 'devil's advocate' make better judgements and are more effective in decision making.[198]

However, accepting conflict as normal is not enough. Intercultural leaders are also expected to resolve conflicts. Morse and Wagner find that a capability for conflict resolution is one of the major factors in measuring leaders' effectiveness.[199] Walton shows that the ability to convert conflict into compromise and consensual agreement is an effective measure of a leader.[200]

---

193 Tsui et al., '"Let a Thousand Flowers Bloom"', 8; Alves, 'Multilevel Analysis', 16.
194 Thomas and Ravlin, 'Responses of Employees', 133–46; Cladis, *Leading the Team-Based Church*.
195 Elmer, *Cross-Cultural Conflict*.
196 Tjosvold, *Working Together*.
197 De Dreu and Weingart, 'Task Versus Relationship', 741–49.
198 Schwenk, 'Effects of Devil's Advocacy'.
199 Morse and Wagner, 'Measuring the Process', 32–35.
200 Walton, Interorganizational Decision Making'; Bass and Bass, *Handbook of Leadership*, 332, 341.

LITERATURE SURVEY AND ASSESSMENT

Some researchers note that transformational leaders are more competent in conflict resolution than transactional leaders.[201]

Intercultural leadership development is also a major research focus. International assignments, conducting international seminars and leading international taskforces are major ways to train intercultural leadership.[202] Research shows that experiential learning, reflection and re-evaluation of experiences brings forth more productive learning results.[203] Damarin suggests that international travelling (not tourism) provides a person with opportunities for cross-cultural observations, and compels him or her to figure out ways of building trust and acceptance.[204] Alternatively, lack of training and lack of preparation of leaders lead to a relatively higher leadership failure rate.[205] Such cultural learning presumes a basic philosophical notion, namely the mutability (capability of change) of human nature.[206]

The preceding studies shed light on the study of leadership in Chinese churches in two respects. Firstly, conflict is always avoided or denied in Chinese communities and Chinese churches. Frequent conflict avoidance occurs but at the expense of ignoring deep-rooted relational and organisational issues, such as dysfunctional leadership styles or not setting personal boundaries. A church with such recurring unhealthy behaviours will eventually become dysfunctional.[207]

---

201 Gibbons, 'Revisiting the Question'; Covin et al., 'Leadership Style'.
202 Oddou and Derr, 'European MNC Strategies'.
203 Kolb, *Experiential Learning*, 20–21; Dodge, 'Empowerment'.
204 Damarin, 'Schooling and Situated Knowledge'; Mendenhall and Osland, *Global Leadership*, 168.
205 Tung, 'U.S. Multinationals'.
206 Kluckhohn and Strodtbeck, *Variations*.
207 Richardson, *Creating a Healthier Church*; Friedman, *Generation to Generation*.

Secondly, leadership development is seldom a priority in the Chinese church. Collectivism is a cultural dimension of Chinese practice; senior pastors and leaders tend to maintain a superficial level of harmony and agreement. Collectivistic pastors do not value individual development. Leaders do not devote time to aspects of relationship building and team development, such as mentoring and modelling.[208] Factors underlying this phenomenon reflect a lack of honest and transparent reflection. This requires further investigation and discussion in my research.

Power and influence in intercultural leadership

Power is a big topic in leadership studies.[209] Leaders can exercise power in many ways, such as in decision making and in controlling the distribution and access to information,[210] and also by regulating resources.[211] Recently, instead of stressing power and authority, some writings have directed the emphasis on the vulnerability, authenticity, weakness and transparency of leadership.[212] This aspect may be a challenge to pastors in a Chinese church. Many senior pastors are perceived as spiritual, godly figures. In order to maintain an image of strong and capable leadership, many Chinese senior pastors tend to hide their weaknesses and vulnerable aspects. Therefore, authenticity and sincerity are not easily seen.

---

208 Stead , 'Mentoring'.
209 Hagberg, *Real Power*; De Pree, *Leading without Power*; Yukl, *Leadership in Organizations*; Shuster 2012)
210 Atwater and Waldman, *Leadership, Feedback*.
211 Yukl, 'Leading Organizational Learning', 53.
212 Goffee and Jones, 'Managing Authenticity', 89; Ancona et al., 'In Praise', 92–94; George et al., 'Discovering', 129–30; George, *True North*; Allender, *Leading with A Limp*.

However, power is not synonymous with influence.[213] Influence is preferable to exercising power and control.[214] Leaders can influence organisations in many ways, such as through organisational collective learning, organisational effectiveness and empowerment.[215]

Cultural dimensions in intercultural leadership

Cultural dimensions (high context and low context, collectivistic and individualistic) have a great impact on intercultural leadership.[216] Rodrigues' research shows that an effective leadership style is determined by specific cultural values, such as choosing the best motivation strategy.[217] For example, a 'directive leadership style will be more effective in those societies with relatively high power distance, collectivism, and uncertainty avoidance'.[218] In situations where changes are made in culturally diverse contexts, Heifetz and Laurie wisely distinguish between *technical change* and *adaptive change*, with the latter emphasising radical changes of people's values, attitudes and habits.[219]

A notable dimension of intercultural leadership is collectivism-individualism, which focuses on the importance and priority of the individual or the attached group.[220] Schwartz argues that the dichotomy of individualism-collectivism may sometimes obscure the desirable root values of individualism

---

213 Bass and Bass, *Handbook of Leadership*, 264–65.
214 De Pree, *Leading without Power*; Banks et al., *Reviewing Leadership*.
215 Yukl, 'Leading Organizational Learning'; Yukl, 'How Leaders Influence'; Yukl and Becker, 'Effective Empowerment'.
216 Hibbert and Hibbert, *Leading Multicultural Teams*, 19–45.
217 Rodrigues, 'Situation and National Culture', 51–68.
218 Pasa et al., 'Society', 565.
219 Heifetz and Laurie, 'Work of Leadership', 128.
220 Triandis, *Individualism and Collectivism*; Hofstede et al., *Cultures and Organizations*.

and collectivism, such as individual interests and collective goals or values.[221] Collectivism-individualism also shapes team members' self-conception as independent or interdependent,[222] which influences the manner of leading.

The notion of collectivism-individualism is an important aspect of the discussion that will follow as it relates to the mutual expectations of senior pastors and younger pastors in Chinese churches. Their differences concerning collectivism and individualism generate miscommunication and misunderstanding.

Another dimension of culture is power distance. Research by Hofstede and Schwartz shows a high power distance culture maintains a hierarchical social fabric.[223] When power differences are huge, autocratic leadership and coercion are more likely.[224] Research also points to differences in the way that power distance shapes team members' understanding of team harmony.[225] Researchers have noted that skilful intercultural leaders, with a thorough knowledge of the host culture, can exercise wise tactics so as to work around the culture of high power distance by excusing themselves from the decision-making meetings.[226]

Power distance is closely related to the individual's assumption about the best behaviour to ensure social order.[227] Thus, in Chinese church settings, the manner in which individual pastors coordinate and socialise with other team members of diverse cultural backgrounds is largely determined by their

---

221 Schwartz, 'Individualism-Collectivism', 140–44.
222 Markus and Kitayama, 'Culture and the Self'.
223 Schwartz, 'Beyond Individualism/Collectivism', 85–120; Hofstede et al., *Cultures and Organizations*.
224 Bass and Bass, *Handbook of Leadership*, 291.
225 Anderson-Umana, 'Differences'.
226 Osland, 'Role of Leadership'; Mendenhall and Osland, *Global Leadership*, 136.
227 Schwartz, 'Theory of Cultural Values', 27.

perceived power distance from other team members. This cultural dimension affects the mode and frequency of communication and engagement.

Communication in intercultural leadership

Communication is essential for intercultural leadership and much research focuses on specific perspectives, such as interpersonal dynamics,[228] cultural identity,[229] cultural adaptation,[230] East Asian perspectives[231] and Christian perspectives.[232]

Language differences and lack of communicative language are the primary issues in leading teams.[233] Lack of language proficiency limits leaders' access to informal social connections, and sometimes, for their own benefit, subordinates may filter or even block information from their language-deficient leaders.[234] Moreover, diction (choice of words and phrases) creates misunderstanding.[235] Researchers also note that, for native monolingual speakers, language is just a mechanism that expresses meaning and reasoning.[236] However, anthropologist Whorf finds that language largely determines how people understand reality.[237] Furthermore, people speaking different languages perceive the world in different ways.[238] Therefore,

---

228 Dodd, *Dynamics*; Lustig and Koester, *Intercultural Competence*.
229 Jandt, *Introduction*.
230 Kim, *Becoming Intercultural*.
231 Yum, 'Impact of Confucianism'.
232 Tucker, *Intercultural Communication*; Moreau, *Effective Intercultural Communication*.
233 Hibbert, 'Enhancing', 29–30; Chen et al., 'Importance of Language'.
234 Peltokorpi, 'Intercultural Communication', 176–88.
235 Hibbert and Hibbert, *Leading Multicultural Teams*, 25–26.
236 Stewart and Bennett, *American Cultural Patterns*; Branson and Martinez, *Churches, Cultures and Leadership*, 115.
237 Whorf, *Language, Thought, and Reality*; Branson and Martinez, *Churches, Cultures and Leadership*, 116.
238 Branson and Martinez, *Churches, Cultures and Leadership*, 116.

the more understanding of language systems people have, the more people can communicate and the more they see the world differently.

Other writers consider the personal qualities that enhance intercultural communication, such as integrity, honesty, character, calling, and even spirituality.[239] Other qualities are also considered, namely personal value,[240] genuine welcoming and hospitality[241] and genuine personal humility.[242]

Servant leadership

Some researchers direct their attention toward servant leadership, particularly in non-profit organisations. Servant leadership and stewardship are different notions. Stewards aim at balancing the interests of all parties, whereas servant leaders target the transforming, building and growing of followers into leaders, even at the expense of their own interests and privileges.[243] Servant leaders share some common qualities with transformational leaders, such as vision, influence, credibility and trust.[244]

Although Greenleaf is a champion of servant leadership, and the concept is well received in the business world,[245] Russell and Stone state that the concept of servant leadership is not well defined and not supported by empirical research.[246] Subsequently, based on literature reviews, researchers have developed lists of

---

239 Webb, *Godly Leadership*; Laniak, *Shepherds*; McNeal, *Work of Heart*.
240 Bordas, *Salsa, Soul, and Spirit*.
241 Foster, *Embracing Diversity*.
242 Collins, 'Level 5 Leadership'.
243 Bass and Bass, *Handbook of Leadership*, 51.
244 Ibid.
245 Greenleaf, *Servant Leadership*; Greenleaf and Spears, *Power of Servant Leadership*.
246 Russell and Stone, 'Review'.

attributes of servant leadership.[247] Moreover, in recent years, empirical studies on servant leadership have emerged, focusing on attributes such as organisational trust,[248] empowerment,[249] leadership development[250] and team effectiveness.[251]

The concept of servant leadership has a strong resonance for Christian leadership. Greenleaf always regarded Jesus as the archetypal leader.[252] Wright develops a theology of servant leadership, listing the prerequisites, principles and power of servant leadership.[253] Roberts' two works lay out the biblical foundations and applications of servant leadership.[254] Åkerlund connects the notion of the servant leadership of Jesus with his mission and obedience to God.[255]

Other works apply the concept of servant leadership to cross-cultural ministry and to developing intercultural leadership in church ministries and mission work.[256]

This review of leadership literature shows proactive research being conducted on the challenges of intercultural leadership. The review also reveals a few challenges to intercultural leaders.

---

247 Russell and Stone, 'Review', 147–52; Winston, *Be a Leader*; Patterson, 'Servant Leadership'; Liden et al. 'Servant Leadership: Development', 173–74; Sendjaya et al., 'Defining and Measuring', 417–18; Spears, 'Character and Servant Leadership', 27–29.
248 Chan and Mak, 'Impact of Servant Leadership'.
249 de Waal and Sivro, 'Relation'.
250 Melchar and Bosco, 'Achieving High Organization Performance'.
251 Liden et al., 'Servant Leadership and Serving Culture'.
252 Banks et al., *Reviewing Leadership*, 108.
253 Wright, *Relational Leadership*.
254 Roberts, *Developing Christian Servant Leadership*; Roberts, *Developing Christian Scripture*.
255 Åkerlund, 'Son, Sent, and Servant.
256 Lingenfelter, *Leading Cross-Culturally*; Jacobsen, *Three Tasks*; Plueddemann, *Leading across Cultures*; Trompenaars and Voerman, *Servant Leadership*.

Firstly, the preceding literature underlines the primacy of knowing the host culture. As suggested by various authors, cultural dimensions impact intercultural leadership in terms of choosing motivational strategies and modes of change management.[257] Effective intercultural leaders will understand and identify personal worldview and cultural dimensions such as collectivism-individualism and power distance. In relation to my study, inattention to collectivism-individualism or power distance creates difficulties in genuine communication and trust. This is particularly relevant to the phenomenon of non-communication among the Chinese pastors.[258]

Secondly, conflicts within intercultural teams are unavoidable and to be expected. Intercultural conflicts should be perceived and addressed in a positive way, as conflicts also produce some benefits to the team. According to various authors, conflicts reveal differences in priority and viewpoint.[259] Conflicts may bring subtle issues to the surface and reveal the alternative perspectives of team members from the minority group.[260] Certain team members may play 'devil's advocate', which helps the whole team to make better judgements and decisions.[261] Therefore, conflict may provide an opportunity to develop a team and improve relationships with colleagues. The willingness to face cultural reality is another important issue in intercultural

---

257 Rodrigues, 'Situation and National Culture', 51–68; Pasa et al., 'Society', 565; Heifetz and Laurie, 'Work of Leadership', 128.
258 Non-communication is one of the significant findings from my interview.
259 Tjosvold, *Working Together*.
260 De Dreu and Weingart, 'Task Versus Relationship', 741–49.
261 Schwenk, 'Effects of Devil's Advocacy'.

LITERATURE SURVEY AND ASSESSMENT

interaction.[262] This is particularly relevant to this study about pastors of Chinese churches.[263]

Thirdly, in order to exercise intercultural leadership, language proficiency is essential and should be given priority. As noted from this literature review, language deficiency limits leaders' ability to improve team connections, and subordinate leaders are tempted to manipulate information and communication in the team.[264] Besides, language largely determines people's worldview and their ways of understanding reality.[265] Therefore, the more understanding of language systems people have, the more they can communicate and the more they come to see the world differently. It is obvious that language proficiency (or deficiency) greatly determines effective intercultural communication, improving the mode and accuracy of communication.[266] It is noted that language plays a significant part in CQ knowledge. Therefore, in intercultural communication, the acquisition of a second language always ensures better communication and the avoidance of misunderstanding.

Lastly, the works on servant leadership show some common attributes of servant leaders, such as integrity, trust, modelling, appreciation of others, communication, competence, delegation, conceptual skills, helping subordinates grow and succeed, creating value for the community, persuasion and foresight.[267] All these attributes converge around the complementary nature

---

262 This is related to my later discussion about insufficient reflection. The determination and capability for reflection relates to CQ metacognitive thinking.
263 As Confucian humanists of traditional Chinese culture are concerned most for harmony, solidarity, stability and peace, they usually avoid and deny conflicts.
264 Peltokorpi, 'Intercultural Communication', 176–88.
265 Branson and Martinez, *Churches, Cultures and Leadership*, 116.
266 Du-Babcock and Babcock, 'Patterns', 161–63.
267 Russell and Stone, 'Review', 147–52; Liden et al. 'Servant Leadership: Development', 173–74; Spears, 'Character and Servant Leadership', 27–29.

of deploying power and exercising influence. Both performance and personhood need to be given equal attention. Therefore, servant leadership could be regarded as a related aspect of intercultural leadership. In relation to my study, intercultural and intergenerational pastors may take Jesus as the archetypal servant leader,[268] better enabling Chinese pastors to cross the intercultural gulf. This, in turn, could provide the necessary CQ drive to reach out to pastors of different cultural backgrounds and to acquire greater language competency.

However, the preceding literature review also reveals certain gaps. The primary absence is the study of Chinese churches and their pastoral leaders. There are a few studies on leadership in the multicultural church and the Asian church in North America, but not the Chinese church in Australia. Therefore, some potential challenges to Chinese pastors are not addressed, such as racism, discrimination, aging and succession. My empirical research and theoretical discussion may join in the dialogue in the hope of finding ministry and leadership insights for the troubled leaders in the Chinese churches of Australia.

Cultural Intelligence

Conceptualisation of CQ theory[269]

The conceptualisation of 'Cultural Intelligence' has been explored and developed over the last three decades. The theory arose out

---

268 Banks et al., *Reviewing Leadership*, 108.
269 I am fully aware that the cultural landscape of second-generation migrants could be discussed and analysed from a number of disciplinary perspectives: anthropology, sociology, cultural studies or leadership studies, for example. In this study, I choose to examine the topic with Cultural Intelligence (CQ) as theoretical framework. This is because of the extensive usage of CQ within the field of leadership studies.

of concern for the competence and performance of expatriates in the context of globalisation.

Study within the field of Cultural Intelligence starts with an exploration of the determinants and factors in regards to the competence and performance of expatriates working overseas, which includes focuses such as corporate selection strategies, personality variables, life satisfaction and organisational structures.[270] The effective components of a global society – adaptability, connectedness, curiosity, empathy and so forth – are still a concern after three decades.[271] The study by Mendenhall and Oddou is one step closer to the formation of an understanding of Cultural Intelligence, inquiring into four dimensions of intercultural competence of overseas managers.[272] The dimension of cultural toughness is only one among the four dimensions.

Lievens and his team track predictors for selecting potential managers for cross-cultural assignments, which indirectly assesses their suitability for working in cross-cultural settings.[273] From an American and global perspective, Lustig and Koester explore various cultural factors and patterns affecting intercultural communication competence,[274] particularly the interpretation of verbal utterances and body gestures across cultures. They also analyse concrete and abstract communication and linear and non-linear (or circular style) communication.

---

[270] Newman et al., 'Determinants of Expatriate Effectiveness'. The literature reviewed in this section mostly concerns the intercultural competence of individuals. There are studies on intercultural competence of organisations (e.g., Van Driel and Gabreya Jr, 'Cross-Level Measurement'). However, the notion of organisational intercultural competence is beyond the scope of this research; my research is more at the individual level.

[271] Wallenberg-Lerner and James, 'Important Components', 18.

[272] Mendenhall and Oddou, 'Dimensions', 40–43.

[273] Lievens et al., 'Predicting Cross-Cultural Training Performance'.

[274] Lustig and Koester, *Intercultural Competence*.

MICHAEL K. CHU

The seminal work on Cultural Intelligence (CQ) is by Earley and Ang.[275] Their theoretical framework of Cultural Intelligence is constructed of cognitive, motivational and behavioural elements. Earley and Ang claim that the concept of Cultural Intelligence is drawn from various disciplines, namely cognitive psychology, cross-cultural psychology, anthropology, sociology and management. Howard Gardner's concept of Multiple Intelligence and Sternberg and Dettermans' concept of multidimensional perspectives of intelligence are acknowledged in the development of the concept of Cultural Intelligence.[276] Subsequently, Earley and Mosakowski state that Cultural Intelligence is acquired from three sources (three components), namely head, body and heart, which refer to the cognitive, the physical and the emotional/motivational respectively.[277]

Ang, Van Dyne and Koh have then developed the final form of the four-factor Cultural Intelligence model: metacognitive CQ (cognitive strategy and coping strategy), cognitive CQ (knowledge about different cultures), motivational CQ (desire and self-efficacy), and behavioural CQ (repertoire of culturally appropriate behaviours).[278] The validity of the measurement and scale of Cultural Intelligence is repeatedly tested and theorised in a chapter written by the same team.[279]

Ng and Earley open up another research direction, an integration or synthesising of two streams of studies, namely culture and intelligence.[280] The cultural/contextual variation of intelligence, they suggest, requires more attention and study. Secondly, the concept of Cultural Intelligence, in particular

---

275 Earley and Ang, *Cultural Intelligence*.
276 Gardner, *Frames of Mind*; Sternberg and Detterman, *What is Intelligence?*.
277 Earley and Mosakowski, 'Cultural Intelligence', 142–45.
278 Ang et al., 'Personality Correlates', 101.
279 Ang et al., 'Cultural Intelligence', 335–39.
280 Ng and Earley, 'Culture + Intelligence'.

LITERATURE SURVEY AND ASSESSMENT

inquiry into the validation of the measurement and theoretical framework of Cultural Intelligence, should be developed. The latter research direction would lead to the full maturation of Cultural Intelligence theories.

In order to improve the four-factor framework of Cultural Intelligence, Van Dyne and her team, after consulting with other related theories, develop the sub-dimensions of the four-factor model of Cultural Intelligence into an 11-factor structure.[281] According to Van Dyne and her team, metacognitive CQ includes some high-order cognitive activities, such as pre-interaction planning, awareness and post-interaction checking. Similarly, cognitive CQ can be subdivided into culture-general knowledge and context-specific knowledge. Likewise, motivational CQ involves intrinsic interest, extrinsic interest, and self-efficacy to adjust. And lastly, behavioural CQ is argued to comprise verbal behaviour, non-verbal behaviour and speech acts.[282] This detailed structure gives a more comprehensive understanding of the four-factor structure of CQ. Moreover, the further expansion of the concept enables more precise measurement and more specific knowledge of cultural orientation.

Researchers also work to understand the primacy and internal dynamics of the four factors of CQ. Among the four factors, Leung suggests that 'motivation is a crucial component of the cultural intelligence model because much, if not all, of cognition is motivated'.[283] Leung further affirms that motivation and cognition are strongly connected, and explains that motivation directs the energy of individuals to understand and learn cross-culturally.[284] This harmonises with the hypothesis of this study that the visceral discomfort derived from differences

---
281 Van Dyne et al., 'Sub-Dimensions'.
282 Ibid., 298–306.
283 Leung et al., 'Intercultural Competence', 494–95.
284 Ibid., 495.

in core values, beliefs or ethnocentric bias are some of the major factors of dysfunctional intercultural communication, resulting in intergenerational conflict among the pastors.

Studying outcome and performance is also a major trend in CQ study.[285] Leung is interested in the empirical evidence for measuring the outcomes of CQ. He suggests that 'motivational cultural intelligence is more strongly correlated with psychological outcomes, and that metacognitive and behavioural cultural intelligence are more strongly correlated with performance outcomes'.[286] As one of the foci of this study is the observable intergenerational conflict among the Chinese pastors, it is important to understand the correlation factors of conflict and their metacognitive CQ.

In Europe, Bücker and his team specifically limit the sample of their research to the Chinese,[287] a study which is therefore quite relevant to my research. The team utilises a two-dimensional model—internalised cultural knowledge and effective cultural flexibility—and their results demonstrate satisfactory levels of reliability and validity. Bücker's study also shows a positive correlation between CQ and communication effectiveness.[288] Besides, Bücker and his team conclude that 'not only expatriates can benefit from developing CQ, but also host country employees who come into contact with foreign cultures regularly'.[289]

---

285 Matveev and Merz, 'Intercultural Competence Assessment', 142–43; Glazer et al., 'Culture Research Landscape', 228.
286 Leung et al., 'Intercultural Competence', 495. It is interesting to note that CQ motivation and CQ strategy are closely related the three main findings of this study, namely, non-communication, language deficiency and the lack of reflection.
287 Ibid.
288 Ibid., 2085.
289 Bücker et al., 'Impact of Cultural Intelligence', 2092. Bücker concludes that CQ is not only relevant to the expatriates, but also to the host country employee. This point is congruent with my interview findings.

LITERATURE SURVEY AND ASSESSMENT

The preceding works and studies show numerous strengths and advantages in the theoretical model of Cultural Intelligence. The research promotes CQ as a robust tool for measuring intercultural competence.

However, there are areas about CQ not yet researched. For example, the relevance and application of Cultural Intelligence in Chinese churches and ministry leadership are yet to be tested. Also, most Cultural Intelligence studies focus on elite groups and top executives and expatriates of international companies; the validity of Cultural Intelligence for the general public is yet to be established.[290]

Application of CQ in globalised business

Knowing that Cultural Intelligence is an effective tool for measuring an individual's capability for performing well in culturally diversified settings is one matter; acquiring Cultural Intelligence is another matter. One dimension of the study focuses on the manner of acquiring Cultural Intelligence. Ng, Van Dyne and Ang suggest experiential learning as a way to develop intercultural leadership.[291]

Studies of the application of Cultural Intelligence in a whole range of work situations have been conducted; for example, its application in global IT contexts, particularly in offshore virtual offices and online meetings.[292] The studies highlight the unique subjective and objective cultures and their importance. Koh and her team correlate and discuss the relevance of the four factors when applied to conflict resolution, problem-solving,

---

290 Livermore and Van Dyne, utilising tests, are collecting Cultural Intelligence data of individuals, but no significant research with the data has been published.
291 Ng et al., 'From Experience to Experiential Learning'; Ng et al., 'Developing Leaders'.
292 Koh et al., 'Cultural Intelligence'; Presbitero, 'Cultural Intelligence (CQ)'.

communication and goal setting.²⁹³ Cultural Intelligence enhances the effective delivery of the preceding tasks.

Cultural Intelligence is also applied to culturally diversified team development. Although CQ is an individual capability, it is intended for team and collaborative work contexts. Koh and her team conclude that Cultural Intelligence provides explanatory power in predicting the effectiveness of cultural judgement, cultural adaptation and task performance.²⁹⁴ Adair, Hideg and Spence research the application of Cultural Intelligence in intercultural work teams.²⁹⁵ Their research shows behavioural CQ and metacognitive CQ has a positive effect on shared values in culturally heterogeneous teams, particularly in the early stages of team development.

Other studies on the application of Cultural Intelligence are documented—for example, studies of Cultural Intelligence application in the selection of global leaders,²⁹⁶ offshore outsourcing 'successfulness',²⁹⁷ knowledge sharing behaviour in university students,²⁹⁸ communication effectiveness and job satisfaction²⁹⁹ and conflict resolution.³⁰⁰

Most of the studies are for global business and international enterprise purposes. However, applications of Cultural Intelligence in church and ministry leadership contexts are relatively few in number.

---

293   Koh et al., 'Cultural Intelligence'.
294   Ibid.
295   Adair et al., 'Culturally Intelligent Team'.
296   Ng et al., 'Beyond International Experience'; Vogelgesang et al., 'Role of Authentic Leadership'.
297   Ang and Inkpen, 'Cultural Intelligence'.
298   Putranto and Ghazali, 'Effect of Cultural Intelligence'.
299   Bücker et al., 'Impact of Cultural Intelligence'.
300   Ramirez, 'Impact of Cultural Intelligence Level'.

LITERATURE SURVEY AND ASSESSMENT

Application of CQ in church contexts

Livermore was the first one to apply Cultural Intelligence to ministry and church leadership, introducing Cultural Intelligence into church settings.[301] Although Livermore includes a twelve-page chapter providing a biblical basis for Cultural Intelligence, it is certainly too brief to be considered a solid biblical base. Livermore also applies Cultural Intelligence to short-term mission trips, which is a showcase work of Cultural Intelligence in a missionary context, yet without a biblical or theological perspective.[302] Livermore further provides some practical implications for leadership in general.[303]

Noticing the Western churches are becoming more multicultural and multiracial, Rah sees the relevance of placing Cultural Intelligence at the forefront of church ministry.[304] Rah advocates the importance and urgency of acquiring Cultural Intelligence, enabling church and parachurch ministries to become more multiculturally adept so as to bear transformative witness to Jesus.

In summary, Cultural Intelligence aims to answer one basic question: why do some individuals function and perform more effectively than others in an intercultural context? Or, from the perspective of this study, why do some Chinese pastors relate to others more harmoniously than other Chinese pastors? Why do some migrant pastors develop teams more effectively than other migrant pastors?

---

301 Livermore, *Cultural Intelligence*.
302 Livermore, *Serving*.
303 Livermore, *Leading with Cultural Intelligence*.
304 Rah, *Many Colors*.

Reflection and conclusion

The preceding literature reviews underline the relevance and significance of CQ for my research. In reviewing, it is clear that CQ is not a perfect theory and has its limitations. At certain points, the theory of Cultural Intelligence awaits clarification. Firstly, a primary question concerns the theory itself. Although the four factors of Cultural Intelligence are proven to be valid assessment determinants, the mechanism of the internal function of the four factors is unknown and lacks careful definition. The question is whether these four factors are of equal weight or whether one among the four factors is the primary determinant. Also, in terms of application, do the four factors carry the same weight in ministry and ecclesiological settings that they do in business and commercial contexts?

A second group of questions focuses on the absence of certain research areas. Not many studies of Cultural Intelligence have been conducted into intergenerational relationships or in the context of intermarriage. Similarly, studies of Cultural Intelligence in multicultural churches, in groups of transnational migrants and in multicultural societies such as Australia, are also scarce. Fortunately, in recent years, subsequent studies have filled some of the missing gaps.[305]

Moreover, the study conducted by Schlägel and Sarstedt reveals that the standard measurement of CQ lacks measurement invariance. Therefore, Schlägel and Sarstedt suggest 'researchers should be cautious when comparing the results of cross-country and cross-cultural research'.[306]

In view of the preceding limitations, various researchers are aware of the research gaps and have suggested a number

---

305   Deng and Gibson, 'Qualitative Evaluation'; Wang et al. 2015, Crowne and Engle 2016, Schlägel and Sarstedt, 'Assessing the Measurement Invariance'.
306   Schlägel and Sarstedt, 'Assessing the Measurement Invariance', 633, 643.

of directions for Cultural Intelligence and intercultural study.[307] Leung, Ang and Tan have suggested that explorations of Cultural Intelligence in relation to personality traits and worldview should be conducted. They have also suggested that the methodologies should shift from self-reported measures to a comprehensive and holistic assessment. Moreover, the focus of research should be moved more towards psychological and behavioural outcomes and the interplay of conscious and non-conscious processes.[308]

Nevertheless, CQ is likely to remain a powerful and essential tool for enhancing intercultural leadership. Studies consistently show that effective leadership requires more than knowledge and information.[309] Effective leadership is shaped by both emotional strength (inspiration and passion) and rational power (reason and logic). 'Leadership concerns the interaction of leaders with other individuals. Once social interactions are involved, emotional awareness and emotional regulation become important factors affecting the quality of the interactions.'[310]

In this regard, Cultural Intelligence, as a multidimensional and multifactor concept or construct, gives a greater understanding of effective intercultural leadership than merely cognitive and affective intelligence. Cultural Intelligence is a holistic and integrated concept, which involves cognitive, affective and behavioural dimensions. Over the last two decades, it has been noted that Cultural Intelligence theories have attracted many subsequent studies and researches. Many studies show that CQ has great explanatory power in cross-cultural relational interactions. Cultural Intelligence theories also reveal a tremendous predictive capacity for intercultural leadership performance.

---
307 Leung et al., 'Intercultural Competence'.
308 Ibid., 509–10.
309 Hughes, *Leadership*; Yukl, *Leadership in Organizations*.
310 Wong and Law, 'Effects of Leader and Follower', 244.

Thus, I regard CQ a useful tool in my study for the following reasons. Firstly, the concept of Cultural Intelligence originates and has been tested through collaboration by Western scholars (Van Dyne, Livermore) and Asian scholars (Ang, Ng, Earley, et al.). Such collaboration avoids theoretical bias towards Westernised perspectives or oriental emphasis. In other words, the applicability of the theory in the global scene and in the international arena is increased. For this research, which targets Chinese migrants in Western social and cultural contexts, the relevance and applicability of CQ theory is highly appropriate.

Secondly, as Cultural Intelligence is a model for developing the intercultural competence of executives and corporate leaders working in an international context, the validity and reliability of Cultural Intelligence are academically assessed. According to Matsumoto and Hwang, the validity of Cultural Intelligence has been academically tested and proven reliable.[311] In other words, other intercultural competence tools are less valuable, less robust and more vulnerable to critical review.[312] Thus, Cultural Intelligence is an effective tool which involves 'the knowledge,

---

[311] Matsumoto and Hwang, 'Assessing Cross-Cultural Competence'. The assessment conducted by Matsumoto and Hwang covers ten different intercultural inventories, such as Cross-Cultural Adaptability Inventory (CCAI), Cross-Cultural Sensitivity Scale (CCSS), Cultural Intelligence (CQ), Intercultural Behavioral Assessment (IBA) and Behavioral Assessment Scale for Intercultural Communication Effectiveness (BASIC), Intercultural Adjustment Potential Scale (ICAPS), Intercultural Communication Competence (ICC), Intercultural Sensitivity Inventory (ICSI), Intercultural Development Inventory (IDI), and Multicultural Personality Inventory (MPQ). The assessment is based on the following criteria: used valid and reliable criterion variables, positive effects from pre–post sojourn or training, extreme group comparison, concurrent ecological validity, predictive ecological validity, incremental validity over demographics, incremental validity over personality, incremental validity over at least one other 3C test, cross-cultural samples (beyond international sojourners in the United States) and mixed methodologies.

[312] Although Matsumoto is the developer of one of the assessed inventories, ICAPS, Matsumoto still concludes that CQ is one of the best inventories (Hammer, 'Clarifying Inaccurate Statements', 3–5).

skills, abilities, and other (KSAOs) factors that are necessary to demonstrate competence' and exhibits adjustment and adaptation outcomes.[313]

Thirdly, one of the main foci of this study concerns the communication among the pastors in Chinese churches. I particularly draw attention to the study of Bücker and his team.[314] While most of the CQ studies are conducted in North America, Europe and some Asian countries, this study is conducted in China. It is particularly relevant to this study on Chinese pastors. Moreover, Bücker and his team assess specifically the impact of Cultural Intelligence on communication effectiveness. The results of their studies show that CQ has a significant positive impact on communication effectiveness.[315] Furthermore, their results also indicate that a higher level of CQ reduces levels of anxiety.[316] Bücker rightly points out that 'cultural intelligence makes people more alert in cross-cultural interactions. It increases awareness of the differences with the other culture and enables the person to make use of appropriate behavioural repertoires and relevant cultural knowledge. This awareness . . . [has] a decreasing influence on the level of anxiety in intercultural interactions'.[317] These study results are relevant to my research.[318]

Lastly, CQ is a relatively new tool for measuring intercultural competence. Various assessments have been conducted in the last few years. CQ has received a positive assessment on both

---

313 Matsumoto and Hwang, 'Assessing Cross-Cultural Competence', 850.
314 Bücker et al., 'Impact of Cultural Intelligence'.
315 Ibid., 2085.
316 Ibid.
317 Ibid., 2077.
318 As non-communication is one of the findings of this research, CQ is highly relevant to my research.

the theory construct and practical application.[319] All these assessments demonstrate CQ as a reliable tool in measuring intercultural competence.

Although the theoretical construct of Cultural Intelligence is far from perfect, the advantages and strengths of CQ certainly outweigh the limitations. CQ is by far the best tool for measuring intercultural competence. It is a valid and reliable tool in understanding human relational dynamics and social interaction across diversified cultures. It is empirically robust, extensively used, stands up under critical review and lends itself to potential application as both a quantitative and qualitative method.

In terms of this study, Cultural Intelligence could be used as a measurement tool of pastors working in Chinese churches. The 20-question self-assessment tool could be easily used to give overall dimensions of strengths and weaknesses (motivational CQ, knowledge CQ, metacognitive CQ, and behaviour CQ) of the pastors' intercultural competence.

Furthermore, as motivation is identified as a primary factor in the four-factor framework, the qualitative semi-structured interview will give special attention in this aspect. The interview findings are likely to reveal the pastors' intercultural motivation. For example, where pastors refrain from communicating with one another, my research will likely reveal the (lack of) motivational factors, such as cultural values or ethnocentric bias. For instance, if the pastors are reluctant to acquire language, the interview will examine their motivational factors (such as experiencing shame) and suggest analysis of these perspectives.

In summary, these points as revealed through the literature review show the extensive relevance and practical application of CQ to my study and therefore justify the usage of CQ as a

---

[319] Matsumoto and Hwang, 'Assessing Cross-Cultural Competence'; Leung et al., 'Intercultural Competence'; Bücker et al., 'Impact of Cultural Intelligence'.

LITERATURE SURVEY AND ASSESSMENT

theoretical framework of analysis in this research. My intent is to show the relevance of Cultural Intelligence in understanding the relationship dynamics and cross-cultural competence of Chinese church pastors. I believe that a research project of this type focused on Cultural Intelligence generates valuable primary data.

CHAPTER THREE
HISTORICAL OVERVIEW

In the literature review, I noted that research and studies on Chinese migrants in Australia are scarce. Although there are some historical accounts of Chinese settlement in the gold rush period and early twentieth century, most of them are limited to certain short periods of time and to a specific sector of people. Chinese migrants and Chinese churches are seldom the focus of study. Chinese Christians and Chinese churches in Sydney are seldom found in the 'suggestions for future research' of research articles. This reflects the inadequacy of theoretical and empirical research of Chinese churches and pastoral leaders. In the absence of candid accounts of generational cultural differences and the shortage of theoretical analyses of the pastoral leadership maze, the real problems experienced by Chinese Christians and in Chinese churches are yet to be unearthed.

Therefore, a historical account of Chinese migrants to Australia and Chinese churches in Sydney is greatly needed. Such a historical study needs to detail the size of Chinese migration, the places of origin of Chinese migrants and the contours of the cultural roots of two generations of Chinese migrants. It should also reveal the social engagement between Chinese migrants and

HISTORICAL OVERVIEW

local Australians and the cultural interaction between migrants of two generations. A historical account of Chinese churches must also identify the traits and roots of the cultural factors that influence ministry development and pastoral leadership. With these things in mind, this chapter traces the historical background of Chinese migrants, the development of Chinese churches and the cultural setting of multi-generational Chinese churches and pastoral leaders in Sydney.

History of early Chinese migrants to Sydney

Australia is a multicultural nation of migrants. One in four of Australia's twenty-two million people were born overseas, and we have more than 270 ancestries between us. Nearly fifty per cent have at least one overseas-born parent.[1]

Any history of Chinese migrants has to be traced back to the mid-nineteenth century. Since 1851, with the discovery of gold at Ballarat, Victoria, Chinese workers and migrants settled in Australia, first in Victoria, then in various regions of New South Wales, such as the Rocky River Goldfield and Bathurst.[2]

Although the gold rush in Victoria was better known, other documents indicate that Chinese gold miners gathered in New South Wales as well. For example, as early as 1866, more than 120 Chinese miners at the Rocky River Goldfield sent a petition letter to the Minister for Lands and Executive Council on 18 April. They asked for the return of Commissioner Dalton as the Gold Commissioner, as they felt that Dalton's presence there could protect them from racial conflict. According to Choi, in the mid-nineteenth century, most Chinese settlers in Australia were in the goldfield. 'In Victoria in 1861, the goldfield areas of

---

1   Australian Multicultural Advisory Council, 'People of Australia'.
2   NSW State Records, 'Immigration from Many Lands'.

Ararat, Ballarat, Beechworth, Castlemaine, Maryborough and Sandhurst had some 24,000 among a total Chinese population of 24,700. In New South Wales in the same year (1861), of a total 13,000 Chinese, about 12,200 of them were in the mining areas—Mount Braidwood, Bathurst, Bombala, Turon and Wellington.'[3] According to Smith, nine Chinese settlement systems within three regions (Braidwood, Tumut and Kiandra) in New South Wales have been identified.[4]

At the peak of the gold rush, the Chinese population in Australia jumped to almost 40,000.[5] Choi's research reveals that 'not all the Chinese in goldfield areas were gold miners; some were scattered around mining towns managing small stores and groceries, or working in market gardens, or keeping cafes and boarding houses. The Chinese population in the capital cities was not large'.[6]

After the gold rush peak years, some Chinese miners returned to China, while other miners chose to move to Sydney, which became the city with the highest Chinese population. According to the Australian Bureau of Statistics, the Chinese in New South Wales in 1901 were recorded at 10,073.[7] 'Chinese were found in most of the suburbs in Sydney . . . even in 1901, but the principal concentrations, both residence and shops, were in the city centres: in Sydney, around the Haymarket-Dixon Street area . . . '[8]

After the Australian gold rush, the number of Chinese migrants dropped. The main reason was a change in government

---

3   Choi, *Chinese Migration*. The figures are taken from Census of Victoria (1861), 22; Census of New South Wales (1861).
4   Smith, 'Hidden Dragons', 209.
5   Mar, *So Great a Cloud of Witnesses*, 1; Choi, *Chinese Migration*, 28.
6   Choi, *Chinese Migration*, 28.
7   Australian Bureau of Statistics, 'Table 72'. The figure is an addition of the settlers from China (9993) and Hong Kong (80).
8   Choi, *Chinese Migration*, 33.

HISTORICAL OVERVIEW

policy. In the early 1900s, the Immigration Restriction Act 1901 was passed, which later developed into the so-called White Australia policy. The White Australia policy was developed as a national ideal, 'a vision of a future Australia inhabited only by "white" people'.[9] The superiority of white Australians to all non-European people 'was nurtured by racial theories, particularly Social Darwinism, at a time of apparent global dominance of European civilisation'.[10]

The White Australia policy required Chinese and Asians to undertake a dictation test for entry to Australia, consequently making it almost impossible to enter.[11] Moreover, the first batch of Chinese in Australia was mostly men, arriving without families, who had left their wives and children in their homelands.[12] The ratio of male and female migrants was disproportionally skewed towards the former.[13] Such a policy lasted for half a century.

In the early 1950s, the Australian government started to restore relationships with Asian nations and planned to erase the negative impressions caused by the White Australia policy.[14]

Steps were taken to accept non-European migrants. In 1957, a policy of allowing non-Europeans with fifteen years' residence in Australia to become Australian citizens was passed.[15] Moreover, the dictation test was abolished. Business migrants

---

9 Markus, 'White Australia', 686.
10 Ibid., 687. See also Yarwood, 'White Australia Policy', 81.
11 NSW Migration Heritage Centre, '1901 Immigration Restriction Act'. According to the 1901 Immigration Acts, all Asians attempting to enter Australia had to go through the infamous dictation test. It was a test of any European language (such as Italian, French or English). It became clear that it was impossible for the Chinese to enter Australia.
12 Kamp, 'Chinese Australian Women', 79. In the early stages of the gold rush, the Immigration Restriction Act allowed the wives of migrants to enter Australia. However, in 1905, the clause allowing the entry of wives was cancelled.
13 Australian Bureau of Statistics, 'Chinese in Australia'.
14 NSW Migration Heritage Centre, 'Object Through Time'.
15 York, 'White Australia Policy'.

were allowed to enter Australia with their wives and children.[16] With families included, Chinese could settle in Sydney long-term. With this, children began to be born in Sydney; hence biological growth became significant alongside migration growth.

As a result, the 'non-English-speaking-background' migrants grew gradually.[17] Statistics show an increase of more than 3,000 Chinese residing in Sydney in less than a decade, in the period from 1954 to 1961.[18]

External factors in Chinese migration to Sydney

After 1970, some external factors contributed to the growth of Chinese migration and settlements. Firstly, in the 1970s, the political instability in certain Asian countries, such as that following the fall of Vietnam in 1975, the civil war in Cambodia, and the Indonesian annexation of East Timor in the mid-1970s, caused a lot of refugees to seek asylum in Australia. Consequently, numerous Asian refugees, many of them being of Chinese ethnicity, were admitted into Australia.[19]

From the 1960s, the Australian government gradually abolished the White Australia policy and instead adopted a policy of Multiculturalism.[20] In the 1970s, the Whitlam government abolished university fees for overseas students. Graduates were allowed to stay in Australia after their study. Thus, upon graduation, a great number of young, highly educated, bilingual (if not multilingual) and skilled professionals became Australian

---

16 Mar, *So Great a Cloud of Witnesses*, 22.
17 Mar, *So Great a Cloud of Witnesses*, 38; Jupp, *Australian People*, 1.
18 Mar, *So Great a Cloud of Witnesses*, 21.
19 Ibid., 38.
20 Department of Immigration and Citizenship 2011.

HISTORICAL OVERVIEW

residents. They stayed, worked and started their families in Australia. This policy was in effect until early the 1980s.[21]

In the early 1980s, Britain and China started several rounds of negotiation on the future of Hong Kong.[22] The Sino-British Joint Declaration was signed in 1984, stipulating that Britain would return Hong Kong to China on 1 July 1997. The signing of the declaration triggered a tide of migration.

The background of the tide of migration should be traced back to 1950. The Communist government ruled mainland China from 1949, and there were several waves of political unrest and social upheaval (such as the infamous Cultural Revolution). Many residents in China (mainly the wealthy and educated) were oppressed by and suffered at the hands of the Communist government. Thus, they chose to escape from China to Hong Kong in the 1950s and 1960s. Now, as 1997 approached, the horrible memory of past oppression triggered a strong urge to migrate to Australia and other Western countries. Therefore, many young Cantonese-speaking families and educated professionals migrated to Sydney. According to statistics, there was a big jump in the Hong Kong migrant community in Sydney between 1971 and 2000.[23]

Towards the end of the 1980s, because of the Tiananmen Square massacre, the Australian government established a

---

21 Megarrity, 'Under the Shadow', 45–46.
22 The background of the negotiation between China and Britain has to be traced back to the mid-nineteenth century. In the mid-nineteenth century, several treaties were signed between Britain and China, leasing Hong Kong to Britain. As the lease of Hong Kong would expire in 1997, the future of Hong Kong was uncertain in the 1980s. Thus, the negotiations were necessary and urgent.
23 Multicultural NSW Hong Kong, 'Birthplace—Hong Kong'.

policy of accepting more Chinese migrants.[24] Thus, 15,000 Chinese students, mostly Mandarin-speaking, were granted temporary visas.

Year of arrival in Australia	Hong Kong (SAR of China) Number	China (excl. SARs and Taiwan) Number
2001 to 9 Aug 2011	7,190	76,084
1991 to 2000	12,620	37,660
1981 to 1990	11,724	27,161
1971 to 1980	4,239	3,817
1961 to 1970	1,126	1,907
Arrived in 1960 or earlier	603	2,688

Table 1: **Number of Chinese migrants arriving in Australia by origin**

From 1980 to the early 2000s, the number of Chinese migrants to Australia increased significantly. Table 1 shows that the increasing rate of migrants from Hong Kong SAR[25] and China was astonishing.

Although migrants from mainland China, Taiwan, Hong Kong and other Southeast Asian countries (such as Indonesia, Malaysia, Singapore, Vietnam and Cambodia) were all ethnic Chinese, their cultural constructs varied.[26] Before the 1980s,

---

24 Callaghan, 'Remembering Tiananmen'. The then Australian Prime Minister, Bob Hawke, shed tears at Parliament House after the Tiananmen Square massacre was broadcast on TV. His sympathy for the Chinese students resulted in the policy of accepting more Chinese migrants.
25 SAR stands for Special Administrative Region. Hong Kong returned to China in 1997 and has been renamed as Hong Kong Special Administrative Region. The reason for using SAR is that Hong Kong maintains a different political, judicial and economic system from communist China.
26 The demographic result of the survey shows that most of the pastors in Chinese churches are Cantonese-speaking. It is plausible to suggest that many Cantonese-speaking pastors are from Hong Kong or the Canton province of China.

HISTORICAL OVERVIEW

mainland China was politically and socially separated from the Western world.[27] China had virtually no business dealings or interactions in the international arena. Migrants from mainland China remained culturally traditional Chinese. However, since Hong Kong had been a British colony for more than a century, social and business interactions between Hong Kong and the rest of the world were common practice. Besides, the education system and English education in Hong Kong brought with them a strong British influence. Therefore, the people of Hong Kong were culturally much less traditionally Chinese.[28] Culturally, Taiwan was in between mainland China and Hong Kong. In this regard, cultural constructs among Chinese migrants were quite diverse. Their levels of the English language also varied. In other words, the cultural distance between Chinese migrants and Australian culture was also determined by their homelands.

History of Chinese churches in Sydney

Today, Sydney has become the most Chinese-populated city in Australia. The establishment of Chinese churches has become a more widely spread phenomenon, especially in the last thirty years, in contrast to the slow development of Chinese churches in the early decades of the twentieth century.

---

27 In early 1979, the then general secretary of China, Deng Xiaoping, introduced and adopted market-economic reforms called *Gaige Kaifang* (which means Reforms and Openness) and advanced a Four Modernisations policy, which included modernisation of agriculture, industry, military, and science and technology.

28 Since 2000, China has undergone high-speed economic development, with a massive increase in international social interaction. Such global social engagement has resulted in a lot of cultural exposure to the Western world.

MICHAEL K. CHU

The establishment of the Chinese Presbyterian Church

At the close of the nineteenth century, the leaders of the Sydney Presbyterian Church started noticing the number of Chinese workers and their need for the gospel. In August 1892, the Presbyterian Church in New South Wales held 'a grand missionary musical festival' in the Sydney Town Hall to raise funds to purchase a site for the Chinese Presbyterian Christians. With the continuous support of the Presbyterian Foreign Mission Committee, the Chinese Presbyterian Church (CPC) came into existence in 1893.[29]

In the subsequent decades, the Presbyterian Foreign Mission Committee provided support in two ways: one was with the purchasing of a church hall, another was recruiting Chinese-speaking pastors to minister to the congregation. In terms of purchasing church hall, the first church hall was purchased in 1893 in Foster Street, Surry Hills. In 1957, Fullerton Memorial Church was acquired by the Chinese Presbyterian Church.[30]

In terms of recruiting ministers, the first minister appointed was Rev. John Young Wai, who was also the longest-serving pastor of the Chinese Presbyterian Church.[31] Rev. John Young Wai was recognised as an energetic pastor, teacher, evangelist and organiser. He was also known as a good fundraiser. He converted and baptised more than thirty new believers.[32] By the early 1960s, the 200-member Chinese Presbyterian Church had her own minister and church building. The church was now virtually a self-supporting church.[33]

---

29 Chinese Presbyterian Church 1994.
30 Mar, *So Great a Cloud of Witnesses*, 4, 22.
31 Ibid., 63.
32 Ibid., 4–5.
33 Ibid., 25.

HISTORICAL OVERVIEW

The two decades after 1960 were marked by the continuous growth of the CPC. One of the contributing factors of the continuous growth was the faithful, devoted and vigorous service of two ministers, Rev. David C. K. Tsai and Rev. Philip Fong. They were enthusiastic in gospel proclamation and gospel ministry. The service of these ministers improved the quality of ministry and stability of pastoral leadership.

Another factor was that Rev. Tsai could speak and preach in various Chinese dialects, such as Mandarin and Swatow. The languages were essential tools in teaching, nurturing and caring. That the congregation could access the word of God in their heart language was a determinant step in their spiritual growth.[34]

Moreover, stable membership also allowed the pastors to select and equip certain church members to become lay leaders. The continuous leadership development was crucial in sharing pastoral ministry. With the assistance of faithful lay leaders, the minister could concentrate on preaching, teaching, leadership and pastoral care. This showed that the quality of the leadership determined the quality of pastoral ministry.[35]

Formation of Chinese ministry in the Central Baptist Church

Before the Chinese Presbyterian Church was founded, a Baptist church was opened in Bathurst Street in 1836, with John Saunders, who had travelled from London to Sydney, as their first pastor.[36] With his enthusiastic effort and devoted faithfulness, John Saunders laid a solid foundation for the church. It was known

---

34 Ibid., 27.
35 Ibid., 33.
36 Prior, *Some Fell on Good Ground*, 28–41; Manley, *Heart of Sydney*; Hughes, *Baptists in Australia*.

to be a church 'strong in evangelism, missionary enterprise and outreach into the community'.[37]

The Bathurst Street Baptist Church later moved to 619 George Street and was renamed the Central Baptist Church on 9 October 1937.[38] As the location of the church was close to Chinatown and the University of Sydney, a Chinese fellowship for Chinese settlers and overseas students was formed at the Central Baptist Church, and gradually became a significant ministry of the church.[39]

A few events can be seen as milestones of the Chinese ministry at the Central Baptist Church. In 1964, about thirty members attended the first 'Chinese Sunday School', which for years was known as 'The Asian Department'. In 1971, Rev. Edward Yu was ordained as the first Chinese minister and served the church until 1994. In 1993, the first Cantonese service commenced on Sunday mornings. Subsequently, Rev. David Tse was appointed as the senior pastor in 1996, and has become 'the longest serving Pastor of the Church'.[40]

It was remarkable that such an established and well-developed local Australian Baptist church would appoint two ethnic Chinese pastors as their senior pastors. The reason, it seemed, was mainly due to the evangelistic and strategic

---

37　Gilchrist and Thompson, *Brief History*.
38　Ibid., 254; Prior, Some Fell on Good Ground. In the late 1960s, small fellowship groups were set up in some Baptist churches, such as Stanmore Baptist Church, Ashfield Baptist Church and Randwick Baptist Church (Fung, UCEC *(Brief History)*).
39　As recalled by Rev. Joseph Fung, in the late 1950s, the Chinese fellowship attracted some Chinese members and overseas Chinese students. Generally, about forty Chinese attended the fellowship regularly.
40　Gilchrist and Thompson, *Brief History*.

HISTORICAL OVERVIEW

foresight of the leaders and the faithful ministry of mission-minded members.[41]

Gilchrist and Thompson rightly remark that the Central Baptist Church had the heart of the gospel as their vision.

> The past is recalled, but the people of God must always look away to God's future. The past is to be remembered with gratitude, but the need of the present and the challenges of the future beckon. The Church is still 'in the heart of Sydney' and still with the heart of the Gospel, and still for the hearts of the world.[42]

The Central Baptist Church indeed did not neglect the heart of the gospel to the Chinese, a heart derived from their proximity to Chinatown.

The Chinese Christian Church and the West Sydney Chinese Christian Church

In the mid-1960s, another Chinese church was formed. Four elders from the Chinese Presbyterian Church observed the need for gospel proclamation and spiritual nurturing among the ever-increasing Chinese migrants.[43] They also noticed that some converted Christians did not want to join a church with a

---

41 Although Central Baptist Church has developed a strong Chinese ministry, the church has never claimed that they were a Chinese church. The Chinese congregation was simply a Chinese ministry among many ministries in the local Baptist church.
42 Gilchrist and Thompson, *Brief History*.
43 The four elders were T. Y. Lin, T. C. Chen, T. Liao and A. Wong (Chinese Christian Church, *Moving Forward*, 15).

Presbyterian denominational background and beliefs.[44] As cited in one report:

> Because of denominational divisions, complacency and language difficulties, wonderful opportunities to cultivate spiritual advancements and Christian works among the believers were sadly missed, and organised efforts to spread the Gospel among the unbelievers were lacking. The need for an Interdenominational and independent Church to fulfil this urgent need weighed heavily in the hearts of many devoted Chinese Christians.[45]

In August 1965, the Chinese Christian Church (CCC) was formed, which was an 'interdenominational' church with congregational governance.[46]

The church recorded fast growth in the first few years. In the first year, the church met at the AMP auditorium at Circular Quay, and the attendance jumped to more than one hundred.[47] Gifted overseas preachers were invited to proclaim the Bible message, such as Dr Leland Wang, Dr Hong Sit and Rev. Wilson Wang. The power of God's word changed and transformed many people's lives.[48] In 1967, the Chinese Christian Church decided to

---

44 Chinese Christian Church, *Moving Forward*, 15–18. As a matter of fact, some early leaders and members of the Chinese Christian Church Sydney were from a Baptist church background. Besides, the first baptism of the Chinese Christian Church Sydney was held at Central Baptist Church, instead of the Chinese Presbyterian Church.
45 Chinese Christian Fellowship, 'Report of The Executive Committee' 2.
46 Congregational governance signifies that the major decisions are made by the members in general meetings. The day-to-day decisions are made by the board of deacons or board of elders, which are led predominantly by the lay leaders. The pastors are expected to provide ministry guidance and advice only. Such church governance is adopted by most independent churches in Sydney.
47 Chinese Christian Church, *Moving Forward*, 20.
48 Ibid., 20–22.

HISTORICAL OVERVIEW

purchase a church from the North Sydney Congregational Church at a price of $110,000.[49]

In terms of leadership, a few years after the inception of the CCC, for various reasons, the four founding elders stepped down from the key leadership positions, and younger members were encouraged to take leadership.[50] As the new younger leaders were more dynamic and energetic, and had a strong background with the Overseas Christian Fellowship (known as OCF),[51] they laid a solid Bible foundation for the newly established church.

Before the close of the 1970s, another new Chinese church was planted. In the early 1970s, the Chinese Christian Church's church hall became overcrowded; the attendance increased from 150 to 240 within a three-year period, from 1975 to 1977.[52] A new church plant was suggested. As a result, a new church, the West Sydney Chinese Christian Church (WSCCC), was established at Strathfield to serve local Chinese migrants. In 1978, the first meeting was held at the Burwood Gospel Hall, and in 1983 the Strathfield Uniting Church was bought as a new church venue. The West Sydney Chinese Christian Church became independent in January 1982,[53] and the key leaders of the new church were Rev. Wilfred Chee, Hock Leng Hiu, Peter Chen, Pak Lim Chu and Lim Kim Bew.[54]

---

49 Ibid., 27–28.
50 T.Y. Lin passed away in 1971. A. Wong returned to CPC and resumed his elder position. T.C. Chen and T. Liao decided not to serve in the key leadership team (Chinese Christian Church, *Moving Forward*, 33).
51 As recalled by Joseph Fung, the key ministry of the Overseas Christian Fellowship in the 1960s was Bible study. OCF members benefited from various faculty members of Moore Theological College (including Broughton Knox, Peter O'Brien, Peter Jensen and Alan Cole). OCF became a platform for leadership training.
52 Chinese Christian Church, *Moving Forward*, 37.
53 Ibid., 38.
54 Information taken from a personal conversation with Rev. Chris Chua on 16 July 2015 at North Rocks.

Both the Chinese Christian Church Sydney and the West Sydney Chinese Christian Church started with a monolingual (English) service. In the 1980s and 1990s, as Chinese migrants continued to enter Sydney, the churches set up Cantonese and Mandarin services to meet the needs of Cantonese-speaking and Mandarin-speaking migrants.[55] Numerical growth was prominent among the Cantonese-speaking and Mandarin-speaking congregations.

The process of establishing branch churches, and later becoming independent churches, was smooth and pleasant. Although the West Sydney Chinese Christian Church became independent, both the Chinese Christian Church and the West Sydney Chinese Christian Church continued to work closely together for a number of years, undertaking joint ministries such as the Joint Missionary Committee.[56] The establishment of the West Sydney Chinese Christian Church was of critical significance to the Chinese churches in Sydney, so that establishing branch churches became a new paradigm or model for planting new churches.

Period of church planting

By the end of the 1970s, the three existing Chinese churches (the Chinese Presbyterian Church, the Chinese Christian Church and the West Sydney Chinese Christian Church) paved the way for many new churches. Since the early 1980s, the growth of Chinese churches in Sydney has been remarkable. By 2016, around one hundred new churches had been established, which included denominational churches, such as Presbyterian, Alliance, Baptist, Anglican, Evangelical Free, Lutheran, Salvation Army, Uniting and

---

55 Chinese Christian Church, *Moving Forward*, 38.
56 Ibid.

the Ling Liang Church. The growth of independent congregational churches was also astonishing. Initially, some churches were purely monolingual, either Cantonese or Mandarin. As years went by, many churches were Cantonese-speaking (or Mandarin-speaking) with an English service for the second-generation young people. Doctrinally, they ranged from evangelical Bible-believing churches to Pentecostal and Charismatic churches.[57]

Many factors contributed to the church planting phenomenon. One of the factors was the ever-increasing growth of Chinese migration.[58] The huge gospel needs of new migrants were visibly met by their attendance at Sunday services and various church meetings. Migrants were people in transition, undergoing drastic changes in life situation. Therefore, they became more open and receptive to Christianity and started attending church.[59] Churches could play a crucial role in providing physical support and community connection for the migrants.[60] As most new migrants were yet to become acquainted with Australian community and culture, and were yet to learn English, they were virtual outsiders to Australian society. Thus, Chinese churches could be perceived as social safe havens, where they could maintain their Chinese traditions, language and culture,

---

57 Information taken from a personal conversation with Rev. Joseph Fung on 15 July 2015 at Cremorne, and conversation with Rev. Chris Chua on 16 July 2015 at North Rocks.

58 Multicultural NSW Hong Kong, 'Birthplace—Hong Kong'; Multicultural NSW China, 'Birthplace—China'.

59 According to the diaspora missiology proposed by Wan and Tira, missions to migrants can be understood as 'missions at our doorstep' (Wan and Tira, 'Diaspora Missiology', 51–52; Wan, 'Rethinking Missiology'). The notion of 'missions at our doorstep' is characterised by such dimensions as accessibility to people, ample opportunity, a holistic ministry approach and partnership (Wan and Tira, 'Diaspora Missiology', 52). These characteristics become the main driving forces in the rapid growth of Chinese churches.

60 Jackson and Passarelli discuss the role of the church extensively in their work, although the discussion is more within a European context (Jackson and Passarelli, *Mapping Migration*).

at least for the first years of their migration. An immediate effect was that the existing number of churches could not cope with the increasing rate of growth. Thus, many new churches were planted.

Another factor was the generous partnership and support from the pastors of Caucasian churches and principals of local schools.[61] Their support and help were particularly crucial in the pioneering stage of newly-planted churches. Specifically, Caucasian pastors allowed the Chinese groups to meet in their church halls, even at the prime time of Sunday mornings. School principals made available their school halls and classrooms to Chinese churches, for Chinese churches to use for Sunday services and Sunday school classes.[62]

Although granting permission to use their premises certainly added extra administrative load for the churches and schools, their gracious tolerance and hospitable support were a great help to the new Chinese churches.

---

61 This is the concept of partnership in the diaspora missiology suggested by Wan and Tira (Wan, 'Rethinking Missiology'; Wan and Tira, 'Diaspora Missiology').

62 For example, the Chinese Australian Baptist Church West Ryde has been meeting at Marsden High School since 1986. In their early years, 1987 to 1992, Northern District Chinese Christian Church (NDCCC) was using Marsfield Community Church as a venue (Chinese Christian Church, *Moving Forward*, 41). Also, NDCCC has been using Epping North Public School for Sunday school classes since 1992, and Epping Boys High School for Sunday services since 2010. Various Sunday services of the Evangelical Free Church of Australia have been meeting at Chatswood Public School and Chatswood Church of Christ since 1987. Hills District Chinese Christian Church met at Castle Hill Baptist Church from 1992 to 1997. Beverly Hills Chinese Baptist Church used Kingsgrove Beverly Hills Baptist Church as a venue from 1995 to 2002. From 1993 to 2000, Livingstone Evangelical Free Church used Beecroft Primary School, Carlingford High School and North Rocks Primary School as venues for Sunday services. North Shore Chinese Christian Church met at Gordon Baptist Church from 2006 until 2013, when the church merged with Gordon Baptist Church.

HISTORICAL OVERVIEW

Fruits of Chinese churches: Evangelism and mission

The thirty-year growth of the Chinese church in Sydney from the 1980s was not only characterised by church planting; the growth also produced many fruitful results.

From 1980 to 2016, the Chinese churches underwent a period of harvest. Unchurched people were reached through evangelistic rallies, personal evangelism and local mission. Apart from individual churches organising their own evangelistic meetings in their own churches, inter-church evangelistic rallies of all scales were organised.[63] Well-known gifted overseas evangelists from America, Hong Kong and Southeast Asia were invited to speak at those rallies, and hundreds responded to altar calls.

Various methods of one-to-one personal evangelism were employed by churches, such as *Evangelism Explosion*, *Two Ways to Live* and *Four Spiritual Laws*. Pre-evangelism initiatives were used to reach to non-Christian friends.[64] All these were complemented by the loving care, new migrant support and constant prayer. As a result, numerous new converts joined the Chinese churches.

---

63 Chinese Presbyterian Church, *Chinese Presbyterian Church*, 3. Major evangelistic rallies were jointly organised by Chinese churches once every two years through the Sydney Chinese Evangelistic Association (SCEA), which later developed into the Sydney Chinese Christian Churches Association (SCCCA). These rallies were held at various auditoriums with huge seating capacities, such as Sydney Town Hall, Sydney Opera House and Sydney Showground. This information is extracted from the minutes of the Sydney Chinese Christian Churches Association (SCCCA) meetings.

64 Christian movies and music, outings and picnics, soccer teams and other sports, and parenting and marriage seminars were employed to reach out. Some churches organised quality children's programs, which led many non-Christian parents to place their children in Chinese churches, as the parents wanted their children to make more Chinese childhood friends. Some churches were skilful enough to organise Christian parenting talks in parallel to the children's programs, at which the gospel was shared to parents. As a result, many parents became Christians.

Chinese churches had also become passionate about overseas missions. On 3 June 1990, a meeting on mission was organised by the Overseas Missionary Fellowship Australia (OMF) for Chinese churches.[65] The speaker, James Hudson Taylor III, challenged the attending 650 young people to 'go forth into battle' and to be involved in mission. Forty young men and women made commitments to do full-time mission ministry.[66]

A joint taskforce titled Chinese Churches for Mission was formed in 2004, initiated by Dr Calvin Ma, then national director of OMF Australia. The taskforce was joined by representatives from various mission agencies[67] and the Sydney Chinese Christian Churches Association. It was set up to mobilise Chinese churches for global mission.[68] Two surveys, one on mission involvement of Chinese churches in Sydney, and one surveying long-term ethnic Asian cross-cultural workers from Sydney, were conducted in 2004 and 2010 respectively.[69] Mission training days and mission conferences were organised in 2006 and 2007.[70] With

---

65 Fung, *UCEC Report*.
66 This is taken from a report to the United Chinese Evangelism Committee (which later became the Sydney Chinese Christian Churches Association) by Rev. Joseph Fung to OMF, dated 8 June 1990. (Fung, UCEC Report).
67 OMF, SIM, Wycliffe, the Chinese Christian Mission Australia and the Far East Broadcasting Company
68 This information is taken from the CCFM meeting minutes, dated 16 June 2004, 21 July 2004 and 22 September 2004.
69 Ma, 'Questionnaire'.
70 This information is taken from the CCFM meeting minutes, dated 26 October 2006 and 12 May 2007.

HISTORICAL OVERVIEW

all these events and initiatives, from 1980 to 2000, almost twenty missionaries were sent overseas by Chinese churches.[71]

Moreover, regular short-term mission trips (one every two months) to rural New South Wales were organised by the Chinese Christian Mission Australia. Destinations included Penrith, Bathurst, Orange, Wagga Wagga, Canberra, Albury, Newcastle, Wollongong, Tamworth and Armidale. Every team was comprised of approximately ten members from various Chinese churches.

The aforementioned results were the joint effort of pastors and members of various Chinese churches, as well as of certain passionate mission leaders and preachers, and the constant assistance of mission organisations. This resulted in multiple converts, who, in turn, became members of Chinese churches. It also resulted in sending many mission-minded missionaries overseas.

---

71 To name just a few: Rev. Patrick and Jenny Fung were sent to Pakistan, and Rev. Fung has now become International director of OMF International. Dr Garry and Maggie Fong were sent to East Asia, where Dr Fong works as a medical doctor among minority groups. Rev. Daniel and Dominica Lai were sent to Kenya, in charge of all the administrative affairs. Rev. David and Janice Zheng were sent to Hong Kong to do mission broadcasting into China. Rev. Phil and Irene Nicholson, Rev. Wayne and Angela Chen and Miss Christine Dillon were sent to Taiwan. Dr Lawrence and Liling Tan were sent to Bolivia. Johan and Debbie Linder were sent to Thailand. Jacob Yung was sent to Tasmania. After 2000, there were even more missionaries sent from Chinese churches in Sydney, such as Shirley Jim, Sharon Law, John and Bec Yeo, Rolf and Bonnie Lepelaar, Jacqui Ng, Aaron and Amy Koh, Andrew and Jo Wong, Alex and Naomi Fung, Peter and Kath Lau, Rita and Rohan Minehan, John and Denise Dickson, Mark and Susan Boyley, Calvin and Joyce Ma, Cathy Lau, Grace Chu, Allan and Bronwyn Lihou, Jason and Hiwin Tam, John and Regine Gill, Dave and Jan Martin, Vivian To, Susanna Tse, Hoi Yan Shea, David and Jenn Ng, Moses Truong, Yakim and Grace Morgan, Lee-On Tan and Michael and Joyce Lee.

MICHAEL K. CHU

Fruits of Chinese churches: Young people's ministry

Another prominent result of the growth of Chinese churches was the development of young people's ministry among both Chinese-speaking and English-speaking Christians.

The first annual Combined Chinese Youth Summer Conference (CCYSC) was held in 1991 with full enrolment.[72] In subsequent years, 150 to 200 Cantonese-speaking young Christians from different churches gathered together to learn the Bible. Speakers were invited from overseas to preach expositional sermons.

One of the results of the conferences was the establishment of the Chinese Christian Fellowship (CCF) in 1992, both at the University of Sydney and the University of New South Wales, with the primary target group being Cantonese-speaking students from Hong Kong. From 1993 and 1994, CCF groups were also set up in other universities, such as Macquarie University, the University of Technology of Sydney, the University of Western Sydney, and the University of Sydney, Cumberland campus. The regular weekly meetings were well attended, ranging from forty to one hundred students.[73] CCF was the evangelistic arm of the church, reaching out to the young people on campus. The evangelistic initiatives of the students brought into the Chinese churches many young members, leaders and pastors.[74]

---

72 Fung, *Chairman's Report*, 1.
73 This is my personal recollection, as I have been invited to preach at various Chinese Christian Fellowships since 1992.
74 Many of the then young leaders became pastors in Chinese churches, such as Wilson Fong (CABC—West Ryde), Herbert Chan (CABC—Thornleigh), Daniel Chan (Grace Chinese Christian Church), David Truong (Northern District Chinese Christian Church), Andrew Tung (Gracepoint Chinese Presbyterian Church), Billy Lee (Campbelltown Chinese Christian Church), and Eric Lai (Christ Evangelical Centre). Many others went into full-time ministry and pastoral ministry in Hong Kong and other areas.

HISTORICAL OVERVIEW

The ministry to English-speaking students also bore fruit. The Overseas Christian Fellowship (OCF) aimed at and reached out to Asian overseas students, mainly from Malaysia, Singapore and other English-speaking Asian countries.[75] Many overseas students became devoted Christians and mission-minded leaders and were subsequently involved in Chinese churches as leaders, pastors and missionaries.[76] Also, groups of the Fellowship of Overseas Christian University Students (FOCUS) were set up at the University of Sydney and the University of New South Wales.[77] The weekly Bible-study groups helped Asian and Chinese students grow in their Christian faith. The English-speaking students also benefited from the annual Katoomba Leadership Conference (now known as NEXTGEN conference) which helped raise up English-speaking leaders and pastors. These leaders were trained in local theological colleges. Over the years, almost forty English-speaking Chinese pastors were trained to serve in various Chinese churches and to teach in Bible colleges.[78]

It is noted that all the aforementioned ministries were conducted in two separate language streams, Chinese and

---

75 Mar, *So Great a Cloud of Witnesses*, 28.
76 For example, John Ting later became a minister at CPC. Andrew Lu later became an elder and session clerk at CPC. Bruce Lin later became an elder at the Chinese Christian Church Sydney. Wilfred Chee was the first one from OCF to serve as a full-time minister. Lim Kim Bew later became a minister at the Chinese Christian Church. Joseph Fung planted a number of Chinese Baptist churches and served as a key leader in the Sydney Chinese Christian Churches Association.
77 AFES, 'Evangelical Union Sydney University > Sydney'; AFES, 'FOCUS University of New South Wales > Kensington'.
78 Some of the names are: Kenny Liew, Sam Chan, Andrew Hong, Eugene Hor, Michael Leong, Steve Chong, Sam Mak, Ying Yee, Tom Tokura, Peter Ko, Gary Koo, Peter Lin, Ben Johnson, John Menzies, Duncan Chang, John Dickson, Joshua Ng, Brian Tung, Cam Phong, Denise Chee, Ernest Chiang, David Tsai, David Chen, Alby Lam, Owen Seto, Simon Wong, Andrew Ku, Thomas Lai, Steve Turner, David Martin, Simon Chiu, John Gurusamy, Anthony Dumbrell, Michael Kwan, Sam Chan, Dan Wu, Andy Chung, Kenny Liew, David Truong, Doug Fyfe and Andrew Tipps.

English. As a matter of fact, young people at university are in their formative stage of life, and supposedly more open to cultural learning, such as acquiring new languages and working with people from diverse cultural backgrounds. However, this cultural learning was not happening. The young people in Chinese groups and English groups had virtually zero contact with each other. It was true that *ministry* was blossoming, but the seed of *non-communication* between Chinese and English believers was being sown in these early days.

Fruits of Chinese churches: The Sydney Chinese Christian Churches Association

By 1966, the leaders of Chinese churches in Sydney realised the great need for collaboration. Although at the time there were only two Chinese churches and a few small Chinese fellowships affiliated with some local Baptist churches, they formed the Combined Sydney Chinese Christian Revival and Evangelism Committee; this was all under the leadership of Rev. Wilson Wong, who was then the pastor of the Chinese Christian Church.[79] The Christians joined hands in organising regular open-air evangelistic meetings in Dixon Street, Chinatown. They also organised once-a-year evangelistic rallies and annual family retreats.[80] Meetings were conducted according to the languages of the target groups.

In 1975, through the encouragement of Rev. Thomas Wang of the Chinese Congress of World Evangelisation (CCOWE),[81] the Combined Sydney Chinese Christian Revival and Evangelism

---

79   Fung, UCEC *(Brief History).*
80   Ibid.
81   Rev. Thomas Wang later became the first general secretary of the Chinese Coordination Centre of World Evangelism in 1976 (Chinese Coordination Centre, 'General Secretary').

HISTORICAL OVERVIEW

Committee was re-formed and renamed the United Chinese Evangelistic Committee (UCEC), under the leadership of Rev. Philip Fong, then minister of the Chinese Presbyterian Church.[82] In 1993, UCEC was again renamed—the Sydney Chinese Evangelistic Association (SCEA). In 2003, the association became a government registered body, and was renamed the Sydney Chinese Christian Churches Association (SCCCA),[83] with seventy-five members.[84] One of the objectives was 'To encourage, promote and support the proclamation of the Gospel among the Chinese in Australia and overseas'.[85]

In terms of operation, general meetings were held once every two months, with Cantonese as the main language, and Mandarin and English as auxiliary languages. Three ministry teams were set up according to the languages, namely Cantonese youth ministry, Mandarin ministry and English ministry.[86] All ministry teams organised activities and events to meet the specific needs of their language congregation. For example, the Combined Chinese Youth Summer Conference had been organised in Cantonese since 1991. Yet in 2013, the conference was divided into two language groups, Cantonese and Mandarin, as the number of Mandarin-speaking youth was increasing.[87] The English track also organised training days in various districts to equip youth leaders in Chinese churches.

Occasionally, ministries might be organised with the joint force of all three language teams. For example, in 2015 and 2016,

---

82 Fung, UCEC *(Brief History)*.
83 Fung, 'SCCCA—History'.
84 Law, *Annual Report 2016*.
85 Sydney Chinese Christian Churches, 'About SCCCA'.
86 The Cantonese youth ministry team was led by Billy Lee, the Mandarin ministry team by Rev. David Zheng, and the English ministry team by Rev. Ying Yee.
87 See meeting minutes of the SCCCA—CYM on 12 December 2011 and 17 September 2012.

as 'same-sex marriage' became a hot issue in the political arena and Chinese churches, the three language teams of the SCCCA organised joint initiatives. A forum on same-sex marriage was organised with both English and Mandarin speakers. Petition letters representing all three language churches were sent to the Prime Minister and the Leader of the Opposition. A statement by SCCCA on same-sex marriage was published in newspapers on 18 June 2016.[88]

With the assistance of SCEA and SCCCA, a few new ministries were established to reach out to the needs of specific groups in the Chinese community,[89] such as the Restaurant Mission, Marriage & Family For Christ,[90] the First Light Care Association[91] and the Chinese Theological College of Australia.[92]

In a sense, UCEC, SCEA and SCCCA were catalysts for developing collaboration between Chinese churches and vehicles for promoting mission as well as being a platform for uniting the language congregations of Chinese churches.

These ministries would not have come into existence without the foresight of visionary leaders and pastors.[93] They were not overwhelmed by heavy ministry loads and busyness. Their constant prayerful attention to the needs of Chinese churches contributed to the prosperous development of the ministry. Moreover, such a ministry pattern was not limited to the first-generation pastors. There were a few second-generation English-speaking Chinese pastors working in a similar manner.

---

88 Law, *Annual Report 2016*, 2.
89 Sydney Chinese Christian Churches, 'About SCCCA'.
90 Marriage & Family, 'About'.
91 First Light, 'History of FLC'.
92 Chinese Theological College, 'Birth of the Vision'.
93 Rev. Joseph Fung, Rev. Dennis Law, Rev. Charles Cheung and Rev. Peter Wongso are among the list.

HISTORICAL OVERVIEW

However, it is noted that ministries in those days were organised separately by Chinese-speaking and English-speaking leaders. There was little routine interaction or communication between English-speaking and Chinese-speaking leaders.[94] Pastoral leaders from the two generations rarely communicated their concerns or shared their visions. Not only was there non-communication between these two groups of leaders at SCCCA level, there was also non-communication among Chinese-speaking and English-speaking pastors in Chinese churches. It is believed that if the English-speaking and Chinese-speaking pastors had communicated regularly, it would have minimised the unnecessary conflicts and disputes within Chinese churches. It would also have demonstrated and developed a desirable, healthy mode of pastoral ministry.

Fruits of Chinese churches: Theological education

Over the last thirty years, theological education has enhanced the growth of Chinese churches; at the same time, the growth of Chinese churches also fostered the establishment of a new Chinese theological college.

Local theological colleges contributed to the development of Chinese churches by organising lay-leader training programs. Morling College (Baptist) offered certificate subjects in Cantonese from 2002.[95] Moore Theological College (Anglican) has offered Chinese correspondence courses since 1995. They have even translated six-course textbooks into Chinese, including Introduction to the Bible, Old Testament 1, New Testament 1,

---

94 The only exception was the issue of same-sex marriage. In the last two years, there were some joint seminars and interaction between the Chinese group and the English group.
95 In 2002, I taught the first class of Introduction to Old Testament, which was attended by fifty-five students.

MICHAEL K. CHU

Romans, Theology 1 and Reformation Church History.[96] As early as 1990, the China Graduate School of Theology (from Hong Kong) offered up to four subjects in Sydney for Cantonese lay leaders each year (biblical subjects and ministry subjects).[97]

Although these courses offered solid Bible teaching to lay leaders, the need for training full-time pastors was not overlooked. The local theological colleges have trained many pastors for Chinese churches. Some pastors even received higher research degrees.[98] All this training was in English.

In 1991, as the number of Chinese churches increased, a group of leaders (from Chinese churches)[99] realised the need to train new pastors in Chinese language. Pastors who were not proficient in English could, therefore, be trained to serve in pastoral ministry. In the process of discussion, they negotiated with various local colleges to explore the opportunity of partnership. In 2000, after years of discussion and planning, they decided to set up a new college, the Chinese Theological College of Australia,[100] with Chinese as the main teaching language.[101]

The Chinese Theological College of Australia has indeed met the theological training needs of students who have less

---

96   I was part of the organising team and was responsible for marking papers, translating and proofreading the course textbooks.
97   Again, I was also part of the organising committee of the courses.
98   Elim Hiu was awarded a ThD through Morling College. Pius Li was awarded a DMin through Morling College. Joe Mock was awarded an MTh from Presbyterian Theological Centre (Australian College of Theology 2016). A few others were awarded MAs from various colleges in Sydney, such as Michael Chu, Bob Lee, Albert Leung, Sunny Tse, Joe Lin, Almon Li, Frankie Law, Chris Chua, Joshua Mak, Wai Kwan Fung and Daniel Lai.
99   The group of people included Joseph Fung, Dennis Law, Charles Cheung, Pamela Chan, Michael Wong and Peter Wongso.
100 The first president was Dr Peter Wongso and the first dean was Rev. Ming Leung, who was formerly the dean of Alliance College in Canberra. Dennis Law, Charles Cheung and Joseph Fung became the board members of the college.
101 Chinese Theological College, 'Birth of the Vision'. At CTCA, Mandarin was the official teaching language, with Cantonese as the auxiliary language.

HISTORICAL OVERVIEW

proficiency in English. Unfortunately, however, the students' exposure to English and opportunity for English acquisition are certainly not sufficient. Thus, when the graduates enter into pastoral ministry in Chinese churches, their communication and relations with pastors of other languages can be difficult.

This historical outline reflects how the Chinese church has grown in both quantity and quality. As of 2015, there were over one hundred Chinese churches, incorporating more than an estimated 15,000 members.[102] The evangelistic enthusiasm and outreach activities of the Chinese churches have become strong. In the last century, Chinese churches have changed from being 'receivers' to 'givers', from 'inward-looking' to 'out-reaching'. The newly developed Chinese churches have shown vitality and signs of self-replication, self-government and self-support. Partnership with local churches and colleges have been valuable, even indispensable, and should continue.

In this historical portrayal, two separate language streams within the ministries are distinctly noticeable. Most of the events and ministries were monolingual, targeting a monocultural people group. In terms of effectiveness, they were successful. However, the underlying disadvantage was that the two language groups did not know one another. There was no communication or relationship between the two cultural groups, and no ministry interface or platform was structured between them. This non-interaction stretched from pastors to lay leaders and members. The non-interaction apparently became a norm, which no one would question. In fact, the non-interaction phenomenon was undetected, and it was covered over by the overwhelming ministry successes.

---

102   This is taken from a letter sent to the Prime Minister from the SCCCA, dated 3 August 2015.

MICHAEL K. CHU

Development of cultural roots of Chinese church pastoral leaders

The rapid development of Chinese churches in Sydney resulted in a great need for pastors. Local colleges were the source of English-speaking pastors. These graduates were either second-generation Chinese or mission-minded Caucasians whose desire was to help develop a new generation of Chinese churches. The Chinese pastors came mainly from overseas, from places such as Hong Kong, Taiwan, Mainland China, Singapore and Malaysia. In other words, pastors of Chinese churches can be roughly divided into two groups: the overseas-born pastors and the Australian-born (or Australian-grown) pastors.

It is noted that the cultural background of overseas-born pastors may vary. For example, pastors from Hong Kong, Malaysia and Singapore may have some Western influence, as these three countries had been British colonies, while pastors from Mainland China may have influence from communism and Maoism.

Cultural backgrounds of pastors from Mainland China could be even more diversified. Apart from the largely unregistered house churches in rural China, Fulton documents five types of churches in the cities of China amid the urbanisation of Mainland China in recent years.[103] Fulton's categorisation of churches in China demonstrates the social and cultural differences between rural Christians living at the urban fringes of Chinese cities and the urban Christians living in more cosmopolitan, global, entrepreneurial cities. It is obvious that the wide range of churches in Mainland China are ministered to by pastors of

---

103 Fulton, China's *Urban Christians*, 23–25. The five types of churches are churches affiliated to the Three Self Patriotic Movement, megachurches at Wenzhou, migrant churches (or known as rural church in the city), urban newly formed churches and traditional unregistered urban house churches.

various social and cultural backgrounds, and the cultural values of these pastors are likely to be quite diverse.[104]

However, in spite of their socio-political and historical differences, Mainland China, Taiwan, Hong Kong and some Southeast Asia regions share similar cultural roots.[105] In particular, Fu et al. specify the commonality of the cultural heritage of Hong Kong, Taiwan and China.[106] Leung reviews a whole range of literature on beliefs concerning the characteristics of individuals and social interaction across people of Chinese ethnicity. He suggests that Confucianism 'has exercised major impact on social practices and structures of Chinese societies . . . have the ability to cultivate their morality and self-control'.[107]

In other words, while the cultures of different countries may be shaped by various economic-political ideologies and

---

104   Although Mainland China has been ruled by a communist government for the last sixty-plus years, the extent of the impact of communism and Maoism on pastors from Mainland China is yet to be assessed. For example, although the government of Mainland China is atheistic and the regime has suppressed religions all these years, the numerical growth of Christians is still phenomenal. It reflects that the impact of atheistic communism in China could be quite minimal. According to Matthews' study, even nowadays, Confucianism, by and large, still dominates Chinese people, even the Chinese students here in Australia (Matthews, 'Chinese Value Survey', 121).

105   Fu et al., 'Examining the Preferences'; Leung, 'Beliefs in Chinese Culture'; Cheng et al., 'Paternalistic Leadership'.

106   'Hong Kong, Taiwan and China share a common cultural heritage. People in the three places have in common the same Chinese language; . . . They celebrate the same folklore festivals and observe the same traditional values. Chinese people . . . all worship Confucianism, which is the essence of Chinese culture. Confucian values are preserved through a set of moral guidelines. Emphasising the importance of education, obedience to authority, interpersonal harmony, loyalty to the family, and kinship affiliation as well as individual responsibility, the deeply rooted cultural values of Confucianism still guide individual actions and attitudes in these three Chinese communities.' (Fu et al., 'Examining the Preferences', 33).

107   Leung, 'Beliefs in Chinese Culture', 222.

cultural values over decades or even centuries,[108] the cultural root of ethnic Chinese from various countries maintains similarity. Thus, Chinese pastors can be largely divided into two main cultural groups: the overseas-born are culturally traditional Chinese, whereas the Australian-born are culturally non-Chinese. The cultural roots of these two groups are different.

Cultural roots of older Chinese pastors

The cultural roots of older Chinese pastors are founded in traditional Chinese culture, which stems from Confucianism. From a worldview perspective, Confucianism can be understood as the traditional Chinese person's foundational assumptions and frameworks; assumptions which they make 'about the nature of reality [and] which they use to order their lives'.[109] Often, Confucianism is regarded as the orthodox Chinese culture,[110] and as synonymous with Chinese culture,[111] although Buddhism and Daoism have also had a significant influence in shaping Chinese culture.

Confucianism is a holistic and comprehensive system of thinking or philosophy whose fundamental concern is 'the person and human relationships in this world... The Confucian humanist concern for personal wellbeing, family harmony, and social solidarity, political stability, and universal peace has become a defining characteristic of the Chinese view of the good life'.[112] The core concept of Confucianism is *ren* (also known as *jen*), which refers to harmony and goodness in social relationships, parental

---

108 'Indian intellectuals have continued to draw from the wellsprings of their spiritual lives, despite two centuries of British colonialism.' (Tu, 'Cultural China', 146).
109 Hiebert, *Transforming Worldviews*, 25–26.
110 Yang, *Chinese Christians*, 44.
111 De Bary, *Neo-Confucian Orthodoxy*, 1–2.
112 Yang, *Chinese Christians*, 45.

and filial piety and brotherly respect.[113] The key thoughts behind these concepts are harmony, peace and stability, which explain why traditional Chinese value relationships (*guanxi*) and avoid open disagreement and conflict. In order to save face, silence is a valued virtue (though, at the same time, it can be seen as a symptom of an underlying problem).

Among these core concepts and virtues, filial piety (also known as *xiao* or *hsiao*) is of great value, especially in relationships spanning two generations.[114] Weber regards *xiao* as 'the absolutely primary virtue'.[115] Wang also makes a similar remark that 'whatever else may be uncertain, there was no doubt that loyalty and filial respect were the duties par excellence in traditional China'.[116]

According to Confucianism, in a politically or economically unstable society, everyone should recognise and observe propriety (literally 'politeness'), which pays filial piety to those who are senior in age.[117] This notion of *xiao* extends from family to organisations and the workplace. According to Lewis' study, in workplace teams, the older team members demand trust, loyalty and allegiance from the younger ones.[118] Subordinates are expected to show allegiance and loyalty upward to their department heads and managers.

This obligation of filial piety is not only observed in China but is also observed among Chinese migrants and communities

---

113 Chan, 'On Translating', xxii.
114 Smith, *Confucius*, 62.
115 Weber, *Religion of China*, 157.
116 Wang, 'Power, Rights and Duties', 169.
117 Braswell Jr, *Understanding World Religions*, 71.
118 Lewis, *When Teams Collide*, 267–70.

in Australia.[119] In practice, filial piety means 'taking good care of one's aged parents as the moral duty and is considered a distinctive Chinese family cultural value'.[120] For example, 'Seeking assistance from social welfare for aged parents was seen by many as shameful.'[121] The notion of filial piety constitutes 'five basic relationships'—ruler-minister, father-son, husband-wife, elder-younger brothers, and friend-friend.[122] These five basic relationships imply strong hierarchical levels. Filial piety is regarded as the 'cornerstone of Chinese society, the root of the Chinese family, and the core value of the Chinese consciousness'.[123] In reference to filial piety, 'family unity is more important than individual . . . the will of the ancestor is equated to be a mandate of heaven that must be obeyed without question'.[124] In practice, younger ones are expected to venerate parents in daily life and ensure their happiness.[125] Without any knowledge of or exposure to traditional Chinese culture, younger pastors can never understand and appreciate the Chinese proverb which states 'Under heaven, no parent is ever wrong'.[126]

It is not uncommon that senior pastors, who are mostly overseas-born Chinese, consider the church as their family, following the belief that 'church is a family'. Senior pastors expect their younger pastors to respect and obey them like their children do. In other words, the more senior pastors care, love and look after the younger English-speaking pastors and treat them as if

---

119 Filial piety is observed even among the long-settled ABCs. Even though the cultural values of long-settled ABCs are largely shaped by Western values, they still see their commitment to the aged as a duty (Ngan and Kwok-Bun, *Chinese Face*, 161).
120 Ibid., 160.
121 Ibid., 161.
122 Yang, *Chinese Christians*, 44.
123 Yu, 'Filial Piety', 317.
124 Tong, *Biblical Approach*, 60.
125 Ibid.
126 Augsburger, *Pastoral Counseling*, 164.

they were their children, the more they expect respect, honour, submission and obedience from the younger English-speaking pastors. Unfortunately, not many young pastors are aware of, or appreciate, their senior pastors' unspoken expectations.

The concept of 'family', from the perspective of the younger, English-speaking pastors, is very different from that of the older pastors. Traditional Chinese families were more 'extended' or clan-like, incorporating several generations living together. Yet, nowadays, this older concept of the extended family has been replaced by the model of the nuclear family, which is simply a two-generation family—only parents and children. The relationships in a traditional extended family were a complicated web and emphasised hierarchy. By contrast, in a modern family, freedom and independence are taken as the norm.[127] Egalitarian, democratic and horizontal relationships are valued and practised. So, even though the younger, English-speaking pastors also consider the church as a family, they cannot visualise the practice that the older pastors expect from them. Thus, the cultural roots of the two individual generations give rise to two different, yet easily overlooked, cultural values. The *outward* similarities of the two generations disguise the very different *inward* cultural values.

Cultural roots of Australian-born pastors

The cultural roots and worldview of the younger generation of Australian-born pastors are very different from those of traditional Chinese pastors. As the Australian-born pastors are primarily immersed in and shaped by Western culture and Western worldview, they see the world and reality differently. As suggested by Hiebert, the worldview of Westerners is governed

---

127   Ibid., 204–6.

by empiricism, characterised by a belief in an orderly, categorised world which can be studied by science and technology.[128] Thus, Australian-born pastors tend to value knowledge, equality, individualism, competition and self-reliance.[129] Augsburger identifies the characteristics of a Western worldview as being openly confrontational, intolerant of ambiguity, unguarded in emotional expression and focused on stressing one's rights.[130] Eckersley considers the dominant worldview of Australia over the last twenty years as being that of 'material progress, which gives priority to economic growth and a rising standard of living'.[131] People with such a worldview treasure achievement-orientation and performance; in other words, they are more task-oriented or goal-oriented.[132]

In view of this, the Australian-born pastors' understanding of the notion of 'church as family' is very different. They see the individual as more important than the family unit, and certainly, they would not regard the senior pastors as their parents. They know little or nothing about Confucianism, so they don't appreciate or value hierarchy and authority, and they do not see submission and obedience having any place in relating to the older pastors. They practise achieving goals over familial unity or filial piety. They separate task and relationship and see interpersonal relationships as primarily horizontal rather than

---

128 Hiebert, *Transforming Worldviews*, 337–41.
129 Ibid., 339–43.
130 Augsburger, *Pastoral Counseling*, 66–67.
131 Eckersley, 'Progress, Sustainability'.
132 It is noted that both the Confucian worldview and Western worldview are humanistic in nature. The assumptions of both worldviews are self-centred and egocentric, which deviate from biblical principles. Therefore, these worldviews are to be critically reviewed, in order to formulate a biblical worldview. See Tu, 'Probing the "Three Bonds"'; Hiebert, Transforming Worldviews, 148–50, 285–90; Plueddemann, *Leading across Cultures*, 69–71, 158–80.

HISTORICAL OVERVIEW

vertical or hierarchical.[133] Thus, Australian-born pastors tend to adopt a more direct communication style. For example, they take the Bible teaching at Matthew 18:15 literally, that 'If your brother or sister sins, go and point out their fault, just between the two of you. If they listen to you, you have won them over'. And this always leads to two-generation direct confrontation. However, as Lingenfelter rightly points out, 'most evangelicals fail to see that this text is written to a specific group of people in a specific social environment . . . for specific social action'.[134] Consequently, Lingenfelter suggests some principles for avoiding unnecessary cross-cultural confrontation, including having regard for caution and wisdom, restricting the scope of disagreement, using mediators and developing the idea of a 'feast of peace'.[135]

However, this is only one side of the story. Actually, Australian-born pastors are exposed to two worlds, the Chinese world in their homes and the Australian world at school and in society at large.[136] They experience internal cultural struggles derived from contact with two contrasting worlds, and they have to find ways to integrate or assimilate the two.

Anthropologist Paul Hiebert has suggested that, as a person moves from one country to a foreign country, the person's life undergoes a certain cultural shock, and they experience some confusion and disorientation, which determines the level of satisfaction of their stay.[137] As time goes by, the person adjusts to the culture of the foreign country, and he or she eventually becomes an adjusted bicultural person,[138] as indicated in Figure 1.

---

133 Mok, *Anthropology*, 40–41.
134 Lingenfelter, *Transforming Culture*, 168–69.
135 Ibid., 169–70.
136 In fact, overseas-born Chinese are also exposed to two worlds. However, their cultural identity is not much influenced and shaped by the Australian culture, because their formative years are not in Australia.
137 Hiebert, *Cultural Anthropology*.
138 Ibid., 39–41.

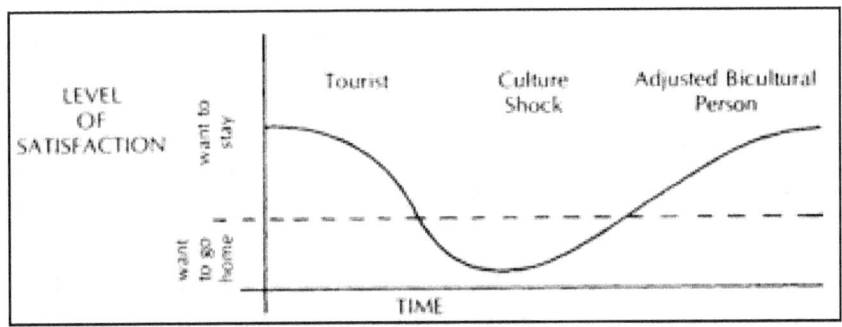

Figure 1: Culture shock is a sense of cultural disorientation to a different society

However, the cultural world of younger, Australian-born pastors is not limited to two worlds, especially in a multicultural country like Australia. They are exposed to the home culture of their parents, the host culture of Australia, the peer culture of their multicultural friends or colleagues, the subculture and the online culture. The result is a hybrid culture, sometimes also known as the third culture.[139]

According to Pollock and Van Reken, 'a Third Culture Kid (TCK) is a person who has spent a significant part of his or her developmental years outside the parents' culture'.[140] Their formative years are profoundly immersed in and moulded by two or more cultures and/or subcultures. In other words, a TCK's cultural identity is a hybrid cultural identity. Sometimes, it is hard to distinguish the components of their hybrid culture.

Over the last few decades, the Chinese churches of Australia (and North America as well) have described the first and second generation in the Chinese church with reference to two terms: 'Overseas-born Chinese' (OBCs) and 'American/Australian-born'

---

139   Tanu, 'Global Nomads'; Gibbons, *Monkey and the Fish*; Pollock and Van Reken, *Third Culture Kids*.
140   Pollock and Van Reken, *Third Culture Kids*, 13.

HISTORICAL OVERVIEW

or Australian-raised Chinese (ABCs or ARCs). However, this simple bi-polar description of the church is both inadequate and inaccurate. It is inadequate because this distinction unhelpfully juxtaposes the two extremes, tending to reinforce generational rivalry. It is inaccurate because such an analysis does not reflect the true picture. The terms OBCs and ABCs should not be seen as a simple dichotomy.

It is here suggested that a 'Cultural continuum' (shown in Figure 2) is a better model for outlining the cultural context of pastors and members of Chinese churches.[141] Every migrant,[142] disregarding their place of birth (Australia or overseas) is in the process of cultural learning and cultural integration. The continuum reflects the fact that the cultural identity of a person is a gradual, evolving process instead of a static and immutable status.[143] In the cultural continuum shown in Figure 2, the location of cultural identity is primarily determined by the number of years in Australia.

---

141 Wong, *Lecture Notes*. The model of 'Cultural continuum' has been adopted and revised from Hoover Wong's lecture notes. Hoover Wong served as a professor at Fuller Theological Seminary, Pasadena, from the late 1980s to the early 1990s. According to Ling and Cheuk, the concept of the 'cultural continuum' was first introduced by Gail Law (Law, 'Model'; Ling and Cheuk, '*Chinese*' Way, 124–5). A similar continuum model is noted in Chun's chapter on bicultural identity (Chun, 'Kingdom-Centred Identity', 250).

142 In fact, everyone, including the migrants and the people in the host country, goes through a certain degree of cultural assimilation, as cultural assimilation occurs when people of cultural diversity interact.

143 This continuum should not be assumed to be moving from left to right, from culturally Chinese to culturally Australian. It does not imply any value judgement, such as that being culturally Chinese is bad and being culturally Australian is good.

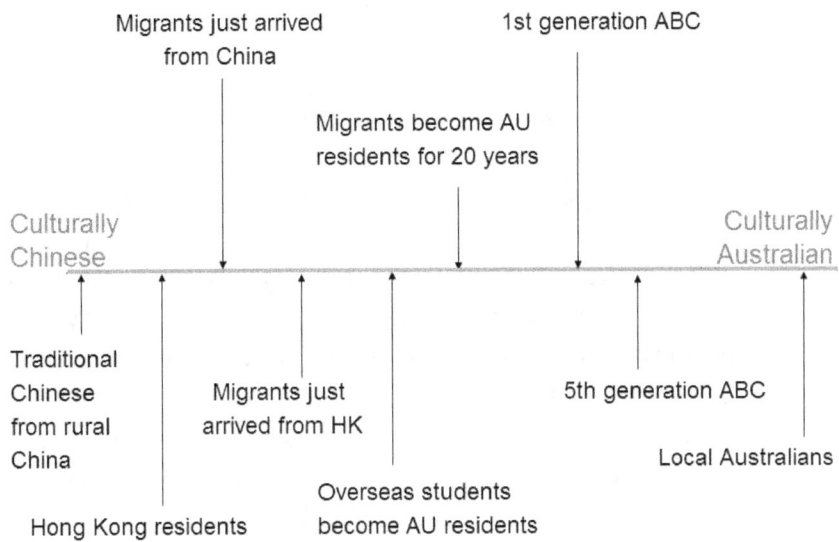

Figure 2: Cultural continuum

For the sake of clarity, the terms in the figure are qualified as follows.

- *Culturally Chinese*. As Confucianism is always regarded as the orthodox Chinese culture,[144] 'culturally Chinese' is basically understood one determined by the worldview and life philosophy of Confucian. Traditional Chinese inherit the 4000-year old teachings from Confucianism, which emphasises harmony, stability, peace and solidarity.

- *Culturally Australian*. Although Australian culture has always been perceived as Caucasian or a European culture, contemporary 'culturally Australian' resists reduction to being merely culturally Caucasian. In a multicultural society

---

144   Yang, *Chinese Christians*, 44.

HISTORICAL OVERVIEW

like Australia, 'culturally Australian' should increasingly be understood as culturally hybrid. For example, a first-generation Chinese couple have three ABC (or ARC) girls, who in turn marry a Vietnamese man, a British man and a Brazilian man. Although all three sons-in-law hold Australian passports and are regarded as Australians, the Chinese couple will relate to three of them in three different ways. After a number of years, three girls give birth to their own children. The Chinese couple now have their grandchildren with even more diversified worldviews and cultures. It is true that all children and grandchildren are regarded as Australians in this multicultural country, though their cultural identity and integration are very different. Such a phenomenon reflects the mixed or hybrid families they come from. Therefore, 'culturally Australian' is not meant to indicate a singularity. 'Culturally Australian' should be understood as a form of cultural hybridity.

- *Traditional Chinese from rural China.* As a traditional Chinese from rural Mainland China has very limited exposure or contact with the Western world, they are basically culturally traditional Chinese.

- *Hong Kong residents.* Hong Kong was a British colony, and the judicial, administrative and educational systems are basically shaped according to British practice. It is now a cosmopolitan city, with residents who still speak some English. Thus, Hong Kong residents are less culturally traditional Chinese.

- *Migrants just arrived from China and migrants just arrived from Hong Kong.* In the first year that migrants arrive in

Australia, the cultural distance between 'Australian culture' and the home culture is different depending on where the migrant has come from. It is assumed that for a migrant from Hong Kong, who has some previous Western exposure, the cultural identity could be more Australian than a person from Mainland China, who has had less interaction with the Western world.

- *Overseas students become AU residents.* When overseas students study in Australia, they spend their formative years in social interaction and engagement with local Australians. This social engagement shapes their cultural identity and cultural values. Therefore, they are more culturally Australian than the other new migrants who lack such formative experiences in Australia.

- *Migrants become AU residents for 20 years.* In general, migrants who have become Australian residents should have plenty of social and cultural contact with local Australian residents. Their cultural learning and cultural identity are more Australian than that of migrants just arrived in Australia.

- *First generation ABC.* First-generation ABCs (or ARCs) are born or raised (educated) in Australia, so their ways of thinking and doing things are basically shaped by an Australian approach. At the same time, the cultural influence from their families cannot be neglected. Therefore, they are culturally more Australian than the previous groups. However, they are not culturally as Australian as a fifth-generation ABC.

HISTORICAL OVERVIEW

- *Local Australians.* Culturally, the Caucasians in Australia have been considered as most characteristic of contemporary Australian, as the White Australia policy had been implemented in Australia in the last 100 years.

In this cultural continuum, the cultural identity of migrants is specifically determined by the length of stay in Australia. It is clearly a simplification for the sake of discussion.

In order to develop a more discriminating model, many other factors or variables are required to take account, such as language acquisition (or the failure to acquire it), immigration history of the family, parental or familial influence, the degree of social interaction, cultural orientation and determination of cultural assimilation.[145] The experiences of cultural integration by migrants is also an important factor. For example, learning outcomes from those experiencing a Confucian educational model (traditional Chinese) and those experiencing a Socratic education model (mostly Western) are likely to be very different.[146]

Language acquisition (English, Chinese or other Chinese dialects) determines the confidence, willingness and degree of social interaction, as well as ensuring opportunities for reaching out to people of other cultures and providing prospects for gaining social capital (education, social resources and social networking). All these may help the new migrants in gaining intercultural

---

145 Ling and Cheuk, *'Chinese' Way.*
146 Socrates' educational pedagogy used dialectical questioning to teach geometry to Meno's slaves, who was totally uneducated and illiterate (Plato, *Plato's Meno*). This approach is contrasted with Confucianism's direct teaching. These two different ways of education result in two different learning outcomes. For example, Socrates' approach encourages students to question, to evaluate, and to doubt, hence produces self-generating knowledge. The Confucian approach stresses learning outcomes of behavioural reform and pragmatic learning. See Tweed and Lehman, 'Learning Considered', 90–92.

competence and accelerate their cultural integration, which as a result shifts their cultural identity towards culturally Australian.

Marriage may also determine the location of cultural identity. The ethnic background of a person's spouse (Caucasian or Chinese, for example) and the number of years of marriage influence the degree of intercultural engagement with the spouse, and these influence the location of the cultural identity on the cultural continuum.

Thus, the cultural continuum can be a useful tool to locate the cultural identity of both younger and older pastors. To be more specific, the cultural continuum is a tool to locate the degree of their cultural hybridity. Every pastor can locate his or her cultural identity on the cultural continuum according to their number of years in Australia, in conjunction with the other variables. The pastor's acquaintances can make a similar assessment of him or her, to either affirm, fine-tune or amend the pastor's self-assessment.[147]

Interim conclusion

The preceding discussion sets out to show that multiculturalism is precisely a reference to a political theory or a social policy. It is helpful in understanding the migrants' social and political status and rights. However, the usage of cultural hybridity theory in this discussion is not with reference to social policy or a social condition. Rather, it is used to better predict an individual's likely

---

[147] This model is not meant for precise assessment of cultural identity. Although no model is perfect, it is a model for pastors to roughly locate their cultural identity along the line of continuum. This is particularly helpful for a team of pastors with diversified cultural backgrounds. After they distinguish their own cultural identity, they may then proceed to discuss the proper ways of intercultural interaction. This model of cultural continuum had been used in the semi-structured interview with the pastors, and they all indicated that the model was helpful for them to understand their own cultural identity and those of other pastors.

cultural identity. This provides the necessary rationale for the use of CQ as an analytical tool.

Yang perceptively points out that the English word *Chinese* can denote Chinese people (not the Chinese language) in several Chinese words: *zhongguoren, huaren* and *huayi*. 'Zhongguoren refers to a citizen or citizens of the Chinese state; *huaren* refers to a Chinese person or persons living outside China with or without Chinese citizenship; and *huayi* refers to person or persons of Chinese descent, especially those born of Chinese parents outside China.'[148]

As a person starts constructing their cultural identity, they have to consider their citizenship (of Communist China, democratic Taiwan, Hong Kong SAR or Australia), their language, their allegiance to Chinese tradition and their acceptance of cultural rituals and ethnicity. This shows the ambiguity and complexity (and perplexity) involved in the cultural identity of Chinese migrants and their descendants. This disorientation or confusion particularly impacts the second generation of younger, English-speaking pastors, as they have to deal with two generations (the culturally Chinese migrant generation and the culturally Australian younger generation) of cultural diversity from time to time. It is true that the primary group they minister to are second-generation church members. At the same time, they have to interact and cooperate, and sometimes negotiate, with the migrant-generation leaders, parents and senior pastors.

However, biblically speaking, the mandate for both the senior pastors and the younger English pastors is to give total allegiance, not to their church nor to their culture, but to Jesus and his calling.

Against this emerging understanding of the broad questions that face the cross-cultural pastoral leadership teams of Chinese

---

148   Yang, *Chinese Christians*, 163–64.

churches in Sydney, it is necessary to specifically examine Chinese pastors' intercultural competence and their interaction dynamics across cultures. We now turn to a focused investigation of current situations and related factors, with special reference to Cultural Intelligence. In short, we now turn to our research process.

CHAPTER FOUR
SOCIOLOGICAL INQUIRY

Research methodology and research method

Intergenerational conflict in Sydney Chinese churches is more than a domestic issue. The intergenerational clash derives from a specific historical setting and socio-cultural context. It is believed that pastoral leaders with certain cultural competencies could mediate for the concerned parties of diversified cultural backgrounds.

The purpose of this research is to explore the lived experiences of the pastors' intercultural competence, often characterised by constant conflicts, and to explore certain ways of enabling them to restore harmonious working relationships.

This study utilises a hermeneutic phenomenological methodology. According to Gribch, 'Phenomenology is an approach which attempts to understand the hidden meanings and the essence of an experience together with how participants make sense of these'.[1] The approach attempts to describe certain

---

1   Grbich, *Qualitative Data Analysis*, 84.

aspects of the lived experience of a person as it appears and aims at 'examining entities from many sides, angles, and perspectives'.[2]

Phenomenology can be largely divided into two streams, namely descriptive phenomenology and interpretative phenomenology.[3] The two streams of phenomenological approach represent two branches of epistemology, that is, positivism and constructivism. According to researchers committed to an interpretive phenomenology, people understand and perceive their own experience, their relationships and the world in their daily life. They give meanings to, define and interpret every matter and event they encounter. Such lived experiences become their perceived reality. 'Phenomenology deals with the way people make sense of their world and how they construct their everyday life.'[4] Phenomenological research does not only interpret the world and its social reality. It also provides an explanation, perception and interpretation of the person's interpretations. As they interpret the world, they act, react, respond and behave according to their understanding and perception of the world.[5]

Rambo and Reh give six elements of interpretative phenomenology: observation, description, empathy, understanding, interpretation (seeing the phenomenon from a researcher's perspective) and explanation (viewing the

---

2 Moustakas, *Phenomenological Research Methods*, 58.
3 From a constructivist perspective, advocates of interpretative phenomenology believe there is no such thing as pure description. When it is applied as a research methodology, all description is already an interpretation. As Heidegger states, 'the meaning of phenomenological description as a method lies in interpretation' (Heidegger, *Being and Time*, 62). In other words, Heidegger saw the description in itself as a form of interpretation because it presupposes engagement with a phenomenon. The term 'interpretative phenomenology' is sometimes known as 'hermeneutic phenomenology' or 'hermeneutical phenomenology'. These terms are used interchangeably hereafter.
4 Sarantakos, *Social Research*, 44.
5 Bryman, *Social Research Methods*, 27.

phenomenon from existing theoretical perspectives).[6] In view of these, my research is more focused on the final three elements: understanding, interpretation and explanation. By 'understanding', I mean that I collect the interviewed pastors' different perceptions of the two-generation culture. By 'interpretation' and 'explanation', I mean that I examine the deep-seated factors shaping the level of the intercultural competence of the pastors.

In addition, my study is also generative in nature.[7] By 'generative', I mean that I will develop certain practical strategies or transformative actions to improve the level of the intercultural competence of the pastors. Thus, such an interpretative phenomenological approach will help me to articulate an *intrapersonal* worldview and *interpersonal* processes of migration experiences and intergenerational conflicts. It will provide me with a stronger explanatory framework to understand the various cultural aspects of intergenerational conflicts among the studied pastors, aspects such as cultural identity, cultural values and intercultural competence. Interpretative phenomenology will enable me to explore innovative ways to improve the pastors' intercultural competence.

In undertaking this research methodology, this study adopts mixed research methods, involving both quantitative and qualitative inquiries.[8] Such a research method provides me with measurable data or evidence of observable behaviours. It also examines the inner world and unexpressed voice of human life.

Mixed research methods can be further divided into three main categories. The first is equal-status mixed research, in which

---

6 Rambo and Reh, 'Phenomenology of Conversion'.
7 Swinton and Mowat, *Practical Theology*, 51–52.
8 According to Creswell, three major types of research methods are adopted in social inquiry, namely qualitative research, quantitative research and mixed methods (Creswell, *Research Design*, 15–16).

equal weighting is given to both qualitative and quantitative elements. The second is quantitative dominant mixed research, in which priority is given to the quantitative component. The third is qualitative dominant mixed research, in which priority is allocated to the qualitative component.[9] This research will give special emphasis to qualitative investigation.

In summary, the research methodology of this inquiry is hermeneutic phenomenology. And sequential-qualitative-dominant mixed inquiry is utilised as the research method. In real terms, the process of the research is twofold. Firstly, it involves a questionnaire; secondly, it is followed by a semi-structured one-on-one interview.

Theoretical framework

As the focus of this research is on the relevance and application of Cultural Intelligence (CQ) to pastoral leadership, the research is based on the theoretical framework of Cultural Intelligence.

Cultural Intelligence is 'an individual's capability to function and manage effectively in culturally diverse settings'.[10] Cultural Intelligence focuses on an 'individual's ability to grasp and reason correctly in situations characterised by cultural diversity'.[11] Cultural Intelligence is a multidimensional concept, or an aggregate construct, of metacognitive, cognitive, motivational and behavioural dimensions.[12] The four dimensions of Cultural Intelligence (sometimes known as four factors) are illustrated in Figure 3 and defined as follows:

---

9   Johnson et al., 'Toward a Definition', 123–24.
10 Ang and Van Dyne, 'Conceptualization', 3.
11 Ibid., 4.
12 Ibid., 4, 7.

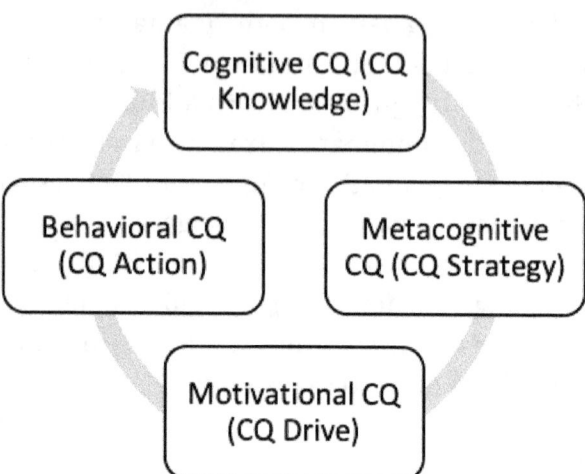

Figure 3: Four factors of Cultural Intelligence

- *Metacognitive CQ*, which is sometimes known as CQ strategy, refers to an individual's capability for conscious intercultural awareness, which enables the individual to 'consciously question one's cultural assumptions, reflect during interactions, and adjust one's cultural knowledge'.[13] Metacognitive CQ allows a person to promote 'active thinking about people and situations in different cultural settings; to actively challenge rigid reliance on culturally bounded thinking and assumptions . . . and to adapt and revise their strategies' appropriate to the settings.[14] Thus, metacognitive CQ is about conscious higher-order reflection.
- *Cognitive CQ* focuses on cultural knowledge of intercultural norms, practices and conventions, which includes knowledge of cultural universals and knowledge of cultural

---

13 Ibid., 5.
14 Ibid., 5.

differences.[15] Cultural universals refer to universal fundamental human needs; whereas these fundamental needs, which vary from culture to culture, evolve different cultural systems, such as 'economic systems, social systems, educational systems, political systems, systems of communication and systems of supernatural belief'.[16]

- *Motivational CQ*, which is sometimes known as CQ drive, refers to the capability of directing appropriate attention, drive, effort, and magnitude of energy towards learning about and functioning in diverse cultural contexts.[17] The amount of attention and energy is determined by 'the expectation of successfully accomplishing the task, and the value associated with accomplishing the task'.[18] In other words, people with higher motivational CQ show higher interest and confidence in performing intercultural assignments.[19]
- *Behavioural CQ*, which is sometimes known as CQ action, refers to the capability of displaying appropriate verbal and nonverbal actions in intercultural interactions.[20] Behavioural CQ is a critical (or the most critical) component, as all the other three CQ dimensions must be converted into this—the only essential feature of human interaction. And, according to Hall, nonverbal behaviours are especially critical, as nonverbal behaviours impart meaning in subtle ways, such as tone and gesture, social class structure and economic structure, timing and space boundaries and so on.[21]

---

15   Ibid., 5.
16   Ang and Van Dyne, *Handbook*, 6.
17   Ang and Van Dyne, 'Conceptualization', 6.
18   Eccles and Wigfield, 'Motivational Beliefs'; Ang and Van Dyne, *Handbook*, 6.
19   Deci and Ryan, *Intrinsic Motivation;* Bandura, 'Social Cognitive Theory'.
20   Ang and Van Dyne, 'Conceptualization', 6.
21   Hall, *Silent Language*, 92.

A person with high behavioural CQ is able to adjust their outward intercultural behaviours.[22]
Apart from this conceptualisation of the four dimensions of Cultural Intelligence, Ang and Van Dyne emphatically distinguish Cultural Intelligence as an intelligence capability, in contrast to personality, temperament and characteristics, although it is noted that some personality traits may be related to Cultural Intelligence.[23]

Cultural Intelligence is not only a well-defined theory; the validity of the Cultural Intelligence Scale (the four-factor CQ scale, CQS) as a measurement of Cultural Intelligence has been academically tested.[24] Research has been conducted into CQS generalisations, including generalisation across samples, generalisation across time, generalisation across countries and generalisation across methods.[25] In addition, separate research has been conducted to test the discrimination validity, incremental validity and predictive validity of CQS.[26]

The results show that the robust four-factor structure of Cultural Intelligence is supported by empirical evidence.[27] Moreover, the results show that 'the four-factor structure is theoretically stable across samples, time and countries'.[28] The research is also able to predict using both the self-report and peer-report approaches.[29] Finally, three categories of validity (discrimination validity, incremental validity and predictive validity) of CQS were also confirmed by the research evidence.[30]

---

22   Ang and Van Dyne, 'Conceptualization', 7.
23   Ibid., 8.
24   Van Dyne et al., 'Development and Validation of the CQS', 16–40.
25   Ibid., 22–31.
26   Ibid., 31–34.
27   Ibid., 34.
28   Ibid.
29   Ibid., 35.
30   Ibid.

As the four-factor structure of Cultural Intelligence offers a strong explanatory qualitative theory and the four-factor CQS is a valid measuring scale, I adopted Cultural Intelligence as a theoretical base for my research. Firstly, the Cultural Intelligence Scale (CQS) is adopted to measure the level of the intercultural competence of the pastors. And secondly, the design of the interview questions and the collection of the interview data are governed by, and the discussion of the interview is based upon, the theoretical framework of Cultural Intelligence.

Empirical research

This research has to answer three questions. Firstly, what is the level of intercultural competence of pastors of Chinese churches in Sydney? Secondly, what are the factors and root issues shaping the level of intercultural competence of these pastors? And lastly, what resources and creative ideas can improve the intercultural competence of these pastors?

The first step of this research, which is a questionnaire survey, answers the first research question, assessing the level of intercultural competence of the pastors. The second step of this research, which is a semi-structured one-on-one interview of the pastors, addresses the second and third research questions—exploring the factors shaping the level of intercultural competence of the pastors and considering ways to improve the intercultural competence of the pastors. Therefore, data from both steps of the self-reporting research approach are essential in this study.

My research method is designed to harmonise with the philosophy of phenomenological study. The purpose of this study is to listen and collect the 'insider' voice of the pastors' lived experiences.

Questionnaire research design

Firstly, I use a quantitative survey to aim at understanding the level of the intercultural competence of the pastors in Chinese churches. The quantitative survey is self-assessing or self-reporting in nature. It allows the researched participants to measure their own intercultural competence.

Secondly, in the qualitative semi-structured interview, through questions and prompting, the participants were allowed to develop further their 'insider' voice, an interpretative voice from their perspective and perception. Through the semi-structured interview, the pastors may share their own understanding of their intercultural competence. The pastors may also explain the relationship between their intercultural competence and the occurrence of intergenerational conflicts. Their voices are collected as data and listened to and interpreted by the researcher. The data collected are analysed to search for meanings in relation to the participants' demographic and sociocultural contexts. As the data collected are interpreted and shaped by the experiences and understandings of the researcher, who is considered a constructivist, the data are not made into a generalisation as the positivists do. Yet, the richness of the data can extend the insight and perspective of the researcher, who, after the study, can reconstruct lived experiences of the social reality.

The first step of my research was drafting the questionnaire. Both Livermore and Van Dyne have developed a Cultural Intelligence test based on the Cultural Intelligence four-factor theoretical framework.[31] The obvious difference between their tests is the number of questions. The survey by Livermore consists of fifty-four questions, whereas the twenty-question survey by

---

31   Livermore, *Cultural Intelligence*; Van Dyne, '20-item, Four Factor CQS'.

Van Dyne is much shorter. As my sampled pastors were busy with ministry, it was better for them to complete a shorter survey—within fifteen minutes. Therefore, this study adopted Van Dyne's Cultural Intelligence test.[32]

An already-designed questionnaire for Cultural Intelligence self-reporting was found on Van Dyne's website and also in her book.[33] It is readily available and free of charge for any participant;[34] for the questionnaire questions, see Appendix A. In order to understand the participants' social and cultural background, I preface the questionnaire survey with demographic questions. A number of demographic questions preceded the questionnaire questions, as shown in Appendix B.

The second step concerned the sampling. About 150 pastors work in Sydney. Some of them serve in parachurch organisations, rather than churches. Some have recently resigned and do not yet have a new position. Some are serving in non-paid pastoral positions and some are serving part-time. It was estimated that one hundred pastors would respond to the invitation to complete the questionnaire. This figure constituted a representative sample of the pastors of Sydney's Chinese churches. In terms of language, the sample covered the Chinese-speaking and English-speaking pastors. In terms of age, the sample ranged from young to old. And in terms of gender, the sample covered both men and women.

---

32 The twenty-question Cultural Intelligence Scale (CQS) developed by Van Dyne has been supported by strong theoretical research, which includes generalisability across various factors, such as time, countries, and methods (Van Dyne et al., 'Development and Validation of the CQS'). The validity and reliability of the Cultural Intelligence survey have been assessed and confirmed by independent researchers (Matsumoto and Hwang, 'Assessing Cross-Cultural Competence'; 867–69.
33 Van Dyne et al., 'Development and Validation of the CQS', 389.
34 Van Dyne, '20-item, Four Factor CQS'.

SOCIOLOGICAL INQUIRY

An invitation to participate in the survey (via email or hard-copy letter) was sent to contactable pastors. A cover letter was attached, along with the information sheet for the research. Assurance of anonymity was given to all respondents. The participants did not need to identify their names and churches.

This survey used the Likert-type seven-point scale, as shown in Table 2. The figures shown are comparative figures, ranging on the scale from one to seven. The respondents were given twenty statements. They read each statement and selected the response that best described their level of agreement.

1	disagree very strongly
2	disagree strongly
3	disagree
4	neither agree nor disagree
5	agree
6	agree strongly
7	agree very strongly

Table 2: Likert-type seven-point scale

The instructions for completing the questionnaire were outlined before participants filled in the questions. The duration of the survey would be less than fifteen minutes. The completed questionnaire was summarised in Excel format. Fifty days were given for the participants to fill in the survey forms. Over the fifty-day period, two reminder emails were sent out to prompt those respondents who had agreed to complete the survey.

After the cut-off date for the questionnaire, the collected data were analysed. The analysis was a two-fold process. Firstly, demographic information was analysed, with special attention given to gender, age, years in pastoral ministry, language spoken at home and positions/roles in church ministry. Secondly, the data were analysed according to the four factors of Cultural Intelligence. The objective was to investigate and compare the distribution of data according to the four factors of Cultural Intelligence and the participants' demographic backgrounds. It was assumed that the observed trends and comparison would give some clues to the subsequent individual interviews. The findings of the survey and analysis are reported and discussed in the latter part of this chapter.

Semi-structured interview design

After the first quantitative research stage, the inquiry proceeded to the second stage, the semi-structured one-on-one interviews. Each interview aimed at understanding the phenomena of the pastor's cross-cultural and cross-generational experiences. It also aimed to explore the factors affecting the phenomena and to investigate possible solutions for improving intergenerational and intercultural relationships.

As I resolved to adopt a hermeneutic phenomenological approach as the methodology of this study, I was cautious and alert to the philosophy and principles of hermeneutic phenomenology in the process of designing and conducting the study.

I was also aware of the possible confusion that might arise from conflicting data findings using quantitative and qualitative methods. This might affect the validity of the research's findings. Therefore, instead of blending the results of the quantitative and qualitative studies, I planned to present the results separately, and emphasis would be given to the qualitative semi-structured one-on-one interviews. This would minimise or even prevent the confusion of any conflicting findings.

SOCIOLOGICAL INQUIRY

As I assumed the frequent conflict between the pastors in Chinese churches was because of the low level of the pastors' intercultural competence, interview questions were drafted with intercultural competence as the focus of discussion. As the participants had completed the questionnaire, they had some prior knowledge of Cultural Intelligence. I could engage with the interviewees using the four-factor framework of Cultural Intelligence by examining and discovering the primary factors and deep-seated reasons for the pastors' conflicts according to their demographic backgrounds.

A number of questions were posed during a one-hour semi-structured interview. The list of questions is attached in Appendix C. The questions reflected a three-fold objective: *examining* their previous experiences in acquisition of cultural competence, *exploring* contextual challenges in acquisition of cultural competence and *seeking* practical ways and approaches of improving Cultural Intelligence.

All questions asked were open-ended and nondirective. Questions of phenomenological inquiry were aimed at understanding the experiences and situations encountered by participants. Follow-up questions were asked, inquiring for clarification and description of the recounted experiences of interviewees. In phenomenological research, the interest of the interviewer is on more than just the *past* experiences recounted, but also on the *present* experiences here and now, a *present* interview.[35] Therefore, participants were also asked questions about how they perceived and reflected upon the factors and causes underlying the recounted situations and experiences.

In terms of sampling, twelve pastors were invited to do one-on-one interviews. The interviewees were chosen from among the pastors who had participated in the Cultural Intelligence

---

35   Englander, 'Interview', 34.

assessment survey. Two advantages of this are noted. Firstly, the chosen pastors, after the questionnaire, had at least some minimum knowledge of Cultural Intelligence. Secondly, because they were interested in the research topic, they were more willing to disclose their lived experiences, even the unpleasant experiences.

Certain criteria were established in order to carry out the selection. Pastors were selected at random according to their languages spoken at home, roles serving at church, gender, and four age groups (25–40, 41–50, 51–60, 61 and above).

The proportion of twelve pastors recruited for an interview out of 150 Sydney Chinese pastors was regarded as a fair representation. Thus, after I had considered the combination of selection criteria, pastors were invited according to the following six categories:

- Two senior pastors, one English-speaking, one Cantonese-speaking
- Two non-senior pastors, aged 50–59
- Two female pastors, one below 50, one above 50
- Three young (50 or below) English-speaking pastors
- Three young (50 or below) Chinese-speaking pastors—one Mandarin-speaking, two Cantonese-speaking

I sent out an invitation letter and information sheet to them via email. Once they replied and agreed, I sent them the consent form for the interview and gave them a follow-up phone call to make an appointment. The appointments were confirmed, again by email.

According to phenomenological inquiry, all the experiences and understandings of the interviewees are assumed to be their perception of reality. Thus, the role of this researcher was to facilitate and encourage the interviewees to recollect their memories and recount the stories of their cross-cultural experiences in a pastoral leadership team. This researcher was careful to give due respect to the interviewees, whatever their responses. The purpose of adopting such a position was to relate to the interviewees in *subject-subject* relationships, instead of reducing the interview process to *subject-object* relationships.[36]

Therefore, the attitude of the interviewer in the interview was most crucial. As I wanted to hear genuine feelings and gain a true picture of how they experienced intercultural intergenerational communication, I had to comply with certain principles. For example, in the process of the interview, I stayed neutral and maintained a rapport with the pastors, and I encouraged them to use their own words so that they could make sense of their own thoughts, which in turn added extra depth to my understanding of the issues. Through these skills, I was able to build upon the questionnaire results and findings and seek further information to increase my understanding of their multidimensional experiences.

I intended to take notes of interviewee responses and to record each interview. I asked for permission to take notes and make a recording in the invitation letter. I asked for permission once again before the interview. In the course of the interview, I deliberately put the recording device a distance away from the participant, so that he or she would not be too aware of the recording. I also muted my phone to minimise possible disturbance. In order to ensure the participants' anonymity, I assured the interviewees that the names of the pastors would be replaced by codes in the reporting and thesis writing. All these minor steps, I believed, would help reduce the participants' anxiety, enabling them to give more genuine responses.

After the interviews, emails were sent to the participants to show my gratitude. This was a basic way to pay due respect to the

---

36   Ibid., 24.

participants, showing that they were *subjects* instead of *objects* in the research.

Post-interview analysis

As mentioned previously, the interviews were recorded. They were recorded as sound files and saved in MP3 format on my computer with password protection. The files were copied onto a USB drive as a backup.

After the interviews, a five-step analysis was followed. Firstly, the recorded interviews were transcribed verbatim. The identity of the interviewees in all transcribed scripts was kept anonymous. Instead, codes were devised in order to protect their identities and backgrounds. All transcribed copies were saved in the computer with password protection. Some participants requested that the transcribed records be sent to them for verification, to make sure that their sharing and opinions were correctly recorded. In the process of transcribing, I compared the sound recordings and the written notes so as to ensure the meaning of the participants was accurately recorded in the transcription. Usually, I did the verbatim transcription within a week of the interview.

Secondly, the interview transcripts were coded during the initial analysis of the text. The purpose of this step of coding is to give an overview of perceived topics and themes that had been raised by the interviewees, including issues between the young pastors and the older pastors. One of the clues that helped me to pick the right terminology for describing the topics and themes was to observe the pastors' frequently used words and repeated phrases. I became aware that different pastors communicated certain issues or concepts using different sets of words and terms. Therefore, topics and themes with similar meaning were grouped together for analysis. Another clue was to note the strong emotions or strong words of interviewees during the interviews. It was assumed that incidents with strong emotions carried extra weight in their lived experience. These emotional clues helped me identify repeated patterns and trends with particular themes and topics. Therefore, I did the coding as soon as possible to avoid confusion.

Thirdly, categories were classified and developed against the theoretical framework of CQ. Four coding categories illustrated the four CQ: CQ knowledge, CQ strategy, CQ drive and CQ action. An inventory of pattern coding units was assembled in this coding categorisation and classification. The pattern-items were categorised under the four factors of Cultural Intelligence. Brief quotes from various interviewees were cited according to the pattern-items in order to demonstrate the integrity of coding. The primary interest of this researcher was to present what the data were telling us about each of the four factors of Cultural Intelligence. The inventory provides a summary of dominant issues under the four factors of Cultural Intelligence. The inventory was essential for analysis in terms of comparing experiences of various pastors, addressing questions as to why, for example, certain issues bothered some pastors while other pastors were not a concern at all.

Fourthly, after this initial coding, all interview responses were further classified according to the four categories of CQ. In this step, interview responses were classified using the coding developed in the previous two steps already described. Separate summary charts of every pattern-item were composed. All the interview data were listed in these charts under the specific pattern-items. By reading and studying these charts, the lived experiences, factors and attributed meanings could be highlighted and checked. Analysis of the cultural patterns and relational inclinations of the interviewed pastors was performed. As a result, eighteen charts of pattern-items were compiled.

Selected research results

a. Questionnaire research findings

This report is divided into two parts. The first part is the general summary of demographic data. The second part is the analysis of the Cultural Intelligence scores of various demographic groups. All the data are shown as tables or graphic charts.

Report of demographic data

The purpose of my demographic data is to highlight the background of the survey sample in order to provide a thorough understanding of the data collected on Cultural Intelligence. In total, 105 invitations to full-time pastors to participate in the survey were sent out. Ninety agreed to participate in the survey, though in the end only eighty-four valid responses were recorded. Such a sample was regarded as fair and representative.

The demographic data of this survey are indicated in the following section, which is intended to give an overall distribution of the various groups according to their age, gender, language spoken at home, roles in ministry, and the number of years in pastoral ministry at church.

The distribution according to age is indicated in Figure 4. The largest age group was 51–60, and the group 61 years and above was the second largest. The figures indicated that almost sixty per cent of sampled pastors were above 50 years of age. In a few years' time, if not enough younger pastors join the pastoral ministry, the percentage of pastors above 50 will rise more. This reflects the issue of aging pastors in Chinese churches, and therefore there is a corresponding projected shortage of younger clergy.[37]

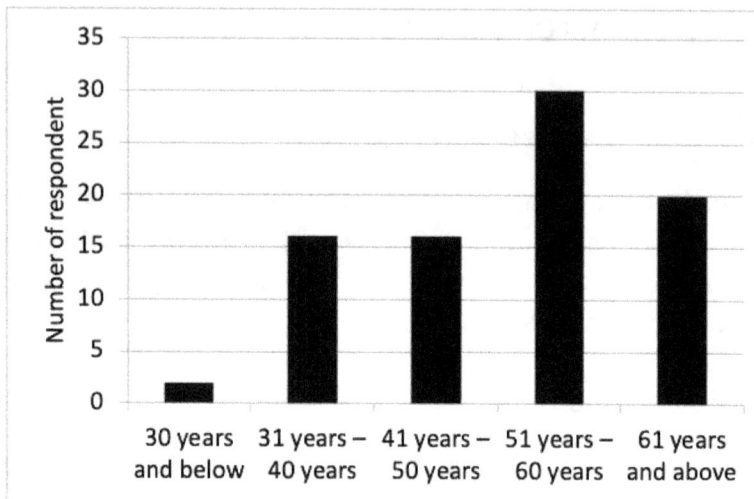

Figure 4: Distribution according to age of researched pastors

This aging phenomenon can be explained with reference to the history of Chinese migration in Sydney. The peak period of Chinese migration to Sydney was in the late 1980s and 1990s. According to the immigration regulations in Australia at the time, the age group 30–40 received the highest points for admission into Australia. That was why many Chinese and pastors migrated to Sydney during that period of time. Twenty years later, that group of migrants is now in the range 51–60 years or above.

Another factor is related to the cultural values of the traditional Chinese. As traditional Chinese culture is characterised by 'high power distance', people respect and listen to those who are senior in age. Besides, pastors in Chinese churches usually

---

37   Weems and Michel, *Crisis of Younger Clergy*, 1–6.

assume the role of teaching and leadership. Thus, Chinese churches prefer to employ pastors of more mature age.

This aging phenomenon is likely to cause further difficulties in regard to pastoral succession. If the above observation of high power distance is true and this group of pastors is getting older, certain crucial issues emerge. One of the issues is whether the older pastors are willing to retire from their existing positions (which include the respect and honour of their congregations). A second issue is the passing on of leadership to younger pastors. Since the older pastors have great influence and are well respected, even if they retire from their pastoral positions officially, they might intentionally or unwittingly become 'power-brokers' or 'shadows of the leader' at church and continue to navigate the ministry in the background. Another issue is whether the younger pastors can earn the trust of the retired older pastors in order to ensure the smooth succession and transition of the pastoral leadership. Although the aforementioned issues are outside the scope of this research, the potential problems cannot be ignored.

The impact of age is also reflected in cultural differences caused by generational differences. The 51–60 age group and the group 61 years and above are the baby boomers, whereas the groups 31–40 and 41–50 belong to Generation X and Generation Y. The worldviews, values and ways of thinking differ significantly among these groups. Generational differences give rise to cultural differences. If older and younger pastors are neither aware of these differences nor relate to one another in accordance with such an awareness, it will certainly increase the chances of conflict.

The gender distribution of respondents is shown in Table 3. The figures showed that the majority of respondent pastors were male. This correctly reflects the profile of pastors in Sydney's Chinese churches. Such a phenomenon impacts the quality of pastoral care, particularly for female members of a congregation. At the moment, the bulk of pastoral care to female members is given by pastors' wives or female lay leaders.

Female	9
Male	74

Table 3: Gender distribution of research subjects

The evident phenomenon of the male majority can be explained from various perspectives. Firstly, it reflects the values of Chinese culture. In traditional Chinese society, males naturally assume the head of social institutions. For example, the father/husband usually makes decisions for the whole family, and the leader of the community is always a man, if not the most senior man. Chinese churches are thus more than the body of Christ; they are also organisations and social institutions. The pastors, who are supposed to be the spiritual leaders of the church, are, unsurprisingly, men.

The second perspective relates to the financial situation of the Chinese churches. In the last twenty years, many Chinese churches have been established by and are comprised of new migrants. Most of the migrants have uprooted their lives from their countries of origin and have moved to Sydney. All they wished for was to survive and settle down in the new country. Thus, monetary giving to the church has not been generous. Therefore, Chinese churches have only been able to employ a limited number of pastors because of limited financial resources. And this, in turn, has meant that the priority of the churches has been to employ male pastors instead of female pastors. This also explains the phenomenon of the disproportion of male pastors in Chinese churches.

It is to be noted that this gender-disproportionate phenomenon might well be a contributing factor to the conflicts among pastors. It can be assumed that most Chinese men, as compared with Chinese women, are less expressive emotionally. On the one hand, when male pastors are offended and feel bad, they are inclined to suppress their emotions, particularly negative feelings such as fear, anger, confusion and frustration. On the other hand, on the receiving end, male pastors are less sensitive and are not as good at picking up on the emotions and feelings of their team members as women might be. Many of the men have not been trained in active listening and non-verbal communication. Therefore, they do not even know when they have offended someone. Thus, negative feelings and emotions accumulate. The next small disagreement might be the last straw, and disagreement might escalate within a short period into irreversibly broken relationships.

The language spoken by the respondents at home is indicated in Figure 5, below. Obviously, the majority language, in this case, was Cantonese. Of the pastors who participated in the survey, fifty-nine of them spoke Cantonese at home (which represents seventy per cent). Nineteen of them spoke English at home. The other six spoke Mandarin at home. This was congruent with the landscape of the Chinese churches in Sydney.

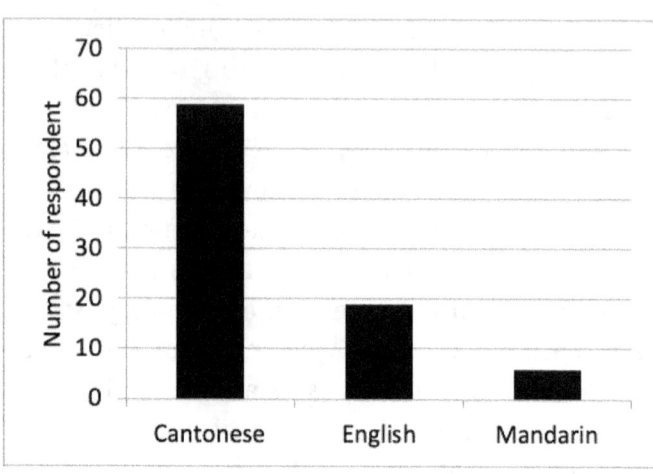

Figure 5: Distribution according to spoken language at home of researched pastors

This phenomenon might be explained by the history of migration and the background of the migrants. In the peak period of migration, the job market and schooling in Sydney were perceived to be better than that of Hong Kong. Since this batch of migrants from Hong Kong were mostly young families and professionals, their primary concerns were job opportunities for the fathers and outstanding schooling for the children. Thus, Sydney became one of the favourite cities for Hong Kong migrants. In accordance with the principle of homophily, more and more migrants from Hong Kong, who were Cantonese-speaking, settled in Sydney. With so many Cantonese-speaking migrants in Sydney, the Chinese churches in Sydney were mostly Cantonese-speaking churches. This explains the high number of Cantonese-speaking pastors.

As Cantonese-speaking pastors are the majority group, and they dominate the Chinese churches in Sydney, I was prompted to further inquire (in the subsequent interviews) whether the phenomenon might impact aspects of their Cultural Intelligence. I wanted to interview the pastors, exploring their level of incentive for cultural learning across language groups, their willingness to adjust to other cultural groups, and their ability to acquire other languages.

This shows one of the strengths of using mixed research methods in a phenomenological inquiry. Without mixed methods, the data collected in the questionnaire cannot provide much insight. Similarly, without mixed methods, there are few hints on how to design the right interview questions for one-on-one interviews.

The distribution according to respondents' roles in Chinese churches is shown in Figure 6. Seventeen of them were serving as senior pastors; the others were serving in various language-based services: Cantonese-speaking, Mandarin-speaking and English-speaking services. Of the pastors serving in the various language-based congregations, as expected, most of them (thirty-six) were serving as pastors of Cantonese-speaking congregations.

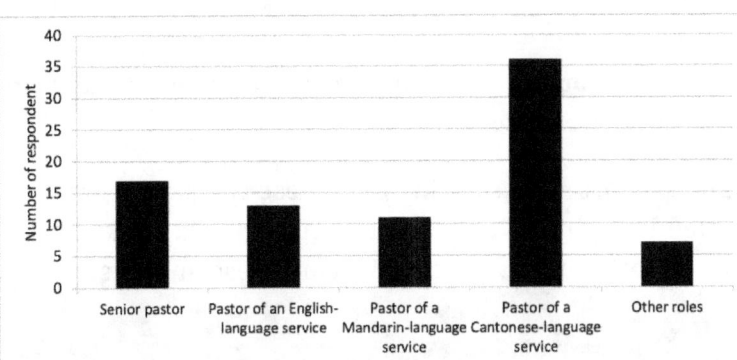

Figure 6: Distribution according to roles in Chinese churches of researched pastors

In order to understand the cultural background of the pastors, the languages spoken in their homes were also identified. Of the seventeen senior pastors, as indicated in Figure 7, two spoke Mandarin at home, two spoke English at home, and the other thirteen senior pastors spoke Cantonese at home. In other words, the key pastoral positions in Chinese churches were occupied by pastors who spoke Cantonese at home. It is plausible therefore that Cantonese-speaking pastors were the chief drivers and decision makers of pastoral ministry, both in terms of the number of pastors and in terms of their pastoral authority, or even power.

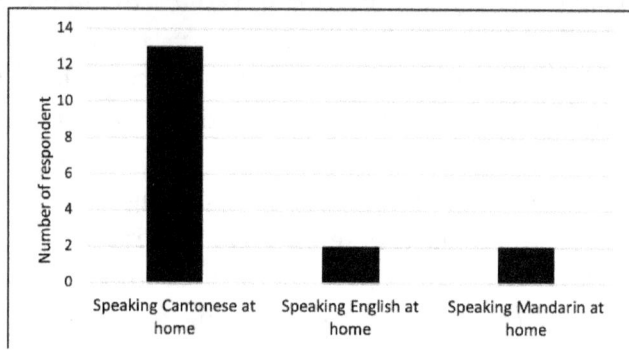

Figure 7: Distribution according to language spoken at home of researched senior pastors

Of the pastors serving in Cantonese-speaking services, as indicated in Figure 8, only two out of thirty-six spoke English at home. The other thirty-four spoke Cantonese at home.

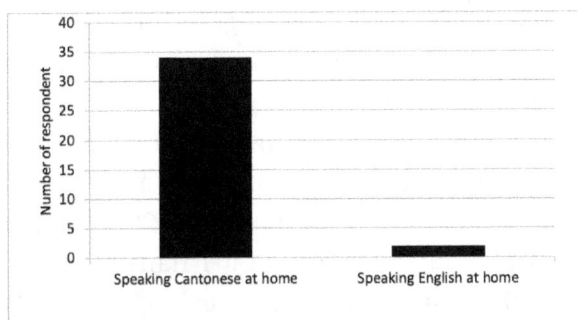

Figure 8: Distribution according to language spoken at home of researched pastors serving in Cantonese-speaking services

We can compare these two sets of data. The total number of pastors speaking Cantonese at home was fifty-nine. In other words, twenty-five pastors who spoke Cantonese at home were serving in other positions. As indicated in Figure 7, thirteen were serving as senior pastors, and, as indicated in Figure 9 below, five pastors who spoke Cantonese at home were serving as pastors of Mandarin-language services. The other seven pastors who spoke Cantonese at home were serving as pastors of English-speaking services, women pastors, adviser pastors or mentor pastors.

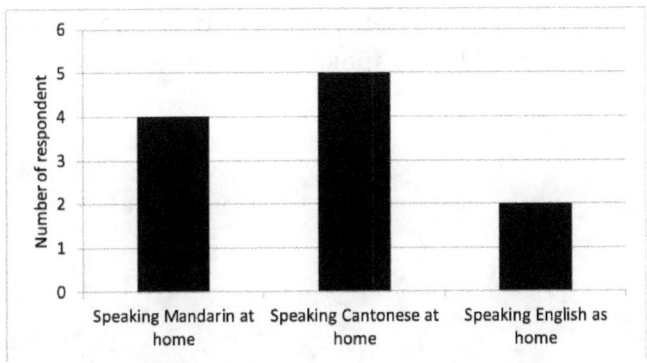

Figure 9: Distribution according to language spoken at home of researched Mandarin pastors

SOCIOLOGICAL INQUIRY

Although the Mandarin-speaking migrant growth rate has been increasing in recent years, the number of Mandarin-speaking pastors in Sydney is not large. This can be explained by the fact that most of the Mandarin-speaking migrants are from mainland China, which is a Communist country with a strong anti-religion policy. Although migrants from mainland China are increasing, the number of Mandarin-speaking Christians remains relatively low, and this is also true of Mandarin-speaking pastors. Thus, some Cantonese-speaking pastors and English-speaking pastors have been courageously taking up the role of pastors for Mandarin-speaking services. They choose to work cross-culturally. This also explains why the general Cultural Intelligence reading of pastors of the Mandarin-language services is higher than that of pastors of the English-language services and pastors of the Cantonese-language services.

The distribution of the age of the respondents is seen in Table 4. Pastors speaking English at home were distributed over all age ranges, though with a concentration in the age range 31–40. Cantonese-speaking pastors were the largest group, with the majority 51 years old or above. Only seven (three plus four) respondent pastors aged above 51 years spoke English at home, compared with forty (twenty-four plus sixteen) respondent pastors aged above 51 who spoke Cantonese at home.

	Speaking Mandarin at home	Speaking English at home	Speaking Cantonese at home
30 years and below	-	2	-
31 years–40 years	-	8	8
41 years–50 years	3	2	11
51 years–60 years	3	3	24
61 years and above	-	4	16

Table 4: Distribution of age groups according to language spoken at home of researched pastors

This phenomenon harmonises well with the overwhelming number of Cantonese-speaking pastors in Sydney. Furthermore, as the pastors speaking Cantonese are older, their learning capacity may be lower. Their vision and drive for developing and mobilising the churches for another level of ministry may be open to question. Thus, the life cycle of Cantonese services or Cantonese churches may be an issue in the future. The ministry of some Cantonese congregations or Cantonese churches might plateau or even go downhill. This issue might also impact the future of Mandarin ministry, as many pastoral positions for Mandarin services are taken up by Cantonese-speaking pastors.

The number of years serving in pastoral ministry at church is shown in Figure 10 and Table 5. A closer examination of the age distribution of the pastors in Chinese churches was revealing. Among the twenty-three longest-serving respondents (twenty-one years' service and above), twelve of them were above 60 years of age, and the other eleven were aged between 51 and 60. They were the most experienced pastors and had longevity in serving as pastors. They are the greatest asset of the Chinese churches in Sydney. Yet their retirement is approaching. The Chinese churches are losing their finest group of pastoral leaders. If this projection is true, the impact on pastoral ministry and Chinese churches will only be intensified.

These results suggest an area for future exploration—regarding the desire for cross-cultural learning and the incentives for cross-cultural adjustment—for pastors approaching their retirement. Some factors might distract or diminish their desire to learn, such as their uncertainty about living standards after retirement, their concerns about the stability of the pastoral ministry in the churches they have served, and their fears concerning the discontinuity of pastoral leadership in the church.

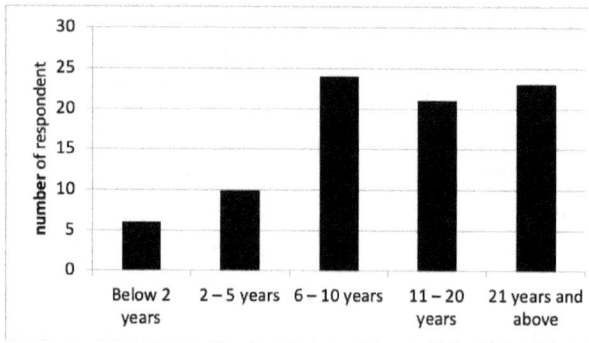

Figure 10: Distribution according to number of years serving as pastors

The demographic data detailed here provide an overview of the distribution of the surveyed respondents. Two demographic features of the pastors have been identified: the average age of the pastors is relatively high, and there is an overwhelming proportion of Cantonese-speaking pastors. The implications for intercultural relationships and intercultural learning will be discussed below.

Report of the score of Cultural Intelligence

61 years and above	12	4	2	2	-
51 years–60 years	11	10	5	2	2
41 years–50 years	-	6	8	-	2
31 years–40 years	-	1	9	5	1
30 years and below	-	-	-	1	1

Table 5: Distribution of age groups of researched pastors according to number of years serving as pastors

The following section is a general summary of the score of Cultural Intelligence (CQ) of the researched pastors. As the intent of this research is to help understand the generational differences and the cross-cultural interactions, the age issue is given special treatment.

The data on the four factors of Cultural Intelligence are shown in Figure 11. As mentioned, this survey used the Likert-type seven-point scale. The figures shown are comparative figures, ranging on the scale from one to seven. One is the lowest score and seven is the highest score.

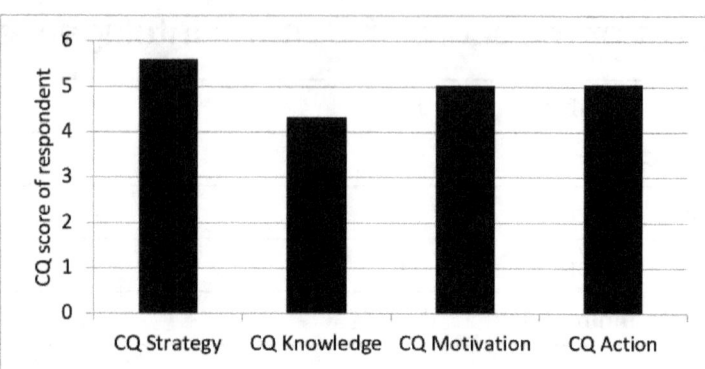

Figure 11: Distribution of four-factor CQ scores of researched pastors

It is noted that the CQ strategy score of the pastors was highest, and their CQ knowledge score was lowest. Apparently, the researched pastors' overall self-assessment of Cultural Intelligence was on the higher side, i.e., above 4. As this was a self-assessment survey, the figure indicated was not an absolute value. It simply reflected their self-knowledge or self-perception of their cross-cultural intelligence.

It is observed that, in comparison with other Cultural Intelligence factors, the CQ knowledge score was relatively low. Serving in a Chinese church in an Australian social context, it would be expected that the pastors would interact and engage with people other than Chinese; however, their cross-cultural knowledge was actually very basic. Therefore, it made sense to explore the reasons for their lower CQ knowledge in the subsequent interviews.

In terms of gender, as indicated in Figure 12, the Cultural Intelligence score of male pastors was higher than that of female pastors. The same trend appeared in all four categories (CQ strategy, CQ knowledge, CQ motivation and CQ action).[38]

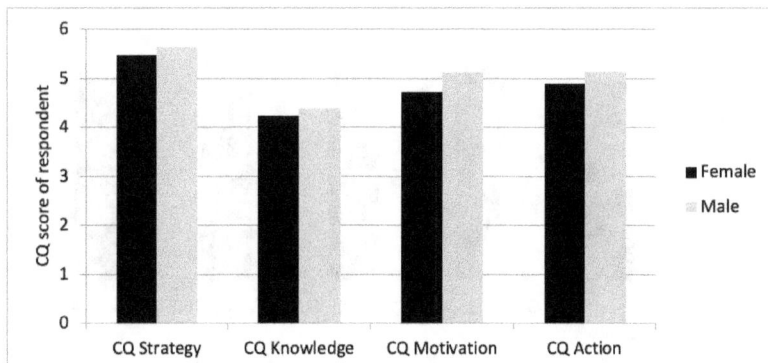

Figure 12: Distribution of four-factor CQ scores according to the gender of the researched pastors

With regard to age, the Cultural Intelligence scores of the respondents are as shown in Figure 13. The Cultural Intelligence scores of age groups 41–50 and 51–60 were among the highest, whereas the Cultural Intelligence score of the group 30 years and below was the lowest.

---

[38] It is noted that not many female pastors were involved in this survey. Out of eighty-four respondents, only nine were female, which represented only ten per cent of the total respondents.

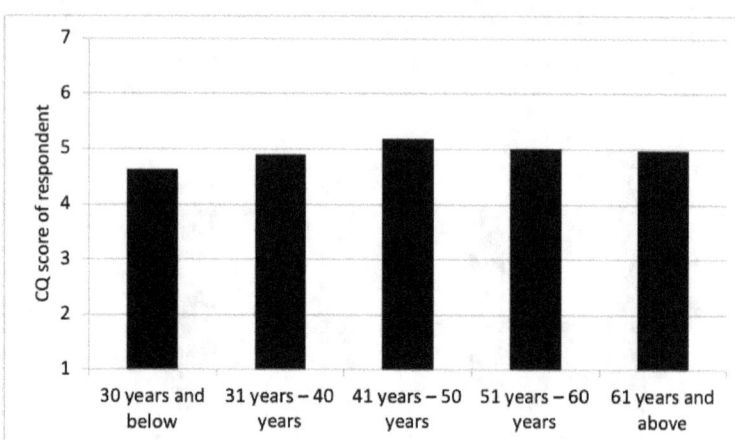

Figure 13: Distribution of overall CQ scores according to the age of the researched pastors

The findings in relation to language spoken at home are indicated in Figure 14. Respondents who spoke English at home scored the highest Cultural Intelligence. In particular, they scored high in CQ strategy and CQ motivation. Of the thirteen pastors of English language services, twelve of them spoke English at home.

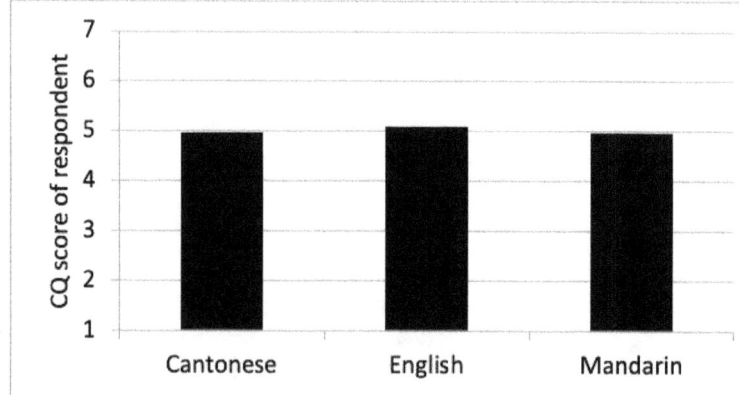

Figure 14: Distribution of overall CQ scores according to the language spoken at home by the researched pastors

It is plausible to assume that pastors speaking English at home always serve as pastors of English services. The Cultural Intelligence score of pastors of English language services was relatively higher. This can be explained by the fact that the governance of Chinese churches is basically controlled by Cantonese-speaking leaders and pastors. Knowing this background, the English-speaking pastors have chosen to work in Chinese churches. Therefore, from the outset, the English-speaking pastors may well have required higher levels of courage and willingness. They may have been mentally better prepared and mindful of this situation when they entered pastoral service in Chinese churches. In other words, their CQ drive and CQ strategy are relatively stronger.

Perhaps surprisingly, the pastors speaking English at home scored the lowest CQ knowledge, as indicated in Table 6. Yet, as Chinese language proficiency and knowledge of Chinese history constitute a main part of CQ knowledge, and the English pastors usually speak limited Chinese (or no Chinese), it makes sense that their CQ knowledge score was relatively lower.

Although the pastors speaking English at home scored comparatively lower in CQ knowledge, their overall Cultural Intelligence score was still higher than the other language groups. In other words, their CQ drive and CQ strategy are exceptional. This phenomenon was subsequently examined in the face-to-face interviews.

SOCIOLOGICAL INQUIRY

	CQ Strategy	CQ Knowledge	CQ Drive	CQ Action
Cantonese	5.6	4.4	5.0	5.0
English	5.8	4.2	5.3	5.2
Mandarin	5.2	4.5	4.9	5.4

Table 6: Distribution of four-factor CQ scores of the researched pastors according to their language spoken at home

The Cultural Intelligence scores relating to roles at church are shown below in Figure 15. It is noted that the senior pastors scored the highest Cultural Intelligence, followed by pastors of Mandarin-language services. As also observed in Figure 16, the language spoken at home by the senior pastors was overwhelmingly Cantonese. However, the Cultural Intelligence scores of the pastors of Cantonese-language services were almost the lowest, as indicated in Figure 15.

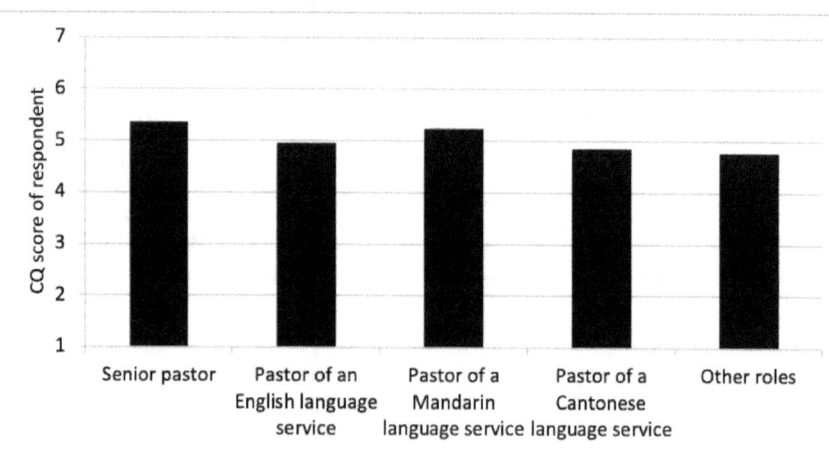

Figure 15: Distribution of CQ scores of the researched pastors according to the roles in church

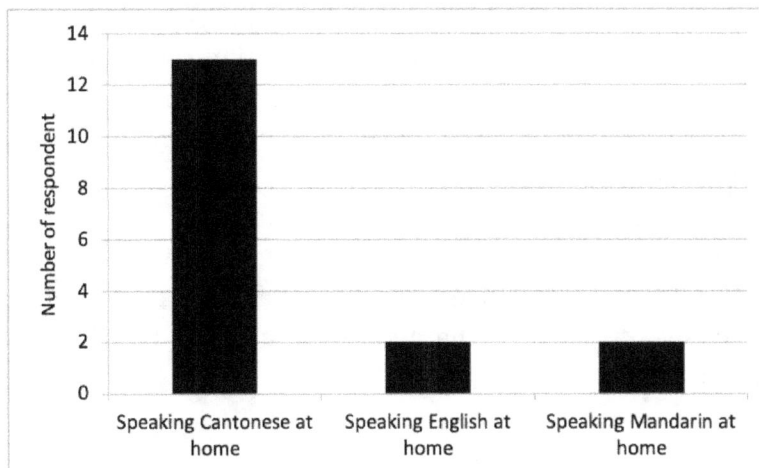

Figure 16: Distribution according to language spoken at home of researched senior pastors

This seeming inconsistency may be explainable by the following. As the senior pastors have to coordinate and lead various ministries at church and maintain the unity and harmony of various language congregations, their communication skills and cultural competence have to be higher; or perhaps over the years of leading church ministry, they have had to improve and acquire higher cultural competence.

Moreover, this phenomenon probably stems from the senior pastors' language proficiency. Usually, in order to perform pastoral leadership effectively, senior pastors in Chinese churches have to be multilingual, proficient in English and Cantonese and/or Mandarin. In particular, pastors with higher English language proficiency improve their social capital, social networks and social acceptance. They have more opportunities to engage with the local community instead of being limited to their ethnic community. A lack of language proficiency certainly affects the performance of their leadership and their ability to earn authority and trust. Besides, with language proficiency, they have a better opportunity to access education resources instead of being limited to Chinese-language information and resources. This thus becomes a major topic to be explored and examined in the subsequent interviews.[39]

The Cultural Intelligence scores of the senior pastors according to the language spoken at home is indicated in Figure 17. The Cantonese speakers scored the lowest, whereas the English speakers scored the highest. In a sense, the figures are still consistent.

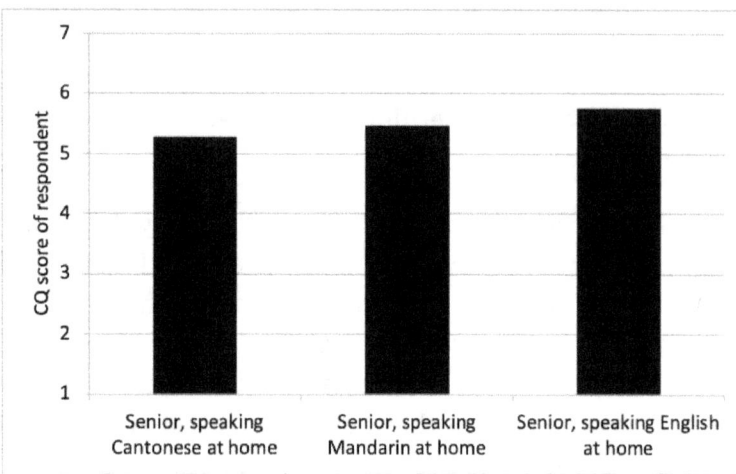

Figure 17: CQ score distribution of senior pastors according to their language spoken at home

Another observation was the comparatively high Cultural Intelligence scores of pastors of Mandarin-language services, as indicated in Figure 15. As also noted earlier, in Figure 9, of the eleven pastors of Mandarin-language services, seven of them were not native Mandarin speakers. The non-Mandarin speaking

---

39 Casey, 'How Shall They Hear?' 146–97.

pastors serving at Mandarin services certainly require a strong CQ drive (their courage, desire and determination). Also, their Mandarin proficiency has to be high enough to preach and provide pastoral care effectively. This too helps explain their relatively higher Cultural Intelligence.

Lastly, the respondents' Cultural Intelligence scores according to the number of years in pastoral ministry at church are illustrated in Figure 18. The Cultural Intelligence scores of the various groups were not particularly different, except that the group serving 2–5 years gained the highest score.

This could be because, in Chinese churches seniority in ministry and hierarchical status are regarded as relatively important, and the 'junior' or 'inexperienced' pastors are expected to submit. In other words, the inexperienced ones have to accommodate themselves in order to survive and maintain harmonious relationships. Thus, it may be that the less experienced pastors have to be more flexible, more aware and more knowledgeable in relating to the other more experienced pastors. However, whether such one-sided submission can endure long is another matter.

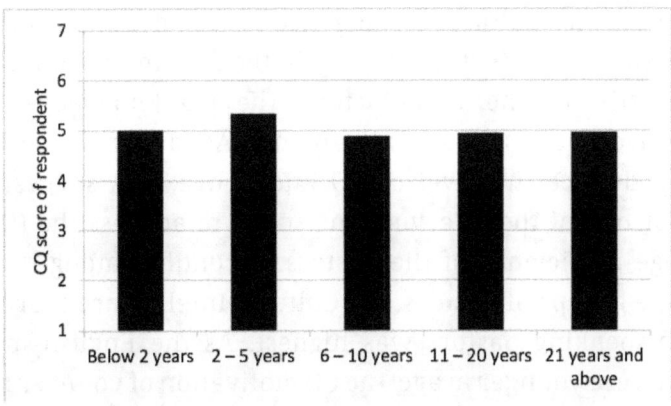

Figure 18: Distribution of overall CQ scores of pastors according to the number of years in pastoral ministry

In summarising the analysis of the quantitative survey, the results reveal the generational differences and cultural differences among the pastors of Chinese churches. The results are consistent with the assumed Chinese cultural values as reflected in cultural behaviours. Moreover, the results verify the hypothesis of this research, that there are deep-seated factors (the four factors of Cultural Intelligence) underlying the constant conflicts and clashes among the pastors of Chinese churches, which could be further examined in the subsequent qualitative interviews.

Face-to-face semi-structured interview research results

As a first step in developing a face-to-face interview tool, the Cultural Intelligence questionnaire survey results were analysed for the purpose of uncovering the cultural dimensions of pastoral leadership in Chinese churches. The purpose of the face-to-face interview was to investigate and follow up certain interconnected dimensions based on the four-factor Cultural Intelligence structure. After the quantitative survey, a number of issues concerning the Cultural Intelligence levels of the pastors were noted, warranting further inquiry in the face-to-face interviews.

Firstly, of the four factors, the CQ knowledge of the researched pastors was relatively low. As language proficiency could influence the level of CQ knowledge, this suggested the need for one of the interview questions to address the (lack of) language proficiency of the pastors. Secondly, among the three language groups of pastors, the Cultural Intelligence score of the English-speaking pastors was highest. As the English-speaking pastors were younger in age, the CQ motivation of younger pastors was addressed by the face-to-face interview questions. Thirdly, among the various roles at church, the Cultural Intelligence score of the senior pastor was the highest. As the senior pastors' role in conflict resolution was crucial, their willingness, awareness and ability to resolve conflict were addressed by the interview questions. Lastly, among the senior pastors, those who spoke English at home reported the highest score. It becomes clearer that the language proficiency of the senior pastors gave them an advantage in resolving conflict. However, intergenerational conflicts among the Chinese pastors still occurred recurrently. Consequently, other factors underlying unresolved conflicts were investigated by the interview questions; these included factors such as cultural learning, observing non-verbal expressions and reflection.

Moreover, as noted already, the percentage of female pastors is quite low. Thus, female pastors' perspectives are not well represented. In terms of pastoral ministry, it is essential to have more female pastors' perspectives. In the first place, in Chinese churches, children's ministries and ministries to the elderly are typically served by female pastors, so the cultural-relevant pastoral input is essential. Moreover, without female pastors' perspectives, the communication dynamics in the pastoral team will be greatly diminished. The discussion in the pastoral team will be dominated by male cultural values, using paternal and authoritative modes. Thus, the need for female pastors is huge.

Although the low percentage of female pastors is consistent with the demographic reality of Chinese churches in Sydney, appropriate caution is needed in discussing and applying the survey results. It is suggested that future qualitative interviews might have to make up for the disproportionate situation. When performing the interview, extra patience and care should be taken in understanding the female pastors' perspectives and their inner voice. It is also suggested that a study with a focus specifically on the Cultural Intelligence of female pastors would be very helpful. The study would extend the scope of research by including female lay-pastors or female elders of Chinese churches in Sydney.

In the following report, it is logically the first step to begin by reporting the phenomenon of intergenerational conflicts among Chinese pastors.[40]

Interview results on intergenerational conflicts

As expected, virtually every interviewed pastor talked about intergenerational conflicts. They shared firstly the causes of conflict, and secondly their ways of resolving intergenerational conflicts. Causes of conflict varied, but the primary factor in intergenerational conflict was cultural-difference illiteracy. One pastor shared:

> The Chinese don't understand the mentality of local born, the younger generation. Thought that they are off the Bible teaching.

More specifically, one of the contributors to cultural illiteracy was differences in mode and manner of communication. An experienced pastor observed:

> Because this is Chinese culture, Chinese tends to speak diplomatic, instead of directly to the point. And this is regarded as polite and virtue. But Western culture is different. If you don't agree, say so directly. We could argue openly, even in the end, we don't agree, still OK. Agree to be disagree.

---

40   Since the responses of the pastors were unedited verbatim recorded, grammatical mistakes are not uncommon.

The same pastor further explained that the issue sometimes involved more than different modes of communication. It was primarily non-communication:

> I personally feel that conflict occurs more among Chinese . . . We don't communicate, but grumbling in heart. When the situation arises, aggravate to the point of animosity. In fact, it could be just disagreement in the beginning but quickly advance to animosity.

Apart from non-communication, intergenerational conflict was also about language difficulties. A pastor recalled his observation of church meetings, that intergenerational conflict was further inflamed by the language differences or deficiencies, which, in turn, evolved into incomplete communication and miscommunication:

> So, in church general meetings, the English leaders shared in English. The Chinese leaders shared in Chinese. Although with translation, the translation is not thorough. And much of the emotional words could not be translated. So, people listened to the grumbling in their foreign languages.

A younger pastor shared his analysis of the communication between two generations in a reflective way, which touched on cultural dimensions and power distance:

> I find that a lot of other conflicts come in terms of communication. How you deal with conflict: Is it direct? Is it indirect? How you work even within a multi-generation context? In the pastoral team, how much do you defer to the elder person because they are older? How much to the younger person? Younger person is forty, they are still seen as the younger

> generation and the young people. That probably is the primary source of conflict . . . in Chinese church second generation feel distance power, and older generation feel disrespected.

A senior pastor reflected on the same issue of power distance, but in terms of hierarchy and submission:

> Another issue is how to handle different points of view. This is related to leadership style. When different points of view emerge, how should we deal with it? This is always an issue. This might be because of hierarchy, or not submissive, or could not communicate or accept each other.

On the same issue, it was recounted that different generations perceived authority differently, either theologically defined or simply as a human device:

> Pastors perceive authority differently. This is just man-made authority, no theological ground. This relates to cultural. Chinese culture requires you do things in certain expected way. Abide by the way, rather than abide by life. Therefore, such expectation (staying in the office more often) could not convince the English pastors theologically.

A younger English-speaking pastor related intergenerational conflicts to cultural perspectives on doctrinal issues, specifically, a rationalistic or devotional and pietistic understanding of doctrine:

> Obviously, it affects doctrine. For example, more rationalistic in the Western mindset, whereas more pietistic in Asian mindset in terms of approach. The devotional life . . . tend to be more important in Asian

and in Chinese approaches of theology. Not just about the rational, but not just about theological discipline. You read the Bible not just for information, but for transformation. Some Chinese pastors will say you guys always reduce things to propositions. Everything has to make sense. Everything is fitting into your system—Calvinism, whatever.

If communication was the primary factor, the logical way to resolve conflict was restoring the communication by using the required language. A woman pastor shared:

> More communication. Once I have more language, I could make more social contact and interaction. I listen to their viewpoint . . . I would not refute. I keep asking questions . . . I have to understand their way of thinking, their source of information.

As listening and understanding enhanced communication, communication could simply mean listening and being seen as willing to listen. A pastor called for more listening:

> At least you allow the other party to speak up, so people would perceive you as a person willing to listen. However, in reality, everyone prefers speak rather listen. Then people would see that you are not willing to listen . . . And this cut off many opportunities of communication.

A senior pastor observed rightly that intergenerational conflict was difficult to resolve, as both parties were stuck in their own cultural mazes and blind spots. Therefore, he suggested that it was sensible to seek input and guidance from an external moderator (such as the Sydney Chinese Christian Churches Association) who would serve as a facilitator:

SCCCA could set up a body, so the local church, in case they have any conflict, they have a body to turn to for help or assistance, or even moderation (not decision).

Another pastor echoed the fact that a facilitator could prompt the right listening process:

Obviously, it is good to have an effective facilitator (an obvious chair) to provoke, to balance, or facilitate for active listening.

A pastor suggested that a metacognitive approach for understanding communication would be an effective way to improve intergenerational communication:

It is process rather result. Probably we need to more aware is a lot of cultural difference has to do with the surface. How you going to approach the questions.

In the course of interviewing pastors, it was confirmed that intergenerational conflicts were obvious and frequent among them. Misunderstanding of cultural differences, non-communication and power distance (hierarchy and authority) were among the main factors. Listening, with assistance from an external facilitator, could help.

Interview results on language learning

As reported previously, communication and relating to one another were seen to be essential in pastoral teams. In relating to other pastors, the most obvious difficulty shared by interviewees was language (English) learning, a topic which impacted virtually every interviewed pastor. Language learning is primarily about CQ knowledge. Ten out of twelve interviewed pastors touched on the issue of language learning and agreed that language is essential in communication between pastors in a Chinese church context. They all agreed that language was an essential tool for connecting with people, and that acquired language capacity was directly proportional to the opportunities for interaction and engagement with others.

One of the interviewed pastors made this point clearly by comparing the different outcomes of his own language capacity and that of his friends when they were in university:

> Perhaps my acquiring language was not bad. I make effort and spent time, and I learnt the language, so my communication with others is easier. I noticed that other students, they were relatively less communication with local. Language is interesting.

In Chinese churches, some pastors are employed to minister to specific language group congregations (such as Cantonese or Mandarin). Although English was not required to perform their pastoral job, there was still a need to acquire English for general communication in their pastoral teams. For example, a Cantonese-speaking pastor observed another pastor struggled with learning English, which weakened and crippled his trust in and his relationships with other pastors:

> Yes, that's true the church employed him to serve as a pastor of that particular congregation. And it doesn't require speaking English. In the end, he was quite difficult. He learnt many hours of English, yet in vain . . . Also, he doesn't trust the English pastors and ministry. He worked for ten years, but in a very unhappy mode.

In fact, deficiencies in language and listening did not just damage relationships among pastors from different language backgrounds; it actually hurt the ministry, particularly in ministry planning and ministry evaluation. A pastor shared:

> So, in the meeting, in the discussion and so on, the person who is from a different culture, they don't say anything. But if you ask them, they don't even understand a word. Even when we try to simplify it, you realise that actually they understood nothing.

The negative impact extended beyond pastoral team meetings; it extended to meetings with lay leaders. For example, language deficiency decreased the quality of discussion and the incentive to exchange ideas in diaconate meetings. One Cantonese-speaking pastor observed:

> That's why the diaconate meeting become dragging and long. Also, if the English pastor speaks in English, the Mandarin pastors or leaders could not understand. People start getting fed up and lost the patience to communicate and listen. Eventually, many decisions made without thorough discussion— immature decision.

In situations of debate, arguing or heated discussion, Chinese-speaking pastors always felt disadvantaged in articulating opinions and in searching for the right words. A Cantonese pastor shared:

> It is also affected by language ability. The language ability affects the ability of articulation. So, in debate, Chinese pastors cannot fully express. Western pastors don't really understand this discrepancy.

A Mandarin-speaking pastor also shared:

> . . . the adjustment is enormous, and the language requirement is at least two languages. And English is necessary, as most of the meeting are conducted in English. So, the pastors with language proficiency are not many. Many are struggling with language, particularly in expressing their point of view. Particularly in disagreement. Therefore, less outspoken in meetings. In fact, they are not quiet. They just don't know how to speak and feel embarrassed.

The sharing here reflected the lived experiences of the pastors in Chinese churches and provided much insight into the two-generation conflicts among pastors in Chinese churches.

There were various factors in facilitating language learning. Most of the interviewed pastors shared their struggles in acquiring English. Certainly, some English language background might have enhanced their learning of English, or at least developed their confidence in learning:

> I worked in international company before, so communication in English is nothing difficult to me. If they are friendly and respect, I could socialise with them.

A senior pastor recalled how his college education in an English-speaking country gave him an advantage in language learning:

> One advantage was that I studied at Canada, so English language is not a big challenge to me. It is a good foundation. Social interaction in English is manageable.

On the other hand, a younger pastor observed the extra struggles of one of his colleagues who had no English background at all:

SOCIOLOGICAL INQUIRY

> I remember a pastor from mainland China. He was ten-plus years older than me. He also attended language class for new migrants. But this was actually a big hurdle for him. He could not accept easily. As he was from mainland China, his English ability was almost minimal knowledge. Thus, he could not really communicate in English in day-to-day life.

Various pastors recalled and suggested ways of improving English. In fact, some of the suggestions were not limited to language learning, but incorporated, at the same time, cultural learning and adaptation. For example, an older pastor shared his past experience:

> Read local paper. Understand the Australian culture. Watch news, that would help him practice the language, speaking and listening. Make time with the English pastor, have a cuppa, talk to one another. Interact.

An older pastor shared his comprehensive experiences in language learning:

> Language is the main part. I am willing and take initiative to mix with people, to acquire English and Mandarin. Observe their daily living and their interests and hobbies. I watch cricket and rugby. Try to know the rules of games. Listen to the radio program. Notice their hot topics, favourite songs, their concerns and local politics. Understand the local government, the two parties and policies, tax, migration regulations. This all helps my living in this society.

Pastors can indeed help one another. One pastor noted:

> If the pastoral team meeting, encourage him to express more. The other pastors have to provide an encouraging environment. Don't laugh at his/her language.

The final remark, 'don't laugh at his/her language', closely relates to 'saving face' or a sense of shame, which is one of the important dimensions of traditional Chinese culture. One humiliating incident (being laughed at) would certainly destroy any incentive to cross cultural divides using a foreign language. This will be discussed further in the CQ drive section.

According to the pastors, if learning circumstances were favourable, language learning could be made easier. The Caucasian and English-speaking pastors might create such circumstances for learning English. One interviewed pastor suggested some minor yet valuable steps:

> To Australians, advise them talk less. As Caucasians tend to talk more, voice out their opinion. So, they better hold their opinion, allow the Asian or Chinese to talk more. Understand their language deficiency. Language deficiency does not equivalent to dumb. Acknowledge that the Chinese are crossing the culture to communicate to the Westerners. Give more allowance, more patience.

Lastly, language learning, according to the pastors, was not seen to be just limited to the Chinese-speaking pastors learning English; it was also about English-speaking pastors learning Chinese. It was true that one interviewed pastor perceptively distinguished between two groups of English-speaking pastors (Caucasian pastors and Chinese English-speaking pastors). These two groups could have two totally opposite learning incentives.

> I suppose the Caucasian pastor, as a foreigner, takes pride in learning Chinese. But the Chinese English-speaking pastors don't take pride of learning Chinese. Instead, they take shame. In terms of identification, they don't identify themselves as Chinese, but ABC (Australian-born Chinese), if not identify with Caucasians.

This was related to the cultural identity of the Chinese English-speaking pastors. If the Chinese English-speaking pastor identified with Caucasians, and regarded themselves as Caucasians, they did not feel shame for not knowing Chinese, and they might be more willing to learn some Chinese. However, if the Chinese English-speaking pastor identified with Chinese culture and identity, and regarded themselves as more Chinese, they felt shame for not knowing Chinese; they were therefore probably less willing to learn Chinese (and even rejecting).

Interview results on cultural awareness

CQ strategy among the researched group primarily entailed cultural awareness. More than half of the interviewed pastors recounted that they became aware of the importance of intercultural learning.

Interviewed pastors shared that the first experience of their awareness of cultural difference occurred when they compared the home culture (culture of the homeland) and the host culture (culture of the new country); they noticed the difference as a majority-minority distinction and an insider-outsider difference:

> Compare with before I came to Australia, I was in Hong Kong, Cantonese-speaking was the majority. But now in Australia, I become minority. I have my own

culture. How do I merge with people of different but mainline culture?

Another source of cultural awareness was their observation of behaviours of those who did not have cultural awareness. Two pastors recalled certain behaviours concerning the lack of cultural awareness of colleagues. A young pastor shared:

> Every pastor has his own cultural background. However, not many of them are aware of their own cultural background, and not aware of the culture of an ethnic church in Australia. I think this is the root of problems. For example, one pastor from China always quote this 'we Chinese always practise like this'.

The 'we' saying of the last remark was revealing. The fact he highlighted the 'we' as the centre of his world implied that the 'they' was peripheral—an interesting yet often unconscious notion.

One interviewed pastor distinguished a two-stage process in becoming aware, moving from 'unconsciously incompetent' to 'consciously incompetent':

> As in cultural learning, the first stage is unconsciously incompetent—I didn't know what I didn't know. But at work, with some knowledge of Australian culture, I become more consciously incompetent. The self-awareness is stronger.

The two-stage process is a useful concept, as cultural awareness is always a gradual route moving of unconscious to conscious, unawareness to awareness and insensitivity to sensitivity. It takes time to move from the unknown to the known.

Unpleasant past experiences or cultural baggage could bring about low cultural awareness or cultural over-sensitivity, which led to overreaction to others' unintentional behaviours. One interviewed pastor reflected on an incident of conflict derived from a sense of inferiority passed down from his previous church:

> Sometimes conflict approaches in very sensitive ways, because I have baggage carried without sensitivity . . . for example, one of the elders in my church was very sensitive the Chinese ministry, feeling like a poor cousin. Even though it wasn't, and we keep communicating it wasn't, but he is very sensitive to that. He did admit that felt that in his previous church. Especially the younger people dismissed the Chinese ministry and . . . those who are older. So, I think that baggage made it much more sensitive. I only realise that in the hindsight why he was so reactive against any hint that.

Racism could also be a cause of cultural baggage. A pastor recounted his experience of racism:

> . . . the whites . . . could not distinguish between mainland Chinese or Hong Kong. They just generalised as Chinese. They have a bit of racism. Their tone and facial expression reflect that. This was quite common in those days. For example, they hinted that your English was not good enough. Or even sometime pretended they didn't understand. Sometimes shout or yell at you. Supposedly, they should accommodate to us customers.

Obviously, in the preceding comment, no explicit racist behaviour was noted. However, the interviewed pastor perceived it as racism. He guessed other people's internal intentions by interpreting their external behaviours, such as tone, facial expressions, hinting at his poor English, shouting and yelling. In fact, as I asked follow-up questions, it became clear that the incident occurred because the pastor jumped the queue at a bank. This was interesting—the pastor was not aware that his own behaviour was the cause.

One more point could be noted. The interviewed pastor did not want to be incorrectly identified as mainland Chinese, indicating that the pastor himself might possibly have discriminatory attitudes towards mainland Chinese.

Although racism was always regarded as an unpleasant experience, racism did not necessarily lead to irrational reactions or revenge. Racism, as reported by one of the interviewed pastors, could actually bring forth cultural awareness and cultural sensitivity, so that he would not want to hurt others in a similar way:

> . . . maybe because I was exposed to racism I came across when I was a kid, I don't want to do that to other people. I don't want other people feel that way, so I am a bit more sensitive in that way, that is the possibility.

Most of the interviewed pastors agreed that cultural awareness and sensitivity certainly enhanced and improved the quality of pastoral ministry. As one pastor reported, cultural awareness was required (and desirable) in pastoral care:

> Pastoral care also requires certain CQ, as it is people ministry. If I am aware people are different, culture, family, and experience are different. Certain cultural sensitivity is preferred.

Cultural sensitivity of the inner aspirations and struggles of new migrants was crucial in preaching the right message with relevance. A pastor shared:

> Promoting cultural sensitivity and understanding. For example, it is very easy to dismiss the migrant

> mentality of needing to have your second generation to do well, and especially, if you are a non-migrant culture, you just think that is wrong priority. There may be things that are wrong idolatry, you haven't understood the struggling migrant family. If you come down very hard—if you send your kids to tutoring then you are being idolatrous—you are not really understanding what struggles that the generation migrants had, why they value education so much. So those kinds sensitivity need to come out in your preaching.

Strategies for improving cultural awareness were the main issues raised in the interviews. If stereotyping was one of the main factors damaging awareness, the way to counter stereotyping was not assuming too much. The intention of every behaviour had to be double-checked before conclusions were drawn, and this required certain attitudes. Two young pastors shared similar viewpoints:

> Be humble and willing to learn. Don't assume what you know your own culture is correct. There are a lot of thing you don't pick up, you need to be aware of.

> We may make some assumptions, but this could be stereotype. They could be exceptions. Assumption needs to challenged.

One pastor suggested that training at theological colleges could certainly help in raising cultural awareness and sensitivity by providing training on Asian culture and Asian churches:

> I think a lot of theological colleges are now being much more aware of culture, not just SMBC [Sydney Missionary and Bible College], even Moore [College].

The second-year course, one thing I do at Moore every year is on Asian culture, Asian churches, and because they want their people to be culturally aware, there is much more awareness than there used to be. I feel like especially, if the pastor comes to work within the Chinese church, they obviously screen out they are at least worthy to be more culturally sensitive.

One pastor shared that ministry structure was another perspective of raising cultural awareness. He suggested church governance and structure should be designed to promote sensitivity and communication:

So, from structures as well. How you set up your church, governance, how you set up committees, what kind of people, what kind of expectation to the committee, in relation to the tasks, the communication between the congregations. And try to establish policies, or practices, that promote cultural sensitivity. I think in my understanding, in Chinese church setting, structurally enabling the lay leaders to be able to take ownership and give feedback, and have a say and have a vote, is quite important.

Interview results on motivation

The drive towards cultural assimilation can be divided into internal and external motivation, that is, self-motivated and circumstance-motivated respectively. Two older pastors recollected their cultural adjustment in their early days, and recounted it as circumstance driven and ministry driven:

We have Mandarin ministry, I also involved in talking to them and preaching. Again, I gradually know them.

SOCIOLOGICAL INQUIRY

> Sounds like it is more about the circumstance forced me to learn.
>
> In earlier days, the adjustment was not easy. However, as I was in the circumstance, it forced me to adjust. When I first attended Chinese Presbyterian Church, though the environment forced me, I still felt I could not mix well with the local born people. The distance from the Western culture was really huge.

A young pastor shared that the church members' respect for him became a motivation to acquire cross-cultural skills.

> How to help people grow, to grow honestly . . . They come by themselves. They come from very far away . . . how do we help them, how do we do that intentionally? Because in their culture, they rely a lot on the minister, they look up to the minister.

Although cultural assimilation was difficult, one senior pastor appealed to the role of pastor, that as leaders of other Christians, pastors were expected to be more self-motivated in adjusting to the culture:

> If we pastors have deficiency, what should we do? We have to make effort to break through this deficiency.

Nevertheless, this pastor affirmed his conviction that the Holy Spirit would help the self-driven pastors:

> As you drive yourself forward, prompted by the Holy Spirit, God will certainly give. I believe this is the right starting point. Without this starting point, others are just theory.

Sometimes, self-driven motivation was triggered by something of higher value. For example, a pastor shared how the beauty of other cultures could be a motivation:

> It is about inspiring the person's need, motivate the person. Because something is greater and more beautiful of others' culture.

Some interviewed pastors articulated their drive for intercultural interaction in terms of curiosity and fun. A younger pastor shared that curiosity kindled his interest and urge to know other cultures:

> Perhaps I am more curious to different cultures, their activities, where to go on holidays. I naturally behave that way and didn't really desire to do the Hong Kong way. Instead, the Hong Kong students were still clinging to their used Hong Kong manners, and they didn't really want to open up to new things.

On the other hand, an older pastor simply admitted that he was not interested in the fun side of intercultural engagement. The 'outsider' feeling could also be because of the language barrier:

> I don't drink. But Friday night, they would drink. If I want to be part of them, I have to drink. I don't enjoy at all. I don't understand their jokes.

In fact, cultural assimilation was not limited to the migrants. It also included the locals' willingness to reach out to engage with the Chinese migrants.[41] Some pastors shared about the willingness of the locals. For example, one older pastor shared his experience of a Caucasian colleague in the 1950s, a time before the multicultural policy had begun:

> Yes, he was nice. That's why he reached out to a new colleague. He knew that we were from a different culture, and he wanted to know us, but I felt uncomfortable. Through this experience, I realise ... the strength of Western culture, willing to reach out to me.

A female pastor shared her impression of her Caucasian senior pastor's readiness to reach out to the Chinese:

> Before he becomes the acting senior pastor, he had a heart for mission. Although he is very Aussie, he is so willing to contact and interact with the Cantonese and Mandarin members. He would even make fun by learning a few Cantonese words. He doesn't agree

---

41 Unfortunately, there is virtually no similar research or published papers on Cultural Intelligence among Australian locals or European Australians to which I could compare my research data on intergenerational Chinese pastors. There is a research paper on intercultural communication and cultural intelligence in the workplace (Martins, 'Intercultural Communication'); however, the study is about hospital and nursing workplaces, not a church setting. Nevertheless, some studies reveal that the willingness of locals is an important factor for intercultural interaction (Deng and Gibson, 'Qualitative Evaluation'; Martins, 'Intercultural Communication'; Tharapos, 'Cultural Intelligence'). Martins specifies that 'stories, different way of life, different attitudes to situations were all part of what motivated people to be willing to engage in intercultural exchanges' (Martins, 'Intercultural Communication', 113-15). Tharapos suggests that 'individuals who are open to new experiences are more willing to move beyond the familiar to the new and unfamiliar' (Tharapos, 'Cultural Intelligence', 46). I look forward to the research of David Turnbull, a lecturer from Tabor Adelaide, whose research is on 'Managing Ethnic Diversity in Local Congregations: A Study of South Australian Clergy and Their Levels of Cultural Intelligence'.

with certain Chinese parenting, he would respect and accept the difference.

In summary, it was noted that the interviewed pastors experienced some cultural assimilation. However, their tone and manner of sharing were not enthusiastic. Quite often they used the words 'I was forced to' or 'I have to', and the factors underlying the drive of quite a few pastors' were 'survival' or 'circumstances'. Among the interviewed pastors, virtually no older pastors verbalised their drive in terms of 'curiosity' or 'fun'. Instead, they felt 'embarrassed' and 'humiliated'.

Interview results on cultural learning

In order to increase CQ knowledge, cultural learning is an important step. Interviewed pastors shared about and identified areas of cultural learning, such as sports, television and radio programmes, festivals, food and popular culture. One pastor from a Hong Kong background shared his pleasant experiences of a team of predominantly Caucasian work friends:

> I have to force myself to involve in local culture, such as watching football, understand their jokes . . . I was invited to join their Christmas and birthday party . . . a lot of food . . . For example, played Australian football, watch football, know their culture. And tried eating meat pie and vegemite.

Another pastor observed the food culture of an Asian group in Sydney, which was in essence an anthropological ethnographic observation:

> Food, a great avenue into a culture. Not just what they eat but how they eat. Are they big family gathering? Are they sitting down with knife and forks? Every

aspect of culture goes about eating, whether they share, whether they use a hand, whether they gather a big round table, and the elderly senior people always expected to goes first, but they also serve the younger ones. How they do food. That can be a window.

The same pastor also observed the language perspective of culture:

> Getting them to notice the language categories. Sometimes asking, assuming you don't speak their language, what the word you use for concepts, like how do you express love in your culture? The words you use for love. Are there different types? Language is a window into culture. Category shapes your brains, boxes, in terms how you classify it, can learn a language, it is almost go into automatically give you greater cultural competence. Even you don't know the language, understanding how that language process it. Even hellos, how does that culture express that hello. Is that just the greeting? Is that 'how are you'? Is that 'have you eaten yet'? Very obvious things that people don't tend to notice, all of that says something about the culture.

As recalled and reflected by an interviewed pastor, the process of cultural learning can be subdivided into a three-step journey—discovery, query and trying:

> I didn't feel the lifestyle was severe difficult. It was sort of discovery. People here walked on the street without wearing shoes. I queried whether the road was hot. But I felt okay. Even I would try walking on the street without shoes. Quite funny. It was a way eye-opening.

Thus, the three-step learning process was a pleasant (fun and eye-opening) experience, which in turn perpetuated his cultural learning.

Cultural learning requires time, persistence and repetition in listening and trying. One pastor shared how he forced himself to learn the culture:

> More listening, listened to news, radio. Even I didn't fully understand, I forced myself to continue. One or two hours a day. Even recorded the radio program and listened. Exposed myself to their culture. This lasted for more than six months . . . Do what they do.

One effective way to learn a culture was to immerse oneself in and engage with the culture. A younger pastor recalled his multilevel experience of homestay as a student, an experience which impacted him in subsequent decades in Australia:

> And I lived at Adelaide for one and a half year. Not many Chinese there. I have to force myself to involve in local culture, such as watching football, understand their jokes. That was a nice family. I was invited to join their Christmas and birthday party. Italian family, a lot of food. Very useful. Compared with other friends, I became more Australian and acquired better English than average. Helpful to me in terms of merging into Australia culture.

As the pastor looked back at his experience of homestay, he agreed that it was an enjoyable experience. But from the outset, he had to force himself to be involved. In other words, CQ knowledge is related to CQ motivation.

One of the behaviours of CQ action was observing and imitating modified verbal behaviours. Pastors reported that, even though they could speak some English, they could not understand the verbal expressions mixed with slang and spoken in a strong Australian accent. Moreover, in some social interactions, Chinese pastors could not appreciate the humour and jokes. However, the pastors were aware of this and took proactive steps to acquire the slang and an Australian accent. A senior pastor reported:

> But I'd pay attention to the Australian expressions, watch the TV drama, Australian and Mandarin, their slang. Special terminology. This might be related to ministry. Or certain Australian pronunciation. Try to speak like them more. Choice of word.

The learning process was not easy though. Ongoing listening to and asking people to repeat were the keys. Another young pastor shared:

> It helped me in a sense I took courage to speak English. If I didn't understand what others said, I'd listen patiently, or asked them to repeat.

Interview results on cultural reflection

Cultural assumptions and stereotyping contributed to the misunderstanding and misinterpretation of external behaviours. Apparently, the interviewed pastors were aware of this. One of the interviewed pastors noticed the likelihood of other pastors assuming too much:

> As young pastors always want to perform with results. Have many assumptions, which might be wrong. May need to reflect on the assumption of external behaviours.

A pastor pointed out, perceptively, that not reflecting on routine practices of the church could impact the efficacy of ministry:

> Sometimes it is non-thinking. Always out of non-reflective. You go to church for many years and having this kind of lunch is our common practice. But you didn't think deep, according to the previous church practice. What do you want to achieve? How is it perceived at the receiving end?

In terms of intercultural learning, instead of being driven by self-initiative, a pastor might choose to be driven by ministry needs. It was more a *reactive* rather than a *proactive* approach, which indicated a lack of self-reflection.

Such non-reflection also occurred in the context of college study. One pastor shared about his experience of cultural learning at theological college:

> At SMBC, they also taught cross-cultural subjects, but from a Westerners' perspective. How does Westerner see Asian? From such subjects, I noticed that I seldom reflected on my own Asian perspective. As they told me their understanding of Asian, that was good.

Apparently, although he knew that the taught knowledge was from a Westerner's perspective, this pastor simply accepted the knowledge passed on to him without further reflection.

The first step in developing a practice of reflection is an awareness of the assumptions and stereotypes. One pastor did not like the idea of learning cultural profiles, as that might reinforce cultural assumptions and stereotypes:

> Learn from cultural profile, from which we may make some assumptions, but this could be stereotype. They could be exceptions. Assumption needs to challenged.

A young pastor suggested the importance of meeting people and allowing others to discuss and give opinions:

> Spend time understanding, meeting, talking to rather than assumptions. Many people have broader assumptions like Chinese do conflict this way, Western in that way. That can be just assumptions and unhelpful. Sometime you put on grip on people.

One interviewed pastor suggested that some reflective questions could be asked to help another pastor who was confused about certain cross-cultural behaviours:

> The question I'd ask, 'Internally what's going on?' For example, he was upset. I'd ask questions such as the source of his upset. On the content, on the speech, on disrespect. Help him to distinguish the matter or the manner.

Although the interviewed pastors made some good suggestions about training new pastors to reflect, they themselves were not good at practising reflection and they did not generally see their need for reflection. Furthermore, half of the interviewed pastors did not even mention reflection.

Conclusion on interview results

In the interview research, pastors acknowledged that intergenerational conflicts were common among the Chinese pastors, and that the four factors of Cultural Intelligence might provide a framework to understand the phenomenon. Three major issues stood out.

Firstly, of the four factors, the pastors were most concerned about and interested in CQ knowledge, particularly the issue of language. They shared that their lack of communication or avoiding communication was because of a deficiency in English. They shared about their struggles in learning English.

They suggested many ways to acquire language. Thus, I make recommendations on improving language/English for pastors at the end of this research.

The second area the pastors were concerned about was CQ drive. In the interview, significant time was given to discussion of the determination, willingness, calling of God and certain spiritual qualities (such as humbleness). One interesting point was noted—that the interviewed pastors were more concerned with their colleagues' CQ drive, subtly revealing that they thought they themselves had a high enough CQ drive.

Thirdly, it was noted that, of the four factors of Cultural Intelligence (CQ knowledge, CQ drive, CQ strategy and CQ action), the interviewed pastors shared least about CQ action or CQ behaviour.

Overall, the interviews showed that pastors were willing to share their intercultural and intergenerational conflicts from the multicultural context. Many of them reflected that this was their first time sharing on such an interesting topic. I observed that they showed new signs of hope that harmonious relationships could be restored.

CHAPTER FIVE
RESEARCH ANALYSIS

The focus of this research has been to examine the deep-seated factors underlying the constant intergenerational conflicts among pastors of Chinese churches in Sydney. In the research interviews, the pastors honestly admitted to the frequent occurrence of intergenerational conflicts. As traditional Chinese are usually inclined to deny disagreement and conflicts, the fact of the admission of these conflicts is already one big step forward.

Chinese pastors' migrant experiences are complex, including ecclesiological, spiritual and organisational aspects, among other things. This analysis takes a socio-cultural approach. In this section, the analysis focuses on the intergenerational conflicts among Chinese pastors. It is based on the interview findings, using the four factors of Cultural Intelligence as a structure. The discussion also engages with the cultural dimensions and cultural values of two generations. The purpose of this analysis is twofold. Firstly, it categorises and discusses the deep-seated factors behind the intergenerational conflicts. Secondly, it explores ways of resolving conflicts.

According to the interview findings revealed in the last chapter, intergenerational conflicts are caused by a number of factors. In summary, they are non-communication, language difficulties and the lack of reflection on cultural differences. The following will discuss these three aspects in turn.

Non-communication and cultural values in intergenerational conflicts

In the interviews, many pastors reported that their team members did not communicate (or that there was not enough communication), both in pastoral team meetings and in their social interactions. The interviewed pastors recounted that the senior pastors tended to make decisions without proper discussion and without any exchange of ideas. The pastors also indicated that senior pastors usually hold absolute power and authority and request unlimited submission from subordinates. Hasty decisions by the senior pastors were sometimes seen by the younger pastors as a symptom of, and even a synonym for, a lack of communication. In the interviews, the young pastors also complained that the senior pastors did not care for them. The young pastors felt that they were treated as employees and hired hands instead of colleagues.

I have noticed that most Chinese pastors are godly, Bible-believing, God-fearing, and gospel-driven men and women. By nature, they are people of love and care. Some of them are extroverts and willing to talk and communicate. Thus, their non-communication is out of character.

Such a phenomenon can be interpreted through the lens of cultural dimensions such as power distance and individualism-collectivism.[1] Concepts of high context and low context are also of great relevance.[2]

---

1   Hofstede et al., *Cultures and Organizations*.
2   Hall, *Beyond Culture*.

RESEARCH ANALYSIS

Power distance is defined as 'the extent to which the less powerful members of institutions and organisations expect and accept that power is distributed unequally'.[3] In other words, in a society of high power distance, people do not expect or demand anything beyond their social status and their position in the group. They dare not desire anything at all.[4] In high power distance communities, unequal status and hierarchical structure are seen as normal, natural and intrinsic. In such organisations, decisions are made by a few leaders. Power is centralised in a few perceived heads in the hierarchy. Subordinates simply follow instructions and take orders.[5]

Lingenfelter points out that it is important to distinguish between hierarchy and power.[6] In other words, just because a leader is regarded as the top of the heirarchy, it does not mean he will unreservedly abuse his power. If the leader is from a majority group and/or dominant group, it is reflexively possible for the leader to define 'the right way' of behaviour for the group and 'correct those deficits'.[7]

Hofstede understands that people in collectivist societies 'are integrated into strong, cohesive in-groups, which throughout people's lifetime continue to protect them in exchange for unquestioning loyalty',[8] while individualist people relate to others in the society loosely. Individualists value personal time, privacy, freedom and contentedness with one's position in life. Moreover, individualists value close, sincere friendship, whereas collectivists do not need to make specific friendships, as friendship is predetermined by the family, clan and group

---

3   Hofstede et al., *Cultures and Organizations*, 61.
4   Ibid., 63.
5   Ibid., 73.
6   Lingenfelter, *Leading Cross-Culturally*, 93.
7   Hibbert and Hibbert, *Leading Multicultural Teams*, 49.
8   Hofstede et al., *Cultures and Organizations*, 92.

membership. Instead, filial piety is more highly valued.[9] Moreover, studies show that countries that score high on the power distance index score low on the individualism index, and vice versa.[10] Hofstede also notes that in individualist societies people tend to communicate orally or verbally. They perceive silence as abnormal, whereas conversation is seen as the social norm. On the contrary, in collectivistic society, being together is emotionally sufficient. People don't feel the need to talk much as long as information has been transferred.[11]

High-context communication, as defined by Hall, is 'one in which most of the information is either in the physical context or internalised in the person, while very little is in the coded, explicit, transmitted part of the message'.[12] A high-context person, according to Plueddemann, communicates by paying attention to the subtleties of a real-life setting. A high-context person observes physical setting, body language and tone of voice, whereas a low-context person greatly relies on explicit communication, precise words, concepts, principles and ideas.[13]

Understanding these cultural dimensions makes much sense of intergenerational conflicts among the pastors in Chinese churches. The senior pastors and younger pastors come from two different cultural roots. The senior pastors are from a traditional Chinese culture, and they are basically collectivists. They work happily within the Chinese cultural structure. The cultural root of traditional Chinese is primarily Confucianism, which teaches five reciprocal relationships.[14] These hierarchical

---

9   Ibid., 100.
10 Ibid., 102.
11 Ibid., 108.
12 Hall, *Beyond Culture*, 91.
13 Plueddemann, *Leading across Cultures*, 78–79.
14 The five reciprocal relationships are ruler-minister, father-son, husband-wife, elder brother-younger brother, senior friend-junior friend.

reciprocal relationships reinforce high power distance.[15] In these relationships, 'the senior person is expected to provide support and encouragement for the lower-status person, whereas the lower-status person is expected to give loyalty and respect to the senior person'.[16]

However, the younger pastors do not operate with a purely traditional Chinese cultural structure. The younger pastors (both Chinese-speaking and English-speaking) are of a hybrid culture or a third culture. The cultural values of the younger pastors are a mixture of traditional Chinese culture and English/Dutch/German-speaking (EDG) culture.[17] They are more individualists, with lower power distance. Their mode of operation is not identical to that of their senior pastors and is shifting between the Chinese culture and EDG culture.

House et al. identify four factors influencing the power distance of a society: society's predominant belief system and religion, its democratic tradition or government, the existence of a strong middle class, and the proportion of immigrants.[18] It is noted that these four factors exist in Australia and contribute to the comparatively lower power distance ranking of Australian culture.

When most younger pastors enter pastoral ministry in a Chinese church, they somehow know that they have to submit to older pastors and senior pastors. Therefore, the young pastors tend to respect and submit to their senior pastors' leadership and let them make final decisions, but they do not do it

---

15 Plueddemann, *Leading across Cultures*, 97.
16 House et al., *Culture, Leadership, and Organizations*, 523.
17 The EDG term denotes the group of people with English/Dutch/German-speaking, low-context, individualist-culture background, a group that includes their descendants in the USA, Canada, New Zealand and Australia. The term is borrowed from Hibbert (Hibbert and Hibbert, *Leading Multicultural Teams*, 21).
18 House et al., *Culture, Leadership, and Organizations*, 518–26.

unquestioningly. They ask clarifying questions, they voice their opinions and reasoning, they explore other alternatives and they even suggest unconventional solutions. Although eventually they are prepared to submit to their senior pastors' ideas, the younger pastors might openly and vocally query the senior pastors. These behaviours are normal and sensible to younger pastors. However, the senior pastors or older pastors do not see the younger pastors' behaviours in the same way.

In regard to cultural values, the power distance of senior pastors and young pastors is clearly different. From the perspective of senior pastors, who are characterised by high power distance, 'asking questions may be interpreted or regarded as criticising and blaming, and therefore may be prohibited'.[19] The senior pastors perceive the younger pastors' asking of questions and voicing of different opinions as disobedient, disrespectful, distrustful and even rebellious. Senior pastors interpret these behaviours as challenging their authority and undermining their leadership, whereas the younger pastors simply expect full participation and productive communication. They think such behaviours show their cooperative teamwork and complementary partnership.

Moreover, senior pastors, who are collectivists, expect unquestioning loyalty and filial piety from other members of the pastoral team. They demand full trust from the young pastors. They dislike and disapprove of the continuous patterns of questioning and debate by the younger pastors.

Furthermore, the collectivistic senior pastors, who value the cohesiveness of their in-group, consider the church as a family. They consider anyone in their team as their family members or even 'children'. The young pastors are God-given 'children' to their families, clans or tribes, and they themselves are 'parents' of the clans. In a family or clan, parents would not

---

19   Plueddemann, *Leading across Cultures*, 99.

fire their children! Although they dislike the behaviours of the young pastors, the senior pastors feel reluctant to dismiss them. The relational strategy of the senior pastors is thus to avoid, even completely, physical contact or communication with the younger pastors. They minimise communication with the younger pastors, using the fewest words possible to convey most messages. To achieve this, the best mode of communication is giving orders and instructions without kind words of respect or encouragement. All the senior pastors require of the young pastors is to take orders and follow instructions. Thus, the younger pastors, at the receiving end, notice the senior pastors' behaviour of non-communication, and feel distanced from them. They do not feel like they are being treated as family members or children. On the contrary, they feel like they are being treated as employees and labourers.

In addition, the senior pastors do not rely on explicit verbal communication, and they normally speak minimally or even use silence. Most of the time, they choose to communicate non-verbally. They prefer hinting and prompting indirectly, hoping the young pastors can understand the unspoken message, a message that seems very obvious to the senior pastors. By contrast, the younger pastors, who are from a low-context culture, seldom take note of the context, specifically the body language and facial expressions of their unhappy senior pastors. And as their mode of communication is explicit verbal conversation, they indiscreetly keep asking and questioning. In fact, the less the senior pastors speak, the more the young pastors ask. The senior pastors feel annoyed and are even more reluctant to speak. The young pastors feel confused and are even more likely to speak. The urge of the senior pastors for verbal communication decreases, whereas the urge of younger pastors for verbal communication increases. It is a deadlock situation, which can escalate within a short period of time.

Listening is another important dimension in intercultural communication: 'Cultural differences in how people engage in listening are a reality, so you need to recognise and respect such culturally based differences in listening style'.[20] Brownell suggests that 'effective listening reduces costly misunderstandings'.[21] Thus, good preachers or speakers are not necessarily 'good communicators'. They may be simply 'good transmitters' and not 'good listeners', paying no attention to listening. Cultural backgrounds impact the 'what' and 'how' of listening. Low-context people listen primarily for facts and concrete information, whereas high-context people take extra note of the form of the speech, such as tone, voice volume, diction and facial expressions.[22] Westerners tend to show they are paying attention to the speaker by making the sound 'mm-hmm'. However, this technique is not evident in most cultures.[23] Similarly, the behaviour of direct eye contact as a way of engaging in attentive listening is not a common custom in many Asian cultures.[24]

Therefore, listening is not listening *literally*. Listening refers to listening to the content and the form of the message. This is what McLuhan suggests with his well-known aphorism that 'the medium is the message'.[25] Listening includes attentive observation, taking note of what has been said and even what has *not* been said. Traditional Chinese are expert at this. Unfortunately, the young pastors, who are unfamiliar with traditional Chinese culture, cannot pick up these sorts of clues. They listen to what

---

20   Morreale et al., *Human Communication*, 160.
21   Brownell, 'Creating Strong Listening Environments', 6.
22   Samovar et al., *Communication Between Cultures*, 391.
23   Asante and Davis, 'Encounters'.
24   Samovar et al., *Communication Between Cultures*, 392.
25   McLuhan, 'Medium is the Message'.

RESEARCH ANALYSIS

is said, and only what is said. They do not listen to the demands and expectations behind the unspoken words and the unfinished statements. They do not understand the clues hinted at by the body language of the senior pastors.

Moreover, intergenerational conflicts always occur in decision-making contexts—the *who* and the *how* of decision making. In high power distance communities, such as Chinese churches, important decisions are only made by the top leaders or the senior pastors, and only trivial decisions are allowed to be made by the subordinates, the younger pastors.[26] However, it is the senior pastors who decide which matters are important and which are trivial. For the sake of efficiency and convenience, senior pastors tend to make decisions on most matters, if not all matters. And usually, the senior pastors do not explicitly explain the basis for making the decisions. Sometimes, the younger pastors are not even informed about the decision. As younger pastors are of low power distance, they feel confused about why they are not involved in the process of decision making. They feel bypassed and perceive that their pastoral roles are being considered insignificant and unnecessary.

Moreover, there are various levels of decisions, such as official decisions, agreements in principle and verbal consents.[27] In Chinese churches of high power distance, because the senior pastors are well respected by the lay leaders, the senior pastors are allowed to implement any policies and decisions simply with verbal consent from lay leaders. By contrast, the young pastors are required to have formal approval in writing before proceeding with anything. They have to go through proper procedures and lines of reporting. Younger pastors notice the differences in treatment, and they feel that the senior pastors are 'more equal

---

26 Plueddemann, *Leading across Cultures*, 106.
27 Ibid.

than others'; they voice the unfairness and fight for their own rights and justice.

In Chinese churches, intergenerational conflicts are also caused by miscommunication derived from nonverbal communication. High-context older Chinese pastors employ plenty of types of nonverbal communication in their relating to others. Moreau categorises seven types of nonverbal communication: paraverbal methods (using vocal apparatus), stillness or silence, physical characteristics, proxemics (spacing), chronemics (timing), kinesics (body movement), and artefacts and environmental factors.[28] By contrast, the low-context younger pastors cannot pick up on any of these. They only take the face value of the spoken words. Thus, in daily interaction with their senior pastors, the younger pastors perceive double-meanings or contradictory meanings from their senior pastors. Their intercultural communication is seldom effective. Younger pastors often feel confusion and frustration in understanding their senior pastors. As these negative feelings accumulate, they cannot help speculating on the hidden agendas and motives of their senior pastors. Distrust slips into the pastoral team. The end result can be disastrous.

Therefore, intergenerational conflicts arise from the pastors' cultural illiteracy. Both older pastors and younger pastors are not aware of the modes of communication of their counterparts, modes of communication that are largely shaped by their existing cultural values.

In this regard, senior pastors are not non-communicative as such. It is only that their non-oral and non-verbal communication is incomplete communication. Similarly, the verbal communication of the younger pastors is also half communication. They overlook and pay no attention to the non-verbal messages. Thus, both sides

---

28   Moreau, *Effective Intercultural Communication*, 115–26.

need to widen the scope of their modes of communication. Older senior pastors need to employ more verbal communication and make their message audible and intelligible so that their messages and good intentions will not be misunderstood or neglected. Similarly, the younger pastors may need to pay extra attention to the non-verbal messages of their senior pastors. They may need to ask questions and rephrase the spoken words of their older pastors, or double-check with their senior pastors with questions such as, 'Is this what you mean?'[29] When the pastors meet, their discussion should therefore not be limited to the issues, but should also discuss and review their communication patterns and modes—which is their metacognitive CQ. Higher metacognitive CQ will improve their communication and will minimise intergenerational conflicts.[30]

Biblical passages could be used for the purposes of reflection. Moreau takes Genesis 23 as an example of a high-context conversation. It is a negotiation between Abraham and Ephron the Hittite for a burial site for Sarah.[31] Both parties in the negotiation, Abraham and Ephron, are from a high-context culture. Abraham explicitly indicates his intention of purchasing the site, whereas Ephron verbally offers to give Abraham the site as a gift. However, Abraham reads between the lines and understands that what Ephron says simply signifies his intention to sell the site, with a price in mind. In the end, after several rounds of conversation, Abraham agrees to the price term and buys the site from Ephron. Both Abraham and Ephron understand the meaning underlying the verbal conversation, and both follow the unspoken rules of negotiation of that culture by observing formal bargaining protocol. Eventually, the deal is done, and most of all,

---

29   Readings on non-verbal communication are helpful. For example, Ueda, 'Sixteen Ways'; Moreau, *Effective Intercultural Communication*, 135–36.
30   More discussion on ministry implications will be elaborated in chapter 6.
31   Moreau, *Effective Intercultural Communication*, 132–33.

face is saved. In this example of high-context communication, 'both knew the words to say, which words to ignore, and which ones had a particular meaning and how to understand them'.[32] Thus, reading the Bible with a purpose of reflection on cultural values sheds new light on human dynamics.

Language deficiency and CQ knowledge in intergenerational conflicts

From the interviews, it was noted that (English) language deficiency was a deep-rooted factor in intergenerational conflict.[33] Most of the interviewed pastors agreed that English was essential in working harmoniously as a team. They did not have enough language to communicate, to advocate and to clarify. Some pastors could not even listen or understand, and thus could not follow the flow of discussion.

In conflict resolution, language is an important dimension. As disagreements and conflicts involve strong emotions, using one's own heart language is preferred. However, whether to use Chinese or English always creates another disagreement!

According to Cultural Intelligence theory, language proficiency is an indicator of high cognitive CQ or CQ knowledge. 'Language skills serve as a fundamental instrument in acquiring

---

32 Ibid., 133.
33 This researcher is fully aware that language deficiency is only one of the factors of intergenerational conflicts. There are many other factors, such as personality clashes, different ways of communication, different expectations and unmet needs. As this study focuses more on the cross-cultural aspects of intergenerational conflict, the discussion centres on factors such as a sense of honour/shame or guilt, power distance or seniority, trust and relationship (Augsburger, *Conflict Mediation*; Chen et al., 'Determinants of Conflict Management'; Elmer, *Cross-Cultural Conflict*; Leung, 'Some Determinants'). That the issue of language deficiency has been brought to the fore in this section is not meant to rule out other factors.

cultural knowledge, such as an understanding of economic, legal, and social systems of different cultures'.[34] Language deficiency may diminish social activity and one's contribution to intercultural conversation.[35] However, language proficiency may help in accommodating people with less language ability, which, in turn, may enhance leadership.[36]

In international communication, English is always regarded as the common instrumental language for team discussion and the basic social language. Thus, English proficiency impacts participation in an intercultural team. For example, language fluency allows a team member to take part in a discussion, in-group interactions and decision making. He or she is more likely to be regarded as being more talented.[37] On the contrary, 'limited language comprehension and fluency may create a sense of remoteness and disconnectedness, which can exclude individuals from each other's view'.[38] Therefore, English fluency is critical in developing intercultural competence and minimising intergenerational conflicts.

Language level also impacts the capacity for articulation, which is an essential quality of leadership. At the pastoral team level, some communication requires a high level of articulation—areas such as vision formation, transferring vision, negotiation, policy-making and communication with difficult people. It requires articulation with the right language to debate and defend viewpoints. Moreover, pastors are required to preach from the Bible in an articulate way as a way of mobilising church members.

---

34 Shannon and Begley, 'Antecedents' 43.
35 Du-Babcock, 'Topic Management', 551.
36 Ibid., 552.
37 Shannon and Begley, 'Antecedents', 43.
38 Marschan-Piekkari et al., 'In the Shadow', 435; Shannon and Begley, 'Antecedents', 43.

Although many pastors understand the negative consequences of language deficiency, learning English is perceived as too difficult a task. There are various reasons for this.

The first factor is related to theological education. English is the common language used in pastoral team meetings in Chinese churches. In many discussions and debates, pastors need to use biblical terms and doctrinal language to express their thoughts and opinions. However, many Chinese-speaking pastors were trained in Chinese-speaking theological colleges back in their homeland (Taiwan, Mainland China or Hong Kong), and they were seldom exposed to theological terms and biblical terms in English such as justification, eschatology, millennium, Ecclesiastes, consubstantiation, Nebuchadnezzar and Deuteronomy. All these terms are of multiple syllables and are difficult to pronounce and spell. As the Chinese-speaking pastors are unfamiliar with the English biblical and theological terms, they are very anxious about speaking in English, let alone debating in it. In fact, they hardly understand what the other pastors say. The theological background of pastors impacts their communication or non-communication.

The second factor is related to the cultural learning background. Some pastors studied in English-speaking countries when they were young. Others, before they became pastors, worked in international companies. So, these pastors have some English communication background. However, other pastors do not have much English language background, or have even zero background: they have to grasp the language basics, such as grammar, vocabulary and common usages. The learning process can be very overwhelming. It's possible that non-achievement in language learning in the first months of migration destroyed their desire to learn, and they eventually gave up learning altogether. As language learning is always through exposing and immersing oneself in the world of that language, their withdrawal from that exposure deprives them of their opportunity for language learning.

This second factor is related to the third factor, which relates to shame and face—a unique feature of Chinese and certain Asian cultures. This can be regarded as an aspect of motivational CQ, a negative motivation. A sense of shame and saving face deters some Chinese from admitting their difficulties and incapability with language learning. This especially applies to the Chinese senior pastors, who are always regarded as leaders with high power distance, at the top of the social hierarchy. Leaders are expected to be teachers or trainers, to be consulted and learned from. Now, the senior pastors' lack of language may be perceived as incapability or failure. Furthermore, the older senior pastors have to learn English from their younger pastors, who are their subordinates and are junior in age. The younger pastors are at the lower end of social hierarchy. This reverse movement is certainly losing face, and older pastors cannot endure such humiliation.

Church pastors may like to reflect upon the notion of shame in the light of the Bible. For pastors, shame means dishonour and worthlessness. But, as suggested by Pattison, Christians should consider less their own shame, and consider more Jesus' glory.[39] Considering the glory of Jesus is the only way of delivering Chinese pastors from the bottomless pit of shame culture. The process of learning is humiliating and humbling, but the end result—gaining cognitive CQ and intercultural competence, which in turn are beneficial to gospel ministry—is an honour, an honour for Christ's sake.

The fourth factor is related to motivational CQ in relation to survival. Nowadays, there are quite a few Chinatowns (or major Chinese communities) in Sydney. Therefore, Chinese who

---

39 Pattison, *Saving Face*, 102–11.

do not have English proficiency can stay in the ghettos of their Chinese communities and churches. In a sense, they do not need to acquire any English at all. In the case of Chinese pastors, they can just harbour themselves in Chinese communities and Chinese churches; these become cultural and ethnic ghettos. Therefore, Chinese pastors can still survive with very limited English. Thus, their motivational CQ is not high at all.

This is also related to their self-perceived cultural identity. Research shows that, as migrants experience the confusion of cultural identity (torn-between cultural identities), as well as a sense of disconnectedness with their homeland and a sense of social isolation, they might choose to retreat back to their homeland culture and their own ethnic group.[40] In the case of some Chinese pastors, if they choose their homeland culture as their cultural identity, they do not consider Australia their home. They maintain their Chinese ways and manners. Their motivation in learning language is greatly reduced.

The last factor concerns language learning in relation to the cultural dimension of individualism-collectivism. According to Hofstede et al., research findings indicate that 'languages spoken in individualist cultures tend to require speakers to use the "I" pronoun when referring to themselves; language spoken in collectivistic cultures allow or prescribe dropping this pronoun. The English language, spoken in the most individualistic countries, is the only one we know of that writes "I" with a capital letter'.[41] This could be another difficulty for some Chinese pastors, who are more collectivists, in trying to speak English. It is unconventional for them to utter a sentence starting with 'I', such as 'I feel so and so', 'I like so and so' or even 'I love you'. Some traditional Chinese feel unconventional in expressing such awkward sentences.

---

40   Jackson, 'Shock of the New'; Horton, 'Mother's Heart'.
41   Hofstede et al., *Cultures and Organizations*, 112–13.

Thus, that group of Chinese pastors may find it is difficult to speak English in certain conventional Australian ways.

Christians may consider how to let the Bible shape their cultural thoughts and behaviours in learning a language. In the Bible, God repeatedly communicates with his people orally, in the language comprehensible to the hearers, such as to Adam and Eve (Genesis 3), Moses (Exodus 3), Jacob (Genesis 28) and Saul and Ananias (Acts 9). The Bible specifically portrays how the Lord speaks to Moses: 'The Lord would speak to Moses face to face, as a *man* speaks with his friend' (Exod 33:11). Jesus even speaks to people in their own dialect (Mark 5:41). In fact, the Bible encourages language learning lest we become outsiders or foreigners to each other. Paul said, 'If then I do not grasp the meaning of what someone is saying, I am a foreigner to the speaker, and he is a foreigner to me' (1 Cor. 14:11).

Lessard-Clouston's article can be brought into the discussion of language learning. He sees language learning as a redemptive activity.

> Language learning can be a redemptive activity which God uses to bless people . . . We in language education need to understand the redemptive aspects of language learning as reflected in Christ's incarnational approach to ministry and his sacrificial work on our behalf. Missionary language learners and teachers can reflect the redemption we have experienced.[42]

If pastors are to participate in God's redemptive plan, language learning is inevitable. Chinese pastors' English acquisition is, in essence, a participation in God's salvation plan.

---

42   Lessard-Clouston, 'Seven Biblical Themes'.

Some Chinese pastors might argue that as the church employs them to do the Chinese (Cantonese or Mandarin) ministry, they do not need to learn English to perform their pastoral ministry in the Cantonese or Mandarin congregations.

Ostensibly, this is a good reason not to learn a language. However, such an excuse can be reviewed and scrutinised under the four factors of Cultural Intelligence, particularly CQ drive. The preceding reasoning reflects the pastors' language learning is ministry-driven, which is an external drive, a drive from *without* instead of a drive from *within*.

Such reasoning reflects the person's very limited view of ministry. Pastoral ministry is never a lone ranger ministry. Pastoral ministry is always team ministry, a ministry of collaboration, which involves envisioning and planning, liaison and coordination, review and evaluation. All these pastoral activities involve a common instrumental language, which is usually English. Therefore, language deficiency limits the possibility of collaborative teamwork and team development. Language deficiency also increases the risk of miscommunication, misunderstanding, and conflicts with other pastors and leaders.[43]

Moreover, although the congregations ministered to by Chinese-speaking pastors mainly consist of Chinese migrants, the cultural identity of the Chinese migrants is not purely traditional Chinese. Their cultural identity is culturally hybrid. The longer they live in Australia, and the more they interact with Australian society, their cultural identity is less influenced or constituted by their 'Chinese-ness'. They are in the process of changing

---

[43] Similarly, such a language requirement also applies to the mission world. Missionaries working in certain mission fields have to learn the language of the local people. Moreover, as the missionary is part of a missionary team, the members of which come from various corners of the world, the missionary also needs to learn the instrumental language of that team, which is usually English. However, such a discussion is beyond the scope of this research.

and shifting away from traditional Chinese culture. Also, the recipients of pastoral ministry in Chinese churches always include two generations, the migrant generation and their children's generation. Pastoral care, guidance on Christian parenting, and Christian education at home involves enormous understanding of the two generations. Without the languages of both generations (Chinese and English), there is no real understanding of their needs and their struggles.

Of such a person, Filbeck rightly points out that 'by not learning to interact with members of the group through the language of the group, he cannot, in reality, learn the network of values, meanings, interests, concerns, and labellings which are wrapped up in the elaborate form of that language'.[44] Therefore, escaping language learning does not only jeopardise ministry effectiveness and efficacy, but it also deprives a pastor from realistically serving the congregation with cultural relevance.

However, language learning is more than ministry-driven or driven by an external drive; language learning is preferably driven internally. For example, as seen in my interviews, some pastors see the beauty of other cultures. They have a sense of curiosity and discovery in getting to know new cultures. Some other pastors experience fun in the language and cultural learning process. All these pleasant experiences and feelings can be ascribed to an internal drive in language learning.

The primary internal drive of pastors is God's calling into ministry. Ministry is driven by God's calling. In a cross-cultural setting, the *process* of language learning is regarded as doing ministry: 'the determination of learning language shows one's interest in the people God calls to serve; it also shows one's need to learn from that specific group of people'.[45] Thus, learning a

---

44   Filbeck, *Social Context and Proclamation*, 51.
45   Willis, 'Learning to Speak', 436.

language is not just a ministry, it is primarily incarnational ministry.[46] It is a way to 'demonstrate a learner's attitude toward the host culture and communicate to the people that their language is important not only to you but to God as well'.[47] Thus, English learning is preferably internally driven, driven from within by God's calling. It becomes clear that cognitive CQ or CQ knowledge (English acquisition) is greatly influenced by motivational CQ or CQ drive (God's calling).

It is noted that language learning should be reciprocal. By reciprocal, I mean language learning is required by both generations. The older senior pastors should acquire as much English as possible, and the younger pastors should at least pick up some Chinese, either Cantonese or Mandarin. This mutual effort is indispensable in strengthening teamwork and team development. Although it is obvious and understandable that some older pastors will never acquire sufficient ministry-level language competency, acquiring a social level of language may be considered. Reciprocal language learning may produce two advantages.

In the first place, the determination and effort in language learning by pastors from one language group may result in the encouragement to learn language by pastors from the other language group. For example, as Chinese pastors notice the willingness and effort of English pastors in learning Chinese, the Chinese pastors feel encouraged to learn a bit more English, and vice versa. Secondly, learning a language at a social level could allow the older senior pastors to provide some pastoral care and ministry appreciation to the younger English pastors. This, in turn, increases the English pastors' incentive to place trust in

---

46 Todd, 'Incarnational Learners'; Brewster and Brewster, 'Language Learning'.
47 Moreau, *Effective Intercultural Communication*, 78–79.

RESEARCH ANALYSIS

their older senior pastors. The older senior pastors may also gain confidence in leading a pastoral team.

Obviously, language learning takes time. It is understandable that older pastors may require more time in English learning. Thus, the younger English pastors should allow the older pastors time to pick up the English. Patience, visible encouragement and practical assistance are required.

The more language is acquired, the more the older senior pastors can be involved in verbal and oral communication. And the younger pastors can gain a new window into understanding the traditional Chinese culture and worldview. Efforts by both generations would certainly minimise intergenerational misunderstanding and conflict.

In summary, language learning is essential in pastoral ministry, in team collaboration and in minimising intergenerational conflicts. Language learning benefits the person's intercultural competence, and Cultural Intelligence demonstrates God's love to the people the pastors are called to serve and points to the glory of God. The preceding analysis also shows cognitive CQ and motivational CQ are closely knitted. The absence of motivational CQ diminishes the cognitive CQ (language proficiency). The higher motivational CQ provides determination to gain further cognitive CQ.

MICHAEL K. CHU

Insufficient reflection on cultural differences and metacognitive CQ in intergenerational conflicts

Lane points out that conflict is more like to occur in cross-cultural contexts because of misattribution. This refers to 'ascribing meaning or motive to behaviour based on one's own culture'.[48] Bates also points out that a Christian worldview may intensify the perception of incompatibility with others: 'One of the major temptations of Christians in conflict situations is to elevate their position to a matter of principle. This artificial production of a value conflict implies that to change is to compromise'.[49] The underlying issue is that people in intercultural contexts are likely to perceive and interpret others' outward behaviours through their own conventional cultural lens, without *critical reflection*.

According to Cultural Intelligence theory, metacognitive CQ plays an important part in improving intercultural competence and communication. It is about strategic thinking, evaluative thinking, forward thinking and thinking about thinking.[50] It requires reflection, review and evaluation of communication. Dean is right in comparing cross-cultural missionary ministry to cultural pilgrimage.[51] In other words, cross-cultural experience is a pilgrim journey, along which various activities are performed, such as observation, note-taking, reflection, articulating concepts, and regulating communication strategies for future directions and steps. If this process is undertaken carefully, the same cross-cultural mistakes will not be repeatedly committed. The quality and effectiveness of intercultural communication can

---

48 Lane, *Beginner's Guide*, 118.
49 Bates, 'Missions', 97.
50 Earley et al., *CQ*, 48; Gough, 'Thinking about Thinking'.
51 Dean, 'Missionary as Cultural Pilgrim'.

be improved. In the case of Chinese churches, intergenerational conflicts can be avoided, and intergenerational relationships can be restored.

In the interviews with pastors, I noticed the non-reflective character of pastors. Firstly, in the process of coding the verbatim scripts of the interviews, it is to be noted that terms or related words about reflection (such as assess, review, contemplate, evaluate, recollect, compare, consider) are not much used. Secondly, concerning the process of interviewing, I note that pastors did not perform regular reflection. Two incidents in the interviews are specifically illuminating.

A pastor recalled his experience of taking a cross-cultural subject at theological college. Although he realised that the lectures and reading materials were from the Westerners' perspectives, he admitted that he seldom reflected on or considered his own Asian or Chinese perspectives. He simply received and accepted, and he was content with whatever was being taught.

Another incident concerned a pastor discussing his future actions for improving his intercultural competence. His answer was, 'I don't think I have to plan and take certain steps to improve my cross-cultural skill. It comes natural . . . I don't think I'd intentionally . . . Through interaction with them should be good enough. So don't need to take extra steps to learn or equip.' Such a reply did not only show his lack of any intentional plan, it also showed his lack of self-reflection. He performed ministry in a *reactive* mode (be reactive to the urgent needs of people) rather than using a *proactive* approach (contemplate the real needs of people).

Rendle laments that for pastors, the 'daily life of a leader is reactive space, not reflective space'.[52] He sees pastoral leaders responding to the immediate problems and challenges instead

---

52   Rendle, *Multigenerational Congregation*, 118.

of observing the trends, contemplating repeated patterns, and reflecting with a big picture in mind. Such an observation concurs with the experiences of pastors in Chinese churches; they are working competently, but not necessarily reflectively and wisely. This is exactly why Peterson calls pastors to be contemplative.[53] This is also why our Lord Jesus retreats from the crowd and heavy ministry into solitude and prayer.[54] After those retreats from the crowd, Jesus refocuses and readjusts his ministry.

In the interviews with the pastors, I also noted the pastors' non-reflection in the debriefing sessions of short mission trips. Almost all interviewed pastors participated in short-term mission trips. However, when asked about their learning and insight during their post-trip debriefing sessions, they were unexcited. They replied with virtually nothing of significance. They simply could not recall any perceptive or reflective questions their team leaders or facilitators asked. Apparently, the orientation of their trips revolved around finishing the tasks and ministries assigned, without considering developmental outcomes gained from the trips. In a sense, the experiences of the mission trips had been a waste.

Supposedly, short-term mission trips are prime opportunities for experiential learning.[55] A mission trip is a moment of experience in which one can observe and reflect, and the post-trip debriefing is an excellent opportunity for in-depth learning by reflective discussion and explorative conceptualisation. On a mission trip, members usually go through a certain amount of cultural shock and undergo cross-cultural experiences. Kohls offers steps to think through the trip experiences: knowledge of the host country and culture; logical reasons behind strange and

---

53 Peterson, *Contemplative Pastor*.
54 Mark 1:35–39, 6:45–46, 14:32–42; Luke 6:12.
55 Kolb, *Experiential Learning*.

confusing things in the host culture; talking to a host national.[56] Barna highlights a number of things that can be reflected upon in the debriefing, such as assumptions, language differences, nonverbal misinterpretations, preconceptions and stereotypes and moments of high anxiety.[57]

Reflection is important and beneficial to adult learners' self-learning. Little's research shows that 'if they are reflectively engaged with their learning, it is likely to be more efficient and effective'.[58] Fanning and Gaba suggest that reflection is the cornerstone of experiential learning and the cornerstone of lifelong learning.[59]

Chinese pastors may consider reflecting on intergenerational conflict from the perspective of cultural values. Moreau highlights the relationships between individualism-collectivism and intercultural conflict by distinguishing instrumental goals and task goals.[60] Moreau notes that individualistic people tend to focus on task goals by solving a problem, achieving a specific goal and getting the job done. They separate instrumental goals from task goals.[61] To individualistic people, conflict is only an idea; it is never personal. However, collectivistic people are concerned with interpersonal relationships. They do not separate the instrumental goals from the task goals. And, most of all, collectivists see conflict as personal.[62] Lustig and Koester remark that 'the distinction, therefore, focuses on conflict about ideas versus conflict about people'.[63]

---

56 Moreau, *Effective Intercultural Communication*, 219–20.
57 Barna, 'Stumbling Blocks'.
58 Little, "Learner Autonomy'.
59 Fanning and Gaba, 'Role of Debriefing'.
60 Moreau, *Effective Intercultural Communication*.
61 Ibid., 332–33.
62 Ibid.
63 Lustig and Koester, *Intercultural Competence*, 269.

Reflection on intergenerational conflicts can be performed in relation to three aspects: causes of conflict, confrontation and resolving conflict.

Decision making is one of the major causes of intergenerational conflicts in Chinese churches. In such churches, the younger pastors, who are more individualistic, simply focus on the discussion of, and decisions about, certain issues and agenda items. To the younger pastors, once a decision is made, it is supposed that the decision will be carried out and be implemented accordingly. However, the senior pastors, who are more collectivistic, are concerned about many other relational and organisational factors, such as relationships with the elders and deacons, the ministry leaders, the power-brokers, brothers and sisters 'with a weak conscience', seekers, musicians and members of different language congregations. After a decision has been made in the pastoral team meeting, the senior pastor may have second thoughts and reverse the decision. If the individualistic younger pastors do not reflect on the cultural difference between them and their senior pastors, they may be upset and feel confused.

Confrontation in conflicts is another dimension which requires pastors to reflect. High-context people (for example traditional Chinese) tend to avoid conflict and deal with conflict indirectly, while low-context people (for example Australians) tend to adopt confrontation and direct conflict styles.[64] Traditional Chinese are inclined to maintain harmonious relationships by avoiding serious conflicts, so as to avoid embarrassing others.[65] The Chinese belief *wu-wei* (non-action) also influences and affects the way that the traditional Chinese deal with conflicts.[66]

---

[64] Chua and Gudykunst, 'Conflict Resolution Styles'; Ting-Toomey, 'Intercultural Conflict Style'.
[65] Yang, '"Yuan".
[66] Leung, 'Beliefs in Chinese Culture'.

In contrast, however, the younger pastors can become very impatient with their senior pastors' avoidance and denial of conflict. This is one aspect both conflicting parties may need time to reflect on.

Sometimes, storytelling can be a powerful way to confront.[67] Nathan the prophet confronts King David about the sin of adultery and murder. The prophets and Jesus tell parables to reveal people's sins.[68] Joab engages a wise woman to become a mediator for King David and Absalom, and the wise woman tells a story for King David's reflection.

Emotions and non-verbal communication in intergenerational conflicts require deep reflection. Such conflicts are enmeshed in substantial emotions which are always expressed in non-verbal manners (such as facial expressions, tone of speech, voice volume, eye contact and body gestures). How both conflicting parties interpret the emotions of one another in verbal and non-verbal exchanges is a huge issue. As the individualistic younger pastors rely more on verbal communication and are more proficient in the English language, they tend towards oral communication. Since collectivistic senior pastors rely more on non-verbal communication, and since their English proficiency is relatively weaker than that of the younger pastors, they more frequently rely on body language. However, the individualistic younger pastors are not good at observing and taking note of the emotional and non-verbal communication of their senior pastors. They cannot grasp fully the emotions that the senior pastors have communicated. Similarly, the less English-proficient senior pastors cannot pick up every single emotional word of their younger pastors. Thus, both parties cannot fully engage in communication.

---

67 Tucker, *Intercultural Communication*, 116–17.
68 Isaiah 5:1–7, Mark 12:1–12, Luke 1.

If, after the conflict, both parties are less emotional—and take time to reflect upon the whole process of conflict, recall the verbal exchanges, recollect the body language and review the interactive dynamics of the dialogue—then there is a better chance for resolving their conflict and for reconciliation. However, if it is not the usual pattern of pastors to reflect, both parties will continue to linger in frustration and confusion and will see themselves as victims and as the offended party; the conflict and relationships will go in a downward spiral.

Another dimension in reflecting upon intergenerational conflict is in relation to third-party intermediaries. In high-context cultures, like the Chinese, if there is any conflict, the preferred conflict resolution style is to use a third-party intermediary as a social resource to resolve the conflicts, so as to maintain harmonious relationships and to preserve face.[69] In low-context cultures, using a mediator is unfamiliar, uncomfortable and unexpected. Low-context people prefer conflicting parties to talk to each other and resolve disagreements directly.[70] Therefore, such cultural differences affect whether a mediator is required in resolving intercultural conflicts. Cultural differences also determine who, when and how the mediator should step in. If a mediator is required and agreed upon, pastors need to reflect on and consider the purposes, roles and functions of the mediator, according to the various cultural-background needs of the pastors.

In Chinese church conflicts, senior pastors are always called in to resolve conflicts. The rationale of asking senior pastors to be mediators is obviously based on power distance.

---

[69] Chang and Holt, 'More Than Relationship'. There is much research on saving face and resolving conflict (Ting-Toomey, 'Intercultural Conflict Style'), self-image and conflict resolution (Neuliep, *Intercultural Communication*), emotionality and conflict (Kochman, *Black and White*), and intercultural conflict styles (Hammer, 'Intercultural Conflict Style Inventory'; Augsburger, *Conflict Mediation*).

[70] Moreau, *Effective Intercultural Communication*, 335.

RESEARCH ANALYSIS

The hierarchical positions of senior pastors, positions which are associated with seniority and credibility, are respected and trusted by both conflicting parties; but only when both parties are from high power distance cultures.[71] However, if the conflict involves two generations—one of which is high power distance and the other is low power distance—the hierarchical role of the senior pastor is in question. And therefore, the mediatory role of the senior pastor is not as effective as it would have been if the pastors were all from a high power distance culture. Moreover, if the conflict involves the senior pastor himself, appointing a mediator can be an even harder problem, as no one in the church is more esteemed than the senior pastor. In that case, a mediator from outside the church would be required.

This socio-cultural discussion shows that there is insufficient reflection by Chinese pastors on cultural differences and metacognitive CQ in intergenerational conflicts.

I recall one of the interviewed pastors, as he recalled his frustration and anger following an experience of abuse and discrimination at a bank. After I allowed him to express his emotions, I inquired further about the unpleasant incident. He finally disclosed that he had been jumping the queue in front of the bank counter. What surprised me was his non-reflection about the incident after so many years; he still felt that he was the victim.

The difference in learning and education approach also contributes to the non-reflection of Chinese pastors. The education approach in China and other East Asian countries is rooted within Confucianism, which is more of respectful learning, that is, 'authorities must be treated with a great deal of respect in order to maintain a harmonious relationship with them'.[72] On the

---

71 Chen et al., 'Determinants of Conflict Management'.
72 Kühnen et al., 'Challenge Me!', 61–62.

other hand, the education approach of the Western world (such as European countries and America) can be traced back to Socrates' dialectic questioning.[73] In the Western world, learning occurs through critical debate, discussion, dialogue and asking questions, which require plenty of interaction and communication. In China and Asia, learning usually occurs through one-way lectures and instruction, diligence and enduring hardship, memorisation and repetition.[74] In other words, the Chinese way of learning does not rely on critical thinking and reflection. Thus, non-reflection occurs more often among Chinese-speaking older pastors.

Thus, pastors should develop a pattern of reflection after performing pastoral ministry. First of all, the pastors should get rid of 'playing victim'. Being hurt in conflict doesn't mean the pastor is on the right side. Besides, 'playing victim' does not produce and ensure a constructive solution; relational distrust merely spirals downwards. In particular, pastors should be encouraged to spend time reflecting on conflict, its causes and ways of resolving it. The time factor is important. Preferably, reflection should be done as soon as unpleasant emotions begin to diminish. The sooner the reflection, the better the memories recalled. The pastors may reflect on areas such as cultural values (for example individualism-collectivism), the course of decision making, the timing and settings of confrontation and any non-verbal communication. These are usually the major areas producing intercultural conflicts. Moreover, talking and debriefing to an unrelated third party about the matter will be helpful. Preferably, the third party should be interculturally experienced. Honest feedback with empathy always gives much insight to the concerned pastor and, in turn, the insight could be

---

73 Socrates method has been widely used education method in American law school. See Ryan et al., 'When Socrates Meets Confucius', 291–92.
74 Kühnen et al., 'Challenge Me!', 62.

used to reflect further for resolving conflict, for restoration and for future avoidance of unnecessary conflict.

Critical reflection is required in using the Bible to resolve conflict. For example, for many Western pastors, Matthew 18 has been used as a primary text for guidance in resolving conflict. However, the context of that passage is about sinning against a brother.[75] In other words, 'using this passage implies that the conflict is due to a spiritual problem and that the person you are approaching is the sinful one. Assumption that conflict arises from the sin of another person rather than from differences in cultural values may sabotage the conflict-resolution process'.[76] The right application of the Bible cannot be achieved without critical reflection.

Nevertheless, there are biblical examples of conflict mediation, such as Jesus being the mediator between God and humankind and Barnabas acting as a mediator between Paul and the Jerusalem church. Abigail also mediates between King David and Nabal, avoiding an imminent war. Paul writes a letter to mediate between Philemon and Onesimus and restores their broken relationship. It is assumed that these mediators would have gone through thoughtful preparation and reflection of the conflict situations before they actually launched into the mediation.

In summary, my analysis shows that the pastors' non-communication, language deficiencies and lack of ministry reflection contribute to intergenerational conflicts, with tremendous consequences. It also shows that the four dimensions of Cultural Intelligence, with special reference to the cultural identity and cultural values of the two generations, provide a

---

75   Cheng, 'Spirituality'.
76   Moreau, *Effective Intercultural Communication*, 331–32.

helpful framework to understand the deep-seated factors behind Chinese pastors' intergenerational conflicts.

In order to foster harmonious and trustful relationships among pastors, it is recommended that Chinese pastors of both generations restore effective communication, acquire language proficiency and develop patterns of critical reflection. Practical ministry implications will be discussed and recommended in the following chapter.

CHAPTER SIX
PRACTICAL IMPLICATIONS

Based on the analysis and discussion of the previous chapter, this chapter aims to draw ministry implications and applications. The purpose of drawing implications is to develop and improve the intercultural competence of the Chinese pastors working in Chinese churches in Sydney. It is believed that improved intercultural competence not only minimises intergenerational conflicts but also increases the cultural relevance and effectiveness of pastoral ministry.

Firstly, I propose recommendations for pastors that can be carried out individually. Secondly, I recommend implications and proposals for Chinese churches (in particular for pastoral teams), theological colleges and mission agencies. Recommendations for Chinese churches, theological colleges and mission agencies address three aspects: communication, language acquisition and metacognitive thinking.[1] Lastly, I conclude with an integrated proposal.

Recommendations for pastors

Equipping and developing intercultural competence of pastors can improve the efficacy of the pastors' performance in pastoral leadership. Clinton suggests beginning where the pastors are.[2] Every pastor has his or her own cultural identity and cultural values. Any leadership theories and practices have to be developed according to one's cultural identity and values. Therefore, knowing oneself is a logical starting point. Some recommendations are as follows.

Firstly, it is suggested that individual pastors complete a self-assessment of their Cultural Intelligence. An assessment report gives the pastors a clear and accurate knowledge of the four dimensions of their intercultural competence and provides information that helps individual pastors to identify their strengths and developmental opportunities. As Cultural Intelligence is a malleable capability 'that may change based on cultural exposure, training, modelling, mentoring, socialisation, and other experiences',[3] pastors can reflect and make use of the information of the report to design a self-development action plan

---

[1] I am aware that many other areas need to be discussed in this ministry implication section. I do not mean to reduce cross-cultural ministry to three areas (communication, language acquisition and metacognitive thinking); however, these are the more significant areas for discussion suggested by the interview findings. Moreover, the focus of this discussion is not cross-cultural ministry in general but intercultural ministry based around intergenerational cultural difference. These are the three most relevant factors towards that end.

[2] Clinton, 'Cross-Cultural Use', 196.

[3] Ang and Van Dyne, *Handbook*, 25.

PRACTICAL IMPLICATIONS

in connection with the pastors' intercultural context to improve intercultural competence.[4]

Secondly, apart from self-assessment of their Cultural Intelligence, pastors are recommended to do a self-assessment of their own cultural values, such as power distance, high context or low context, collectivistic or individualistic and uncertainty avoidance. There are various assessment tools online, and most of them provide post-assessment explanatory reports. Similarly, the assessment of cultural values aims at improving the pastor's self-awareness of the cultural values construct and to identify their personal cultural strengths and areas for development.

As a supplementary suggestion, assessment of Cultural Intelligence capacity and cultural values may also be conducted in the pastors' recruitment process.[5] The Cultural Intelligence assessment is not meant to screen out candidates of different cultural types or those with a low level of Cultural Intelligence. Rather, it is to help the pastoral candidate, once he or she becomes part of the team, to understand his or her own intercultural competence and to understand the cultural distances between pastors. This would certainly enhance future teamwork and mutual understanding within the team.

Thirdly, to be an effective and functional pastor, the pastor has to undergo continuous learning, which results in pastoral longevity, sustainability of ministry, and most of all cultural relevance in pastoral ministry service. Because pastors are adult learners, the effectiveness of adult learning is greatly determined by self-motivation and voluntary participation. The motive of

---

[4] It is noted that Hibbert offers an inventory for multicultural team leaders (Hibbert and Hibbert, *Leading Multicultural Teams*, 223–25). Although it is not entirely a review of intercultural competence, it provides a profile of a leader with intercultural capability. It may be helpful to leaders in a culturally diversified context.

[5] Rockstuhl and Ng, 'Effects of Cultural Intelligence', 217.

adult learning focuses primarily on the learner's 'innate desire to acquire new knowledge, skills, insight or competence'.[6] Therefore, it is suggested that pastors reflect and develop their own intercultural learning motivations or Motivational CQ. The developing of motivation can be achieved by two approaches: firstly, by removing the negative motivations, and secondly, by building positive motivations or passions. Pastors are encouraged to do an honest stocktake of their negative motivations, such as ethnocentric superiority, shame, racism or prejudice, fear of transparency, unpleasant past experiences and risk avoiding. Pastors can then check that their positive motivations include self-efficacy, appreciation, gratification, curiosity and creativity. This process may require a list of reflective questions. Sometimes, a perceptive facilitator or mentor can help pastors to identify and develop motivations.

The recommendations mentioned so far are more about skills. Perhaps reviewing self from the perspective of worldview is more basic. Instead of just outward behavioural change, it is suggested worldview transformation is more fundamental. Hiebert is right in distinguishing three levels of life transformation — behaviour, belief and worldview—in which transformation of worldview is most fundamental and radical.[7] It is because worldview governs and directs people's conducts, convictions and values. The chart of evaluative norms at the worldview level outlined by Hiebert is valuable for pastors to understand self and others in the team.[8] The chart is a helpful tool in reviewing worldview of various dimensions of life. As cultural value is one of the major deep-seated factors in intergenerational conflict, worldviews of different generations should be looked into. Older

---

6   Brookfield, *Understanding and Facilitating*, 11–12.
7   Hiebert, *Transforming Worldviews*, 316.
8   Ibid., 64.

PRACTICAL IMPLICATIONS

pastors are more collective (or group-oriented) and young pastors are more individualistic (or individual-oriented). Thus, it is logical to the understanding of worldview of group-oriented community and individual-oriented community.[9] For example, pastors desire to develop teams and form ministry collaborations. However, different cultural groups may understand the notions of 'team' or 'friendship' differently. Thus, understanding of the level of friendship could be very helpful in understanding and developing ministry collaboration.[10] Therefore, steps should be taken to understand worldviews, so as to improve cultural intelligence. The 3-step approach suggested by Kraft is recommended.[11]

Lastly, the cultivation of inner life qualities should be a fundamental priority.[12] It is believed that an influential leader should have certain personal qualities that attract followers. Leadership skills are less important when compared with the morality and spirituality of a leader. Inner life qualities include showing empathy, gracious encouragement and generous life-giving. These inner life qualities are particularly powerful in a cross-cultural context. However, not many of the existing leadership development programs emphasise the development of inner life qualities; thus, inner life qualities can be regarded as a forgotten but important area of leadership development in Chinese churches. Therefore, a long-term development plan or leadership development program is greatly required.

---

9   Ibid., 21.
10   Ibid., 96.
11   Kraft, *Anthropology for Christian Witness*, 444–46.
12   I specify this point in the very end of this discussion with the purpose of stressing that the morality and spirituality of a Christian leader are more basic and foundational. I am not suggesting that leadership skills are not important. Rather, it is a question of relative emphasis. I just don't want to see pastors and leaders putting the cart before the horse.

MICHAEL K. CHU

Recommendations for churches

Communication among pastors

First of all, having pastoral teams with members of diversified cultural backgrounds should not be regarded negatively as a barrier to mutual learning. Instead, culturally diversified teams should be seen positively; indeed, they are opportunities for and platforms of mutual learning. Working in multicultural settings prompts more learning challenges. As postulated by Shokef and Erez, working in a multicultural team enhances the development of Cultural Intelligence and global identity,[13] and people with global identity are more likely to be intentional in acquiring and functioning in multicultural contexts.[14] Therefore, the best way of improving Chinese pastors' intercultural competence is encouraging them to join and work in a multicultural setting. Various training devices can be structured into the group processing so as to increase intercultural engagement and interaction. Such structures are basically congruent with education theories of collaborative learning.[15]

The starting point is developing an intercultural friendship. Developing friendship has been a resounding aspect of the call to cross-cultural missions.[16] At the 1910 Edinburgh Missionary Conference, Bishop Azariah appealed to the conference delegates for cross-racial friendship, which is more valuable than money and life.

> Through all the ages to come the Indian Church will rise up in gratitude to attest the heroism and self-

---

13　Shokef and Erez, 'Cultural Intelligence', 181.
14　Ibid., 182.
15　Brookfield, *Understanding and Facilitating*, 14–15.
16　Morr, 'Role of Friendship'; Robert, 'Cross-Cultural Friendship'.

PRACTICAL IMPLICATIONS

denying labours of the missionary body. You have given your goods to feed the poor. You have given your bodies to be burned. We also ask for love. Give us friends![17]

Gospel ministry should not be reduced to a mere task to accomplish but should be understood as a loving relationship to cultivate. Thus, pastors in multicultural teams are not just performing ministerial tasks but cultivating relationships between trustful friends. Trustful friendship has to be developed through 'trust-provoking experiences'[18] and 'unstructured time together'.[19] In other words, pastors may need to be prepared to spend time going through certain experiences together.

My observation of Chinese churches in Sydney is that most of the pastoral teams function as work teams. Their orientation is towards tasks, administrative discussion, coordination and task allocation. Such a working pattern does not help intercultural friendship.

In order to cultivate and strengthen intercultural friendship and relationships, it is suggested that pastors organise non-business gatherings, such as picnics, hiking groups, parties, occasions for having tea together, ball games, meal sharing and mini-book clubs (sharing recently-read non-academic, non-ministry books). These non-business gatherings could be organised on alternate weeks, in parallel to the formal pastoral team meetings. These non-business initiatives bring fun, help pastors drop their guards and defence mechanisms, increase mutual understanding and strengthen mutual trust in informal settings. With this trust and understanding, pastors can genuinely share their inner selves, their aspirations and struggles. These are

---

17   Rouse and Neill, *History of the Ecumenical Movement*, 359.
18   Roembke, *Building Credible Multicultural Teams*, 122.
19   Tucker, *Intercultural Communication*, 100.

essential for understanding one another's worldviews, cultural assumptions and cultural preferences. Acquaintance with one another can also improve motivation for furthering intercultural understanding.

Secondly, as already suggested, all pastors are encouraged to do a self-assessment of their Cultural Intelligence and cultural values. Post-assessment workshops may be organised to discuss their assessment reports and results. As self-assessment of Cultural Intelligence and cultural values can be subjective, assessment results can be checked and supplemented by others' feedback and input, which may result in a more complete picture of their Cultural Intelligence and cultural values. Post-assessment workshops are preferably facilitated by external trained facilitators, who are more knowledgeable and professional.

Apart from post-assessment workshops on Cultural Intelligence and cultural values, workshops can be organised for the pastors to discuss other specific cultural topics. The objectives of workshops are to

> increase positive attitudes toward the people of other cultures, increase awareness of the problems that arise in communicating with people of other cultures, increase awareness of participants' own culture values and unstated cultural assumptions, call attention to any counterproductive stereotypes and prejudices toward people of other cultures, assist in preparing people to better adapt to and be more productive during intercultural assignments.[20]

---

20 Kohls and Knight, *Developing Intercultural Awareness*, xii.

PRACTICAL IMPLICATIONS

Workshops with games and exercises, followed by debriefing discussion, have proven effective in developing a strong intercultural team.[21]

It is suggested that pastors utilise the results of their Cultural Intelligence and cultural values self-assessment to design or structure training for intercultural awareness and competence and to make plans to understand the cultural values of juxtaposing. For example, if a pastoral team is more collectivistic, workshops can be organised to understand cultural behaviours and styles of individualistic people. If a pastoral team leans towards low-context culture, the team may gain cultural knowledge of high-context culture through training workshops. Workshops can be designed to understand the communication modes of high-context people (who focus on body language) and low-context people (who rely on verbal and oral communication). The pastors can brainstorm and explore possible interaction dynamics, pitfalls and ways of effective communication of these two groups of people. Case studies and fictitious situations on decision making or disputes can be utilised to stretch the pastors' minds. Before the workshop is over, the pastors can even draft certain ground rules or guidelines on effective communication for their team development. These are non-threatening ways to enhance the intercultural competence of pastors.

Moreover, follow-up action may be formulated after these workshops. Individual pastors can be delegated to write a short 'sharing' article to be printed in the church Sunday bulletin. This follow-up action is two-fold in purpose. Firstly, the lay leaders and congregation are informed, made aware of and shaped unobtrusively and imperceptibly by the concept of intercultural communication. The importance of intercultural communication is emphasised. Through this, the whole church undergoes a subtle

---

21   Ibid.

process of intercultural learning. Secondly, the pastor who writes the article is given an opportunity to perceptively articulate his or her understanding of intercultural communication. The writing process allows the pastor to think through the cultural topic they have been assigned, and writing becomes the best way to present his or her thoughts. This prepares the pastors for future preaching to church members and training lay leaders.

Apart from developing friendship and discussion workshops in order to improve intercultural communication, pastors are encouraged to adopt various communication modes (such as verbal and written forms) in pastoral team meetings. For example, after a discussion between a Chinese-speaking pastor and an English-speaking pastor, a written summary report can be distributed and kept by both pastors for reference and further action. The summary report may include all the major items discussed orally, with outstanding tasks or unfinished issues to be followed up. That would minimise the chances of miscommunication and misunderstanding. The summary report also reduces unnecessary assumptions and speculations; hence, conflict may be minimised.

Nowadays, younger-generation pastors prefer to use online and social media technology for communication (such as email, WhatsApp, text messaging and Facebook), whereas older pastors above fifty tend to stick to face-to-face communication. Pastors may need to understand and adapt to others' preferred ways of communication. Senior pastors may need to learn more communication technologies. The younger pastors may need to adopt face-to-face discussion, which could seem less efficient to them.

It is also noticed that older pastors tend to talk verbosely, whereas younger pastors prefer shorter and more precise

PRACTICAL IMPLICATIONS

communication. Pastors need to be aware of these differences and prepared to readjust their own communication style.

Listening is another important dimension in intercultural communication. Listening is about attitude and mindfulness, giving full attention to the speaker. 'Instead of half-listening while your mind is pursuing other thoughts, focus on the words, trying to identify the purpose of the message and discerning the context from which the message comes.'[22] Thus, practical steps may include withholding immediate reactions, avoiding interruptions, suspending judgement, postponing evaluation and making brief notes. Simple questions for clarification and repetition can be asked in a gentle way, such as, 'Can you help me to understand the reason for . . . ?' or, 'I do not fully grasp the last point—can you repeat that point?' As younger pastors from a low-context culture are concerned more with speaking and take less note of non-verbal behaviours, it is suggested that they learn active listening in conversation, such as avoiding interruptions while the older pastors or Chinese pastors are talking.

It is also noted that there are separate services and house groups for Chinese congregants organised in certain Caucasian denominational churches in Sydney (such as Baptist and Anglican churches). The recommendations made to the pastors of Chinese churches are also applicable in these Caucasian churches with Chinese or Asian migrant pastors. Chinese-speaking pastors in these churches, who are usually assistant pastors of these Caucasian churches, may see themselves as a minority, if not outsiders. As most Chinese-speaking pastors in these Caucasian churches are from high-context cultures and high power distance cultures, they may see themselves as subordinate, and they would submit to every decision unquestionably. They may be hesitant in voicing their opinions. In the long-term, such a communication

---

22   Smith, *Creating Understanding*, 72.

pattern may jeopardise the functioning of the team. I suspect that not many pastors in Sydney have been trained in cross-cultural communication and intercultural competence. Therefore, both the Caucasian pastors and Chinese-speaking pastors may like to improve their intercultural competence by means of the preceding suggestions about developing friendship, assessment, workshops and listening.

Language acquisition

The objective of acquiring language is to improve communication. The suggestions below are not meant to improve the language level of Chinese pastors to a perfect level, particularly for those Chinese pastors whose English language background is limited or non-existent. The foremost concern is to take away the hindrance of language learning; the greatest concerns of adult language learners are reported to be 'worry and embarrassment at being required to speak in front of fellow students', the 'feeling of not being good as a language learner' and 'not able to understand what was required'.[23] In the interviews with the pastors, various pastors reported similar concerns. Thus, the following suggestions are given simply to increase the opportunities of Chinese-speaking pastors to speak in English. The more opportunity to speak, the more likely the Chinese-speaking pastors can acquire improved English.

Firstly, it is noted that some Chinese-speaking pastors in Chinese churches are reluctant to speak English in pastoral team meetings. Thus, it is suggested that various discussion modes be adopted in such meetings. When a discussion item is raised in pastoral team meetings of five or six members, Chinese-speaking pastors, whose biggest concern is embarrassment in speaking

---

23 Nunan, 'Learner Strategy Training'.

PRACTICAL IMPLICATIONS

English, are inclined to keep silent in the discussion. To address this, instead of allowing open, free, spontaneous discussion, the group of pastors could be subdivided first into pairs to have a five-minute preliminary brainstorming session, before regathering to report their ideas from their preliminary discussion. As the preliminary discussion is less formal and is just an exchange of ideas, there is a better opportunity for Chinese-speaking pastors to participate using the English language.

Similarly, after an agenda item is raised in the pastoral team meeting, the English-speaking pastors can be prompted to defer their opinions and let the Chinese-speaking pastors have priority in sharing their viewpoints. Or pastors can be asked to share their opinions round the table, so every pastor has a chance to speak. However, the sequence of speaking may be tactfully organised so that the Chinese-speaking pastor speaks last. This allows the Chinese-speaking pastor enough time to consider and articulate his viewpoints in English. There is a variation of this. One or two days before the meeting, a special agenda item can be conveyed to the Chinese-speaking pastor to let him or her prepare a brief written proposal, which will be read out in front of the whole pastoral team. In summary, various devices can be employed to encourage the Chinese-speaking pastors to speak in English and to increase their confidence in doing so.

In the pastoral team meeting, some Chinese-speaking pastors speak in clumsy and broken English. And perhaps the spoken words cannot fully be comprehended. Other pastors who are more fluent with English should not ridicule them or laugh at them, as that would destroy the Chinese-speaking pastors' incentive and seriously discourage them from participation in the future. On the contrary, the senior pastor or other English pastors may rephrase what the Chinese-speaking pastors said and enquire whether the rephrased expression is what was meant. In this way, Chinese-speaking pastors learn a better way to express that idea in English. Also, the team displays oneness in helping Chinese-speaking pastors to speak in English. I believe the more opportunities there are to speak, the more language is acquired.

Apart from pastoral team meetings, Chinese-speaking pastors can be invited to attend the English services. As the Chinese-speaking pastor is attending the English service as a special guest, he may be asked to give a two-minute informal greeting, a brief update about the Chinese ministry or several prayer points. If the Chinese pastor is confident enough with his English, he can even give a pastoral prayer to the English congregation. The Chinese-speaking pastor can also be interviewed in English to let him or her share something about his or her family or personal issues. Or the Chinese pastor can be invited to preach a short sermon at the English service. Although interpreters can be organised, the Chinese-speaking pastor could be encouraged to preach in English. As the congregation would clearly know that the Chinese-speaking pastor is not eloquent in English, they would always make generous allowance for the Chinese pastor and would be very patient with his or her clumsy English. All these ideas increase opportunities in which a Chinese pastor may speak in English.

Some Chinese-speaking pastors, whose English is of an elementary level, may find speaking English a task too difficult. Thus, listening can be the first step. According to research, listening can be understood as comprehension and as acquisition.[24] Schmidt emphasises the role of consciousness and noticing in language learning by distinguishing between input (what the learner hears) and intake (that part of the input that the learner notices).[25] Therefore, as a starting point, the Chinese pastor may

---

24   Richards, *Teaching Listening and Speaking*.
25   Schmidt, 'Role of Consciousness', 139.

move from input mode to intake mode. When Chinese-speaking pastors visit an English service, they may pay attention and take note of the English usage of the chairperson (service leader), the prayers and the preaching. By this, the Chinese-speaking pastors may be familiarised with English usage through taking notice of certain vocabulary, jargon, terms, expressions, phrases, slang and sayings. These are some practical steps Chinese pastors can take to improve their English.

The preceding suggestions are meant to expose Chinese pastors to the English-speaking environment and will hopefully improve the English acquisition. However, it is noted that there are Chinese pastors over fifty years of age who find English acquisition too difficult a task. If all these ways have been tried and prove unsuccessful, the only way remaining will be to use an interpreter. Preferably, if there is a bilingual pastor in the team, he or she could serve as an interim interpreter. Perhaps he or she may help to clarify unclear opinions.

One difficult situation concerns language usage in resolving conflicts. Typically, Chinese-speaking pastors become emotionally overwhelmed in conflict or dispute situations, and they feel more comfortable retreating back to their first language. In these situations of disagreement, the senior pastor who conducts the meeting may like to slow down the discussion or even adjourn the discussion item for the next meeting. In between the two meetings, the senior pastor may talk to the concerned pastors and find out the issues behind the disagreement.

In serious conflicts or disputes, the church may establish a policy of using interpreters in resolving conflicts, just like interpreters are required in the diplomatic arena and international negotiations. The advantages are two-fold. Firstly, the Chinese-speaking pastors can use their own language, and, at the same time, what they say can be accurately interpreted and listened to. Secondly, as extra time is required for interpretation, it slows down the flow of conversation and dialogue, which may be helpful in calming down the emotions. Preferably, the facilitator or moderator should be bilingual, a person who can manage both languages.

Metacognitive enhancement

Sometimes, if pastors can pick up certain metacognitive or CQ strategies, they can communicate effectively with pastors speaking other languages. A pastoral relationship across diversified cultures is like a detective searching for evidence, who has to trace and make sense of certain confused and ambiguous situations. Livermore suggests that cultural learning includes

> learning some general strategies for how to communicate in ways that are respectful and effective. What are some key ways to ask questions or get information? What are some key phrases that are needed, even if you can't achieve fluency in the language of the other?[26]

Enhancing the pastors' metacognition is another advantage of the suggestion that Chinese-speaking pastors visit an English service. When pastors visit a service other than their own congregation's service, they make cultural observations of that service. It is similar to an anthropological visit. For example, during the visit, the Chinese-speaking pastor can specifically observe and reflect on the singing at the English service. The pastor may observe the number of songs, the music styles, the accompanying instruments, the congregation's singing posture, the use of PowerPoint, the lighting, the sound effects and the use of a choir or a singing team.

---

26 Livermore, *Cultural Intelligence*, 115.

PRACTICAL IMPLICATIONS

As the pastor observes these, he or she can reflect on and consider the criteria and rationale of the various aspects of singing. The pastor may like to write down any observations, reflections, metacognitive questions and speculative interpretations. These are then double-checked with the English-speaking pastor, and the English-speaking pastor can clarify the logic and reasoning behind all this musical organisation. By this process, the Chinese pastor can start to grasp metacognitive thinking.

This kind of metacognition exercise can be repeated with many other aspects of the English service, such as the preaching, the order of service or the relationship dynamics between English-speaking pastors and their congregation. It is believed that pastors' metacognitive CQ is greatly enhanced by such repeated exercises. Furthermore, as the Chinese-speaking pastors show their interest in English ministry by regularly visiting the English congregation and by follow-up discussion with English pastors, the English pastors feel encouraged and supported.

Similarly, metacognitive learning can be acquired in the non-business gatherings of pastors. For example, the Chinese pastors can be invited to have a meal in the house of the English pastor. The Chinese pastor may notice the family interactions and pay attention to the process of having a meal, which is a great avenue into understanding a culture, observing not just what they eat but how they eat. Is the family gathering a big family or a nuclear family? Are they sitting down with knives and forks or chopsticks? Do they share or do they keep silence as they eat? Do they gather at a big round table or a long table? Do the elderly, senior people go first? All these are beneficial for Chinese pastors' metacognitive observation and reflection.

Another way of improving pastors' metacognitive intercultural reflection is to read a book on intercultural leadership or intercultural communication in the pastoral team.[27] The pastoral team may choose to read a specific book in a year. The first forty-five minutes of every weekly pastoral team meeting could be devoted to a book discussion.[28] In this way, pastors not only receive cognitive knowledge input from the reading, but the pastors interact with the author and with the author's expert knowledge on various intercultural issues. Pastors can engage with other pastors across cultures. Pastors may ask questions for clarification of cultural assumptions or worldviews. The pastors may interact, critique and scrutinise the reading with biblical principles. Through the process of reading and discussion, metacognitive reflection takes place.

Subsequent to the book discussion, the results of the conversation can be converted into discussion papers or policy guidelines on various church matters.[29] These papers and guidelines can be distributed to the elders and deacons for further discussion in the board meetings. This writing step has two purposes: one is to consolidate and articulate the pastors' learning, and the other is to start transferring certain learning to other key leaders, which will gradually improve the intercultural competence of the whole church. The orientation of the discussion is contemplation on perspectives of intercultural communication. For example, in the discussion on a book of preaching across cultures, many questions on intercultural dynamics can be asked, such as:

---

27 A suggested booklist for reading and study by the pastoral team is listed in Appendix D.
28 This format can be modified to a monthly half-day discussion, which could allow more meaningful discussion.
29 A wide range of church ministry can be discussed from the intercultural perspective, such as disciple training, preaching programs, prayer ministry, church discipline, house group ministry, mission support (financial and prayer), budgeting, church planting, church architecture and interior design.

PRACTICAL IMPLICATIONS

- Is expositional preaching universally appealing to people of all cultural backgrounds? Why or why not? How is topical preaching or doctrinal preaching valued in a specific culture?
- What sort of preaching styles appeal to Chinese-speaking or English-speaking congregations? Three-point sermons? Narrative sermons? Story-telling sermons?
- Does the cultural background of a congregation affect our choice of biblical books and topics? Epistles? Narrative passages? Psalms?
- To what extent do cultural backgrounds of pastors influence the crafting, logic and delivery of sermons?
- What is the purpose of using illustrations in congregations across different cultural backgrounds? Choice of illustrations? Amount of illustrations?

By reflecting on and discussing these questions, pastors can grasp the cultural metacognitive principles that shape behaviours relevantly and intelligibly for a specific culture. It also helps pastors to mutually understand ministry presuppositions, which are shaped by our cultural values. The pastors may come to understand the extent of the cultural values shaping their ministry design, style and emphasis, aiding communication with other pastors. As outlined by Clinton, knowing the cultural distance and the underlying factors between self and other pastors is crucial in leadership.[30]

Another suggestion to improve metacognitive reflection is personal retreat and journal writing. Pastors may consider taking a number of days away from ministry or going to a retreat centre. During the retreat, pastors may practise extensive reading, contemplation, personal reflection and journal writing. The chosen reading may be on intercultural leadership or

---

30   Clinton, 'Cross-Cultural Use', 196.

intercultural communication. The reading aims at knowledge input and mind-stretching, and the book is read in connection with reflection on the recent intercultural pastoral engagement, both pleasant and unpleasant incidents. After reading, the pastor may proceed to reflection and write journal entries on the pastor's cultural journey.[31] The journal writing is meant to recall events and incidents with cultural implications in the last few years. As the pastor reflects, he or she may recollect their feelings and emotions and review their behavioural reactions. It is suggested that reflection can give special attention to the pastor's own cultural identities, backgrounds and values and the cultural distance between pastors. As the pastor reflects, he or she may focus on his or her thinking styles (analytical, abstract, concrete, intuitive or synthetical), social status, non-verbal language, shame, language competence, logic (linear or analogical), subculture, and cultural type (collective, fear-power, guilt-innocence, high context, high masculinity, or honour-shame). The pastor may re-enact the incidents and events and consider alternative ways of doing things more 'culture-wisely'. After the retreat, reflection findings may be double-checked and shared with pastors of other cultures or an experienced mentor. It is believed that the more reflection is practised, the more cultural self-awareness and metacognitive thinking can be achieved.

Lastly, intercultural training for Chinese pastors is likely to improve the Chinese pastors' metacognitive enhancement. Pastors may be encouraged to attend training workshops on intercultural knowledge, intercultural skills, and most importantly, intercultural thinking. They may gain ways to make intercultural observation and undertake intercultural listening. They may also learn how to ask intercultural questions. They may learn how to review and reflect on intercultural engagement.

---

31 Questions for reflection are suggested in Appendix E.

PRACTICAL IMPLICATIONS

The intercultural training may enable pastors to adjust and plan strategy of intercultural interactions. This would improve the Chinese pastors' intercultural sensitivity and awareness. Most of all, intercultural training may develop an intercultural thinking pattern or thinking habit in their day-to-day intercultural ministry.

Recommendations for theological colleges

Intercultural knowledge

Theological college is a platform preparing and equipping potential pastors. Any input in the colleges will bear fruit in terms of pastoral ministry later in the churches. Therefore, the role of college is crucial and strategic in shaping new pastors.

Firstly, as cultural behaviours are greatly determined by a person's cultural knowledge, the college may consider organising courses on basic cultural knowledge and cultural values. In terms of curriculum, as the cultural scene of Sydney is increasingly diversified, it is preferable that the colleges reconsider and redesign the curriculum on pastoral ministry for cross-cultural contexts in areas such as pastoral leadership, pastoral counselling, church models, Christian education and evangelism in culturally diverse contexts. The colleges might need to revise curricula to offer subjects in areas such as ecclesiology in a diversified cultural society, the theology of migrant churches, the theology of migration and pastoral theology for minority groups.

Secondly, in order to achieve this revised curriculum, the colleges may need to consider the modes of delivery, looking for effective training modes and structures other than lecturing. The Western approach to education tends to minimise relationships and focus on techniques and skills, overemphasising knowledge while neglecting spiritual formation, and assuming linear logic in instruction and learning.[32] However, training models relevant to the Chinese pastors might be through observation, listening, role modelling, storying, informal apprenticeships, retreat or camps, workshops and discipling.[33]

For example, to students of a high-context cultural background, verbal or written approaches may not be effective communication modes to them. Instead, more pictures, charts, tables, figures, graphics and other non-linguistic methods might be more effective. Sometimes, students in theological colleges are asked to do group work or projects. It is suspected that the group involvement and participation of Chinese or Asian students is limited due to their language inadequacy. Therefore, it may be suggested that Caucasian students allow Asian or Chinese students to speak up and share first.

Besides, textbooks and references are mostly written by Western writers with Westernised perspectives, without Chinese or Asian perspectives. Therefore, college lecturers may need to review and update their course outlines and reading lists. Consultation from Chinese church pastors and mission leaders with strong academic backgrounds may be considered.

As every lecturer has his or her own cultural background, collaborative teaching by a team of lecturers from diverse cultural backgrounds is also of great value. Therefore, faculty development of intercultural perspectives is essential for effective training of potential pastors. Moreover, as a way to increase ethnic diversity of faculty of theological colleges, it is also suggested that regular faculty exchanges with Chinese theological colleges would also enhance the abilities of theological colleges to serve growing migrant churches. This is beneficial in two ways. One the one hand,

---

32   Tucker, *Intercultural Communication*, 261.
33   Ibid., 262.

the faculty of local Australian and Chinese theological colleges are allowed to interact interculturally with various academic topics. On the other hand, the cultural exposure of the faculty members from Chinese theological colleges could be also increased.

English acquisition

Many colleges structure their curriculum to encourage Chinese-speaking students to engage with English-speaking students. Three-year pastoral ministry courses provide limited training to improve the Chinese students' English acquisition. However, English learning is a long-term continuous intentional process, so, after college, the Chinese graduates are encouraged to practise their English in church settings, which has been discussed previously.

However, the English level of the pastors trained in Chinese-speaking countries is unsatisfactory. Correct usage of biblical terms and doctrinal language is a specific weakness. Thus, theological colleges may consider organising subjects like 'biblical and theological English'. Such a course would target the non-English-speaking pastors. The course content may include biblical terms and doctrinal language, with special attention to listening, pronunciation and speaking. It would aim to help the overseas-trained pastors to develop their English usage in church and ministry settings.

It is noted that the Chinese theological college in Sydney may need to consider the English acquisition of their students. Apparently, academic activities within the Chinese college are conducted in Chinese, such as lectures, writing essays and student interaction. Such an all-Chinese set-up may equip the Chinese students for pastoral ministry; nevertheless, it is unfavourable and unhelpful to the students' English acquisition. In a sense, the graduates are ill-equipped for future pastoral ministry in Chinese churches with diversified cultures. Therefore, it is suggested that the college injects certain English learning into the curriculum of the Chinese college. For example, the lectures may be conducted in bilingual form, so that the students could be exposed to some English biblical and theological terms. As the Chinese college is attached to a local theological college, and both colleges are using the same building, it is suggested that some joint activities be organised to help the students' English acquisition. The Chinese college may organise regular chapel services with the local college. Students of both colleges could have lunch together. Joint mission teams could be organised to increase the intercultural ministry opportunities. It is also suggested that students of the Chinese college take a certain proportion of subjects at the local college within the three-year course, say twenty percent. By these limited initiatives, the students of the Chinese college would not be deprived of opportunities for English acquisition.

Metacognitive enhancement

As critical reflection is essential for pastors to improve their intercultural competence, training on critical reflection should be developed and incorporated into the students' ministry patterns as early as possible. Apparently, theological colleges focus their training on biblical-theological reflection in their curriculum. However, socio-cultural reflection is relatively scarce. Proposals are recommended below for consideration.

It is suggested that students learn intercultural knowledge from their lecturers. Groups of three students may be assigned to interview a faculty member and inquire about their intercultural journey and experiences. The students may ask about the faculty members' personal discoveries and struggles concerning cultural identity and cultural values. They may inquire about the faculty

PRACTICAL IMPLICATIONS

member's learning journey on international trips and projects. Students may request the faculty member to suggest certain avenues for post-college intercultural learning and to provide a booklist on intercultural studies. The interview results could be summarised as a written report to be copied and presented in class for other students to reference. The students would not only benefit from the specific faculty member they interview, but also take advantage of information shared in interviews with other faculty members.

Annual college mission trips may be utilised to the full extent. Before the trip, the students might be required to do serious preparation research and reading about the people group, their ethnic backgrounds, cultural constructs, demographic information, religious backgrounds and possible ministry implications. The students could interview missionaries or Christian workers (via internet/Skype), missionaries on home assignment, or missionary veterans, to learn some intercultural communication metacognition. As the students arrive on the field on the first day, before participating in any assigned ministry, they could make a basic anthropological observation trip. Instruction on what and how to observe would be given to the students. For example, they might be asked to order food in the food court or restaurant. They could learn to greet local people or ask for directions. In the process, students may make notes on their observations. At the close of a day's observation, debriefing should be organised, and the students may be required to write a one-page reflection. Before the mission trip is over, at least one full day should be devoted to debriefing. It is suggested that the students write a post-trip reflection essay, focusing on a personal future learning plan on intercultural learning. The students may be asked to share their discoveries in the college chapels, sing a song of the specific country, wear their local clothes and provide local snacks for tasting. Written assignments and verbal sharing require the students' deep reflection. These steps can develop the students' capacity for metacognitive reflection.

Another way to help the students to think reflectively is through specific course assignments. Students may be asked to review an evangelistic tract for Chinese people.[34] The assignment can be in two parts. The first part is to critically review the content and format in view of Chinese cultural values (format, theme, cultural assumptions, approach, choice of words, graphic design and amount of information). The second part of the assignment is to rewrite or draft an evangelistic tract for contemporary Chinese. It is a good exercise for reflecting deeply on ministry application and practice in Chinese culture. Similar exercises on cultural reflection can be done for other ministries, such as pastoral visits, funerals, sermons or organising an Easter Sunday.

Colleges might consider developing a course on mentoring and facilitating.[35] As facilitation and mentoring are in great demand in helping younger pastors and pastoral teams to improve intercultural awareness and capacity, the target group of the course could be primarily the senior pastors or lead pastors. The course could be organised with two training objectives, namely enabling and sustaining. Enabling means that senior pastors are trained to enable and equip their younger pastors. Sustaining refers to senior pastors being trained to sustain and support their younger pastors. As indicated in the interview research, younger pastors were yearning for encouragement and support from their senior pastors. An essential ethos of the organised course could be to introduce the mode of mentoring, such as appreciation, affirmation and affection. It is believed that such

---

34   Hesselgrave and Rommen, 'Contextualization', 222–27.
35   Mowry, 'Contextualized/Transactional Model'.

PRACTICAL IMPLICATIONS

a course in itself would be an excellent opportunity for senior pastors to reflect upon their own cultural values and constructs.

Another radical suggestion is that the local theological colleges may consider 'continued education' after graduation.[36] Theological colleges may organise one-year courses with structured intercultural training for recent graduates, particularly young pastors who work in Chinese migrant churches. The course outline may include the study of traditional Chinese culture, Chinese church history, Chinese religions, Chinese worldview, Chinese social structure (marriage, family and filial piety) and even Chinese cultural blind-spots. Certainly, all these topics would be delivered with a biblical and theological critique. Practical tips and case studies could be included in the course, on areas such as working well in Chinese churches, exercising pastoral leadership in Chinese churches, pastoral care for Chinese members, and even conducting Chinese weddings and Chinese funerals. A course of such set-up requires plenty of specialty knowledge; the teaching team would have to be a collaborative team or intercultural taskforce. Apart from the regular classes, experienced Chinese pastors may be recruited and assigned as mentors to every young pastor. Mentors would meet with the young pastors regularly, and the mentors would serve as facilitators to ask the young pastors reflective questions about cultural dimensions. Such a course could require a great deal of human and financial resources. Chinese churches may have to give substantial financial support to keep the course sustainable.

College libraries are great resources for pastors. Libraries may consider increasing their collection of intercultural studies and certain Asian cultures. Some college libraries have a small Chinese collection. However, the collection is quite limited, with

---

[36] The colleges might consider setting up an auxiliary department, or even a small organisation, affiliated with and supported by the colleges.

not many substantial works on Chinese culture and Chinese church history. In the last ten years, more Chinese publications of academic standard have been emerging. Therefore, the college libraries may be more ambitious in extending the Chinese collection. This will certainly improve the teaching and research quality of Chinese studies. Apparently, budget and resources are always major concerns. Therefore, some strategies may be implemented to reduce costs, such as purchasing electronic copies, cooperation among college libraries (in which every college is assigned a certain speciality) and implementing inter-library loan systems.

Theological colleges are institutions for training competent pastors. A college is also a brain, a think-tank for various church issues from theological, biblical and sociological perspectives. It is noted that social research always gives way to biblical and theological studies, both in local colleges and the Chinese college. Therefore, theological colleges are encouraged to promote social research on Chinese churches and ministry. Theological colleges may cooperate with independent social research centres, to conduct major social and cultural research on Chinese churches. Faculty members would be encouraged to adopt and integrate research findings with biblical theological reflection. The faculty members should be encouraged to research and publish articles with reference to cross-cultural contexts. Research articles might be concluded by a section with a consideration of intercultural implications. Faculty members might be encouraged to preach and teach at Asian and Chinese churches. The rationale would be that the faculty members may have more exposure to Asian and Chinese cultures. Some research may invite assistance from some Chinese pastors with research backgrounds, so that the research is relevant to the Chinese cultural settings and ministry needs.

PRACTICAL IMPLICATIONS

Regular academic seminars and symposiums may be organised so that faculty members can present papers regularly. Seminars may possibly bring together expertise from various streams, including interested leaders and potential researchers. All papers presented in seminars and symposiums may be later converted into articles, occasional papers, and even major works. Some of them might be translated into Chinese so that Chinese churches and pastors may benefit from the most recent research.

Recommendations for mission agencies

Mission agencies also play a significant role in developing the intercultural competence of Chinese pastors.

Short-term mission trips are valuable opportunities for Chinese and English pastors to gain cross-cultural experiences, and mission agencies have expertise in this field. The benefits of short-term mission trips to the Chinese pastors are two-fold. Firstly, by immersion in another culture, pastors experience new cultural encounters and their cultural assumptions are challenged. Secondly, short-term mission teams may consist of both young and old pastors, Caucasian and Asian pastors, and Chinese-speaking and English-speaking pastors. Chinese pastors can learn from team members across different cultures, at the pre-trip preparation period, during the trip and in post-trip debriefing and evaluation (see Appendix F for suggested post-trip debriefing questions). Thus, an international mission trip is a condensed and intensive learning opportunity.

It is suggested that mission agencies may organise mission teams just for pastors from Chinese churches. As the teams may include older Chinese-speaking pastors, younger English-speaking pastors, Caucasian pastors and pastors from other English background cultures, such a team is a combination of pastors from culturally diversified backgrounds. It is beneficial to the Chinese pastors in that they can be away from the daily routines of pastoral ministry, and intensively interact with pastors across different cultures. As international travelling induces a sense of curiosity and discovery and the trip process presents a mixture of fun and challenges, cultural learning and intercultural communication are more likely to occur. It is also a great opportunity to learn English, as English may be the only instrumental language used during the trip. Moreover, it is beneficial to the mission agencies, as pastors exposed to the needs of mission fields are more likely to mobilise overseas mission involvement in Chinese churches, which are a great source of potential missionaries.

Apart from mission trips, mission apprenticeship programs are another possible initiative for intercultural communication and metacognitive thinking. Mission agencies may organise one-year or two-year apprenticeship schemes in certain mission fields. The course of apprenticeship would be in effect an informal intercultural education. In order to survive, the apprentice would be required to learn language and intercultural communication. Through daily interaction with people, the apprentice could demonstrate his or her aptitude and character, reflecting his or her reaction to conflicts and disputes. With the field supervisor as his mentor and facilitator, knowledge and awareness of intercultural learning and language acquisition are gained. I believe that willingness to engage with intercultural learning would also be improved.

Mission agencies can provide a resource pool of leaders with cross-cultural expertise. Missionaries on home assignment, missionary veterans and mission leaders are excellent and experienced facilitators and mentors to pastors of Chinese churches. They could be invited to conduct training on

PRACTICAL IMPLICATIONS

intercultural issues for the pastoral teams in Chinese churches. Their experiences with missionaries from other countries are valuable to the Chinese pastors, particularly their struggles, miscommunications, disputes, failures, communication breakdowns and trust issues. Chinese pastors could be inspired by their sharing of intercultural communication, and benefit from the suggested clues for overcoming difficulties. Thus, cultural learning would no longer be a sterile study of rules and conventions, but a common experience to be shared.

Apart from the preceding suggestion about missionaries in general, returning Australian missionaries who have specifically served in Chinese churches in Asia could benefit the Chinese churches in Sydney to a great extent. This particular group of missionaries could serve as interim pastors or mission pastors in Chinese churches. As they are experienced with working in Chinese churches and Chinese culture and are proficient in Chinese language, they could perform pastoral care and relate well with pastors and leaders of various congregations (English, Mandarin or Cantonese). They could develop cross-cultural leaders and disciples for Chinese churches. They could help to improve intercultural competence or Cultural Intelligence among the leaders and pastors in Chinese churches. As they are bicultural or even multicultural, they could make perceptive observations about the conversational dynamics of the pastoral teams, and could provide valuable ways and advice to improve their intergenerational communication.

Training how to facilitate debriefing is another proposal. Many missionaries have experience in leading mission teams, where they need to conduct post-trip debriefings. Thus, they are likely to be skilful and competent in conducting debriefings. Missionaries can provide training to the Chinese pastors on debriefings and on reflection in intercultural encounters.

Miscellaneous

Apart from the separate recommendations for pastoral teams of Chinese churches, theological colleges and mission agencies, these three entities could join hands to develop and strengthen the intercultural competence of Chinese pastors.

It is suggested that these three entities co-organise a consultation for intergenerational and intercultural leadership development for Chinese churches. The consultation may include three streams: biblical-theological perspectives on intercultural leadership development, sociological research on cultural aspects of intercultural leadership development and ministry implications and projections for intercultural leadership development.

The target group of the consultation would be Chinese-speaking and English-speaking pastors, theological college academics and mission agency leaders. The consultation would be primarily conducted in English, with the provision, if necessary, of simultaneous translation from English to Chinese.

The purpose of the consultation would be to outline biblical-theological perspectives of intercultural leadership, to report findings of socio-cultural perspectives from studies on intercultural leadership and to explore various ways to prepare intercultural pastors and leaders for Chinese churches.

Two major outcomes could be anticipated. Firstly, it is expected that the Chinese-speaking and English-speaking pastors and leaders would rekindle a hope for intercultural collaboration in leading Chinese churches. The pastors from Chinese churches would become more willing to form partnerships in ministry by valuing one another and forming mentoring relationships. Secondly, it is anticipated that the theological college academics and mission leaders would commit to providing continuous

PRACTICAL IMPLICATIONS

theoretical support and research resources for Chinese churches. Thus, the ethos of the consultation is to generate momentum for the various leaders to develop a joint workable plan for future Chinese churches.

In the consultation, apart from the speeches and reports, roundtable group discussions may be organised to gather the participants' comments, feedback and responses. In the roundtable discussions, contextualised applications may be collected as well. Some training workshops may be organised in the consultation. Training workshops could be organised on cross-cultural listening, reading non-verbal language, overcoming blind spots in Chinese culture, debriefing and reflection, and understanding cultural values. The workshops could be geared towards training on cognitive CQ and metacognitive CQ, to provide cultural insight and intercultural skills.

People organising such a consultation would have to consider the cultural values of the target groups as well. It is noted that a consultation would be a mode foreign to individuals with a traditional Chinese background. Chinese-speaking pastors often 'observe' from a distance. Their involvement in open discussion and giving opinion in public may be limited. Therefore, a separate discussion group may be organised solely for the Chinese-speaking pastors so they can share at ease in their own language and be free to voice their comments and suggestions. This discussion group may be facilitated by leaders of bicultural background.

After the consultation, it is suggested that SCCCA (Sydney Chinese Christian Churches Association) set up a branch ministry for research and development. The main purpose would be to recruit a group of leaders in Chinese churches to write semi-academic papers for the Chinese churches. Faculty members of theological colleges may concentrate on academic research on intercultural leadership and intergenerational communication. The research and development of SCCCA may convert some academic research into ministry application, with special reference to Chinese churches in Sydney. The ethos of these semi-academic papers is to suggest practical ministry methods with practical feasibility.

Furthermore, SCCCA may consider translating some books and works on Cultural Intelligence and cultural dimensions into Chinese, so Chinese migrants and Chinese churches can benefit by reading, becoming familiar with, and reflecting on the results and findings of Cultural Intelligence research. Hopefully, these translated works can open the Chinese churches and leaders to a huge missing gap in understanding and exercising pastoral leadership.

Other follow-up actions should be organised to enhance ongoing development and enrichment of the pastors and pastoral teams. A book list can be compiled for pastors' ongoing reading. A Bible study schedule on intercultural awareness and mobilising intercultural practices may be suggested for regular pastoral meetings (see Appendix G).

It is also suggested that consultancy may be provided to the leadership teams of the Chinese churches. Facilitators with expert knowledge and experience could lead a one-day workshop on developing the intercultural competence of pastors and leaders. Through games and exercises, discussion and reflection, the quality of teamwork could be improved and conflicts could be minimised and resolved.

The suggestions made in this chapter are intended for the personal growth of pastors and the development of pastoral teams. They can be adopted at any concerned parties' discretion.

CONCLUSION

This research emerges in response to my observation of frequent intergenerational conflicts and disputes between the pastors of Chinese churches in Sydney. I set by postulating two hypotheses. Firstly, I assumed that there were some deep-seated cultural factors behind the conflicts, and that the theoretical framework of Cultural Intelligence could provide an effective way to understand these cultural factors. Secondly, I assumed that the pastors of Chinese churches, who are knowledgeable adult learners, could collaboratively formulate effective strategies to respond to cultural change and cultural diversity to avoid unintended hostility and conflict.

Through my research, I believe that I have demonstrated that these hypotheses are valid. I conclude that cultural factors are more important than other factors (such as spiritual, organisational or personality clashes) in provoking intergenerational conflicts among Chinese pastors. Through my semi-structured interview research, I have demonstrated the primary importance of English acquisition, the relatively weak motivation towards interpersonal and intergenerational communication between Chinese pastors and the relative lack of critical reflection among pastors. My research identifies three highly significant contributors to the constant intergenerational conflicts among the Chinese pastors: 1) non-communication between migrant pastors and second-generation pastors, 2) English language deficiencies and 3) insufficient intercultural reflection.

All these findings and analyses are framed with reference to the four-factor theoretical framework of Cultural Intelligence. It is evident that Cultural Intelligence is a useful theoretical framework for understanding and explaining the cultural perspective of intergenerational conflicts among the Chinese pastors.

This research fills the gap left by most previous Cultural Intelligence studies. I argue that this study contributes significantly to the Chinese churches in the Australian context. It highlights the relevance and argues for the application of Cultural Intelligence in helping Chinese pastors to understand the implicit factors and dynamics of their intergenerational communication. This study has introduced Cultural Intelligence to the Chinese churches, generating initial interest among many Chinese pastors, and it sheds new light on intergenerational relationships from a socio-cultural perspective.

In the following sections, I will highlight the significant achievements of my research.

Literature review

This research began with an extensive and systematic literature review. The literature review underscores the relevance and legitimacy of my topic and its hypotheses, and it introduces the resources I have used in adopting interpretative phenomenology as my research methodology.

Firstly, I note that Chinese churches and Chinese leaders in Australia are overwhelmingly absent from the literature. The literature review also alerts me to the fact that studies of Chinese Christians and Chinese churches are seldom found in

CONCLUSION

the 'suggestions for future research' section of journal articles. In other words, intergenerational conflicts in Chinese churches remain mostly absent from the agenda of academic research. This only serves to highlight the importance and urgency of the problem.

Secondly, most of the studies examine the *inter*relationships between the host culture and the migrant's home culture. However, studies on *intra*relationships of the generational relation dynamics of migrants and Chinese pastors hardly appear. Thus, I remain convinced that my research on intergenerational relationships among pastors with respect to cultural differences helps to fill a significant gap in the literature.

Thirdly, the literature I have reviewed seldom covers cultural assumptions, cultural worldviews and related cultural dimensions such as collectivism-individualism and power distance. Also, although the literature suggests that the language proficiency of migrants is essential and should be given priority, studies on the components and processes of language learning among various generational groups of Chinese migrants are largely missing. Why the Chinese pastors are reluctant and hesitant to acquire English requires further investigation. All these prompted me to examine the cultural factors underlying the difficulty that Chinese pastors have with regard to language learning.

Lastly, most of the works lack the dimension of migrant self-disclosure and self-articulation. Pastors clearly know the biblical teaching on unity. They know that they need to work harmoniously with other leaders. However, in day-to-day ministry, they experience endless differences, disagreements and disputes. The pastors' struggles and agonies, their 'insider' voice and personal perspective on intergenerational conflict, are seldom given attention and listened to. It was pondering how best to fill this gap in research knowledge that led me to consider interpretative phenomenology as research methodology.

In short, the literature review not only confirms the foundational value of my research topic and the value of my research hypotheses, it also prompted me to adopt interpretative phenomenology as research methodology and mixed research methods as the research method.

Historical discussion

In my literature review, I noted that historical study on the development of Chinese churches in Sydney is scarce. Therefore, this project began with background research, tracing the migrant history of Chinese pastors and their cultural roots, which I believe are major factors in shaping contemporary cultural identity, cultural values and intercultural competence. The historical account of the Chinese church in Sydney proved to be rewarding in understanding the numerical and demographic trends of Chinese migrants, including their homelands and their cultural constructs. The historical study also revealed how migrants of different language groups interact. The historical inquiry sheds light on the cultural factors underlying intergenerational conflicts.

In particular, it is exciting to observe the development of Chinese churches, in terms of a growing number of churches. However, my historical research shows that most of the ministries have been conducted in two separate language streams: Chinese and English. The lack of contact between the Chinese-speaking group and the English-speaking group has gradually reinforced the pattern of non-communication between the two language groups. No interaction means no communication, and no communication deprives the two language groups of the opportunity to learn cultural sensitivity, cultural observation, cultural awareness and cultural adjustment. Thus, I have identified non-communication as one of the root issues of endless intergenerational conflicts. It also prompts me to investigate further the cultural factors underlying such non-communication.

My historical study of the cultural roots of Chinese migrants as well as of the second generation also proves to be tremendously helpful. The historical study identifies certain cultural characteristics of a traditional Chinese worldview, such as the concepts of family, filial piety and honour and shame. With the help of Hofstede's theories of cultural values, all these concepts provide effective explanatory tools for understanding the cultural dimensions of intergenerational conflicts. Most of all, the proposed model of cultural continuum that I have developed and refined has proven to be a valuable tool in locating the cultural identity of various generations of migrants. The model of cultural continuum provides a key to examining intergenerational conflict between the pastors.

Although the historical study was originally intended as a background study, it has become clear that it provides a valuable resource for my quantitative questionnaire survey and qualitative face-to-face interview study. In fact, my historical study is a first attempt to outline a comprehensive history of the Chinese churches in Sydney.

Sociological inquiry

Quantitative survey

As the historical study reveals, the pastors of the two language groups do not communicate regularly with each other, and they lack the corresponding cultural sensitivity and cultural awareness. This prompted me to measure the levels of intercultural competence among the pastors I surveyed for my quantitative research.

I have used a quantitative survey aimed at understanding the level of the intercultural competence of the pastors in Chinese churches. With the quantitative survey, I intentionally used the self-assessment approach, because I was especially interested in the self-awareness of pastors. The data collected is analysed to search for meanings in relation to the participants' demographic information and sociocultural context.

Although it is generally assumed that people doing self-assessing survey tend to rate themselves higher than their actual score, it turns out that the Cultural Intelligence scores of the pastors are not particularly high. Therefore, the questionnaire findings, to a certain degree, verify my assumption that the pastors in Chinese churches have relatively low levels of intercultural competence.

One of the more significant discoveries of the Cultural Intelligence questionnaire study concerned the pastors' demographic profile. The quantitative survey contains two astonishing findings: firstly, it confirms the disproportionately large number of Cantonese-speaking pastors in Sydney Chinese churches and, secondly, it reveals that the average age of the pastors is fifty and above, with the majority now approaching their retirement. I am convinced that the disproportionate majority of Cantonese-speaking pastors and the aging of the Chinese pastors are factors working against English acquisition and culture learning. The dominant majority of Cantonese-speaking pastors has diminished the pastors' motivation for acquiring cultural awareness and cultural learning. The older average age of the pastors also explains the lack of capacity for,

CONCLUSION

and confidence with, language acquisition. I speculate that their felt need for acquiring English is relatively low.

If my research were to stop here, the preceding analysis might only be taken as provisional. However, I determined to use mixed research methods, in which the questionnaire survey was followed by a face-to-face semi-structured interview study. This use of mixed research methods is a particular strength in a phenomenological inquiry. Without mixed methods, the data collected in the questionnaire cannot provide much conclusive insight. Similarly, without mixed methods, there are few hints on how to design the right interview questions for the one-on-one interviews. It proves that adopting mixed research methods has been a valuable and highly appropriate research method.

Qualitative research

In the qualitative research stage, I used a face-to-face semi-structured interview. Through questions and prompting, the participants were encouraged to develop further their 'insider' voice, an interpretative voice from their perspective and perception. Through the semi-structured interview, the pastors were able to share their own understanding of their intercultural competence. The pastors could also explain any relationship between their intercultural competence and the occurrence of intergenerational conflicts.

In my qualitative research, I used face-to-face interviews with the pastors as a way of helping me to investigate the relatively low levels of Cultural Intelligence among pastors. Through the face-to-face interviews, two points became specifically noteworthy.

Firstly, the interview findings identified several of the cultural factors implicated in the phenomenon of intergenerational conflict, such as power distance, individualism-collectivism and high-low-context.

Secondly, the interviews also revealed the language deficiency of the pastors and its negative impacts on ministry effectiveness and relationship development.

Thirdly, in the face-to-face interviews, I observed the relatively non-reflective character of pastors. The pastors seldom use terms or related words that hint at the capacity for reflection (words such as assess, review, contemplate, evaluate, recollect, compare and consider). In fact, some interviewed pastors admitted that they did not perform regular reflection.

Thus, in the face-to-face interviews, I have identified and highlighted various factors of the pastors' relatively low motivation for cultural learning, such as communication avoidance, English deficiency and lack of metacognitive reflection. These three are ascribed to the deep-seated cultural factors underlying intergenerational conflicts. These findings verify and confirm my research hypotheses. They are not only helpful to my understanding of the relationship knot between the pastors, but also illuminating to the interviewed pastors.

Important analytical insights

After identifying these three cultural factors (communication avoidance, English deficiency and lack of metacognitive reflection) ascribed to intergenerational conflicts, I further scrutinised them from the perspective of cultural values. As a result, I have been able to shed more light on intergenerational conflict.

Firstly, concerning the communication avoidance or non-communication, I have differentiated the cultural values of older pastors and younger pastors: collectivists versus individualists, people of high context versus people of low context, people of

CONCLUSION

high power distance versus people of low power distance. I have also highlighted certain notions in relation to intergenerational conflict, such as loyalty and filial piety, verbal and non-verbal communication, listening to the content of conversation, and listening to the context. All these have profound value in explaining the cultural dimensions of pastors' non-communication. I have concluded that non-communication is not non-communication *per se*; rather, it is a matter of different modes of communication.

Secondly, concerning the English deficiency, almost all pastors agree that English acquisition is a 'must' in cross-cultural communication. However, many Chinese pastors are hesitant to learn English, particularly the older senior pastors. Therefore, I have examined and analysed the cultural factors deterring senior pastors' acquiring English from a characteristic of traditional Chinese culture, namely shame and saving face. I have highlighted the notion that the older senior pastors usually perceive themselves as 'weaker' persons when they learn English from someone more capable and knowledgeable. It is certainly unbearable for senior pastors, who have always been perceived at the higher end of social hierarchy, to admit their weakness and even 'failure'. It is an entirely shameful process.

I bring attention here to the notion of shame in the light of the Bible. I have borrowed an insight from Pattison, that Christians should consider less their own shame[1] and consider more Jesus' glory. I have suggested that considering the glory of Jesus is the only way of delivering Chinese pastors from the bottomless pit of shame culture. The process of learning may be humiliating and humbling, but the end result, gaining cognitive CQ and intercultural competence, which in turn are beneficial to gospel ministry, is an honour—an honour for Christ's sake and an honour in advancing the gospel.

---

1   Pattison, *Saving Face*, 102–11.

Lastly, I have also examined the issue of the lack of metacognitive reflection, in particular as it relates to the matter of confrontation. From a cultural perspective, I propose that senior pastors of traditional Chinese culture usually avoid confrontation. However, without confrontation, conflicts and misunderstandings cannot be resolved. I am thrilled to highlight storytelling as an effective way of confrontation. The practice of storytelling in confrontation helps to avoid denial of disagreement (sweeping things under the carpet) as well as allowing the senior pastors time and space to critically reflect on the issues contributing to conflict.

I am convinced that the preceding analytical insight can benefit the pastors of Chinese churches. With these insights, the pastors are able to make better sense of intergenerational conflict, can understand the cultural factors surrounding the hesitancy in acquiring English and can go on to find some effective ways to confront these tendencies.

Immediate personal benefit

At the conclusion of this study, I have suggested various ways to improve trustful communication, language acquisition and critical reflection. These improvements will require a collective effort by individual pastors and pastoral teams in Chinese churches, theological education institutions and mission agencies.

Personally, I have benefitted from the journey of this research project in two major ways. Firstly, I am keen to make use of the results and findings of this research project to assist pastors in Sydney, and elsewhere in Australia, to improve their intercultural competence. Although I can provide consultancy and training through seminars and workshops, I personally have had to consider what might be some of the more effective modes of

CONCLUSION

delivering training from a culturally relevant approach. As older pastors do not like being trained in a top-down approach, I have argued for the role of a 'co-pilgrim', to walk alongside the Chinese pastors in the process of intercultural learning. For example, I might organise a cultural anthropology trip with a group of pastors to certain suburbs of distinctive cultures, such as Auburn (Muslim background), Leichhardt (Italian cultural background) or Cabramatta (Vietnamese cultural background). In this way, pastors could observe cultural behaviours and customs of people from other cultures, such as food culture, greeting culture and friendship culture. I would conduct debriefing sessions so that the pastors could share and learn from their cross-cultural experience.

I argue for the value of organised reading groups for pastors, so we could 'read broadly from Urban Anthropology', as suggested by Casey.[2] I would ask perceptive questions concerning cross-cultural issues in the book, connecting what we read from the books with the pastoral situations in our own churches.

Secondly, apart from assisting pastors to improve their intercultural competence, I recognise the need for ongoing research in this area and in related areas. In the course of this research project, I have gained experience and confidence in research, I have learnt both quantitative and qualitative research methods and I have learned the basic steps of historical research. Most of all, I have come to know some colleagues in the academic arena. All of these are essential in my future research activity.

As I have suggested at the beginning of this research, I am an insider to the research, and this positioning potentially weakens my objectivity in research. However, it turns out that the pastors who participated in the research were quite ready to share with me. In fact, they indicated that they felt at ease

---

2   Casey, 'How Shall They Hear?', 205.

and secure enough to share and disclose their inner and private world to me (as an insider). This gives me more confidence in future research. As I reflect on my research journey, I notice that I have some character qualities that may enhance research, such as language proficiency in English, Mandarin and Cantonese. I am also able to ask perceptive questions and follow up questions in a non-threatening manner.

The face-to-face semi-structured interviews demonstrated that the pastors were reasonably ready to share their perspectives, perceptions and concerns. Their readiness might indicate that they have suppressed their 'insider voice' for a long period of time. It only takes some encouragement and assurance for them to pour out their hearts. I regard their shared insights and experiences as an essentially hidden and unexplored resource for the learning and ministry of the Chinese churches in Sydney.

Future studies

Regarding future research directions and research themes, I am eager to see more scholars who are well trained in biblical and theological studies engaging in the research of pastoral and congregational practice. I notice that practical theology has somehow been marginalised. Practical theological research and writing are not the first priority in the academic world. Therefore, I am keen to see the collaborative endeavour of scholars of all disciplines, forming research teams to undertake practical theology in order to make an impact upon the churches.

As this study is unique, or among a very few studies that research Cultural Intelligence in regards to Chinese pastors in the Australian context, I look forward to seeing more studies in the future. Future study may research and compare the Cultural Intelligence of pastors who have dropped out of pastoral ministry

CONCLUSION

with existing pastors. Similar studies might also be conducted in other cities with a high proportion of Chinese migrants or Asian migrants, such as Melbourne, Toronto, Vancouver or San Francisco. Apart from cities with international Asian migrants in the Western context, there are also cities with inter-regional migrants, such as Hong Kong. High numbers of migrants have moved from mainland China into Hong Kong in recent years. The impact on pastoral ministry and pastoral leadership there is tremendous as well.

I recommend a longitudinal study of pastors' cultural competence. Studies might examine the improvement of intercultural competence or metacognitive reflection of Chinese pastors over a number of years in order to investigate the effectiveness of intercultural training. Other longitudinal studies could also investigate the impact of metacognitive reflection on the other three Cultural Intelligence dimensions (cognitive CQ, motivational CQ and behavioural CQ) of Chinese pastors. These longitudinal studies will provide explanations of the attitudes, behaviours and values that contribute to the development of intercultural competence.

I also suggest an inquiry into the cultural perspectives of Chinese pastors and Chinese churches. For example, one of the research focuses could be to trace the history of the cultural experiences and cultural learnings of certain prominent figures or pastors of the Chinese churches. Such a study might investigate how the cultural constructs, cultural identity and cultural values of the prominent pastors have impacted the development of Chinese churches in Sydney over the last thirty years. Similarly, publishing case studies of a few churches with multiple language congregations could be expected to give a fuller understanding of Chinese churches in Sydney. Studies of individual Chinese churches could also compare the Cultural Intelligence of leaders from a large-size church and a small-size church.

One more perspective would be to encourage the study of leadership development of the younger generation within Chinese churches. Research could focus on the three language streams (Cantonese, Mandarin and English) with special reference to leadership development in relation to the leaders' cultural identity and cultural competence. Another focus of research could be an exploration of the cultural factors that might be involved in a collaborative task force to develop young leadership in Chinese churches.

In reviewing the course of this research, I have become more convinced that an effective multicultural leader does not only become a leader; he or she also becomes a witness, a witness to Jesus' truth and grace (John 1:14). I am convinced that key movers are absolutely essential to advocate intercultural learning and to promote intercultural partnership. I am convinced that platforms for intercultural dialogue and understanding are also essential, such as conferences and seminars on cross-cultural leadership development. As international and inter-regional migration continues, the needs for and challenges of intercultural and intergenerational pastoral leadership are tremendous and ever-increasing. Leaders of Chinese churches, indeed all churches on earth, must respond proactively to the challenges and needs. The purpose is to draw all Chinese pastors together for God's glory.

These words from Cahalan and Mikoski helpfully summarise what I have done so far and point the way ahead:

> Practical theologians are unapologetic change agents. Much of our work aims at critically assessing what is destructive and diminishing of our lives and what can

CONCLUSION

be changed in order that individuals, communities or societies can strive toward a more just common good.[3]

May this project be like a mustard seed that is sown and bears much fruit in Chinese churches in Sydney.

---

3   Cahalan and Mikoski, *Opening the Field*, 6.

Appendix A
RESEARCH TOOLS: QUESTIONS OF QUESTIONNAIRE

The Cultural Intelligence Scale[1]

Read each statement and select the response that best describes your capabilities.

Select the answer that BEST describes you AS YOU REALLY ARE (1=very strongly disagree; 2=disagree strongly, 3=disagree, 4=neither agree nor disagree, 5=agree, 6=agree strongly, 7=very strongly agree)

Metacognitive CQ:

MC1	I am conscious of the cultural knowledge I use when interacting with people with different cultural backgrounds.	☐
MC2	I adjust my cultural knowledge as I interact with people from a culture that is unfamiliar to me.	☐
MC3	I am conscious of the cultural knowledge I apply to cross-cultural interactions.	☐
MC4	I check the accuracy of my cultural knowledge as I interact with people from different cultures.	☐

---

1   Van Dyne, '20-item, Four Factor CQS'; Ang and Van Dyne, *Handbook*, 390.

APPENDICES

Cognitive CQ:

COG1	I know the legal and economic systems of other cultures.	☐
COG2	I know the rules (e.g., vocabulary, grammar) of other languages.	☐
COG3	I know the cultural values and religious beliefs of other cultures.	☐
COG4	I know the marriage systems of other cultures.	☐
COG5	I know the arts and crafts of other cultures.	☐
COG6	I know the rules for expressing non-verbal behaviours in other cultures.	☐

Motivational CQ:

MOT1	I enjoy interacting with people from different cultures.	☐
MOT2	I am confident that I can socialise with locals in a culture that is unfamiliar to me.	☐
MOT3	I am sure I can deal with the stresses of adjusting to a culture that is new to me.	☐
MOT4	I enjoy living in cultures that are unfamiliar to me.	☐

MOT5	I am confident that I can get accustomed to the shopping conditions in a different culture.	☐

Behavioural CQ:

BEH1	I change my verbal behaviour (e.g., accent, tone) when a cross-cultural interaction requires it.	☐
BEH2	I use pause and silence differently to suit different cross-cultural situations.	☐
BEH3	I vary the rate of my speaking when a cross-cultural situation requires it.	☐
BEH4	I change my non-verbal behaviour when a cross-cultural situation requires it.	☐
BEH5	I alter my facial expressions when a cross-cultural interaction requires it.	☐

© Cultural Intelligence Centre 2005. Used by permission of Cultural Intelligence Centre.

Appendix B

RESEARCH TOOLS: DEMOGRAPHIC QUESTIONS

Sex ☐ Male ☐ Female

Age range

☐ 30 years and below ☐ 31 years–40 years

☐ 41 years–50 years ☐ 51 years–60 years

☐ 61 years and above

Language most commonly used at home

☐ English ☐ Cantonese

☐ Mandarin ☐ Other dialects _____

Number of years as pastor in all churches

☐ Below 2 years ☐ 2–5 years ☐ 6–10 years

☐ 11–20 years ☐ 21 years and above

Your role at church

☐ Pastor of an English-language service

☐ Pastor of a Mandarin-language service

☐ Pastor of a Cantonese-language service

☐ Senior pastor

☐ Other _____

Appendix C
INTERVIEW QUESTIONS

Questions **examining** previous experience of pastors in acquisition of cultural competence

- You have completed the CQ questionnaire. How do you feel about your result? Satisfied? What surprised you? Or was your self-knowledge confirmed? (Please share and elaborate).
- Think about an experience you've had in cross-cultural learning and understanding. [Encourage storytelling]
- From your experiences, what are the needs for pastors in cross-cultural learning?

Questions **exploring** the contextual challenges of pastors in acquiring better cultural competence

- Can you recall remarks or incidents of cultural interaction that made you feel most pleased? Did anything annoy you?
- From what you observe, what are the main issues which bring disagreement or conflict among the pastors?
- From your experience, what extent of the disagreement among pastors is caused by different ethnicities or cultural difference?
- I am interested in the connection between cultural competence and cross-cultural pastoral leadership. To what degree do the following tasks require greater cultural competence? Explain.

- Handling and resolving conflicts
- Leading or facilitating a discussion
- Envisioning and mobilising
- Preaching and teaching
- Decision making

Let me show you a flashcard showing a diagram of cultural continuum [see opposite page]. When I show the diagram, I explain a few sentences about the diagram. The wording is attached right after the interview questions.] In the diagram of cultural continuum, would you like to locate where you are in the continuum? Where do you perceive your ministry colleagues to be located in this continuum?

Questions seeking practical ways and approaches of improving Cultural Intelligence

- As you reflect on the last several years of being a pastor, have you made any changes or adjustments in cross-cultural competence in coping with a multicultural church setting?
- Did you go through any formal training in cross-cultural communication (such as seminars or workshops)? If yes, please briefly describe the frequency, procedure, setting and content. Did you like this training? How would you evaluate what you learnt in engaging cross-cultural leadership?
- What would motivate you most to seek cross-cultural learning? For example
    - Friends, family, colleagues
    - Written information or pamphlet
    - Media messages
    - Ministry requirement
    - Others

MICHAEL K. CHU

- If a friend comes and asks you about cross-cultural training, what would you say? How would you encourage him/her?
- I am hoping to help pastors improve their cultural competence in dealing with cultural change. What advice do you have for me?

Interview Flashcard

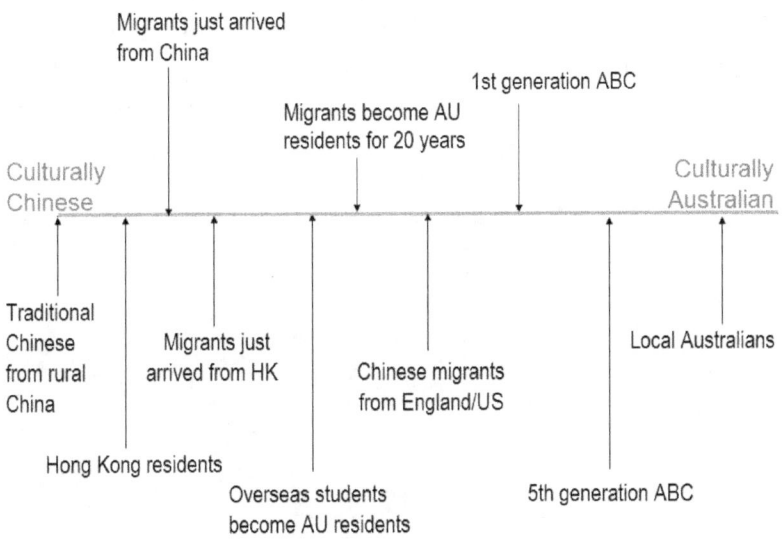

APPENDICES

Cultural Continuum

Over the last few decades, the Chinese churches of North America have been described the first and second generation in Chinese church with reference to two terms, 'Overseas-born-Chinese' (OBCs) and 'America-born-Chinese' (ABCs). However, this polarised distinction of the church is too simple, as if the church has only two groups of people. Cultural continuum is a better model to outline the cultural phenomenon in Chinese churches. The continuum reflects the fact that cultural identity is a gradually evolving process. Cultural identity is determined by various factors, such as the number of years spent living in Australia, the degree of social interaction, one's language proficiency, parental influence and other factors, including personality traits.

Appendix D
BOOKLIST ON INTERCULTURAL LEADERSHIP FOR PASTORS

Note: The book list suggested here is for pastors' reading and for pastoral team discussion. Pastors may choose to read a chapter in their weekly pastoral team meetings. Or the pastors may spare a half-day for book reading. The subject matter of the list includes intercultural leadership, intercultural communication, cross-cultural church ministry and intergenerational conflict. Pastors can learn ministry implications and put them into practice. As the language levels of pastors of Chinese churches vary, priority is given to books that are more readable and accessible. Books marked with * are highly recommended.

Augsburger, David W. *Conflict Mediation across Cultures: Pathways and Patterns.* Louisville, KY: Westminster John Knox, 1992.

*Cha, Peter, S. Steve Kang and Helen Lee. *Growing Healthy Asian American Churches: Ministry Insights from Groundbreaking Congregation.* Downers Grove, IL: InterVarsity, 2006.

Elmer, Duane. *Cross-Cultural Conflict: Building Relationships for Effective Ministry.* Downers Grove, IL: InterVarsity, 1993.

*Hibbert, Evelyn, and Richard Hibbert. *Leading Multicultural Teams.* Pasadena, CA: William Carey Library, 2014.

Hofstede, Geert, Gert Jan Hofstede, and Michael Minkov. *Cultures and Organizations: Software of the Mind.* New York, NY: McGraw-Hill, 2010.

APPENDICES

Ling, Samuel and Clarence Cheuk. *The 'Chinese' Way of Doing Things: Perspectives on American-Born Chinese and the Chinese Church in America.* Pasadena, CA: China Horizon, 1999.

Lingenfelter, Sherwood G. *Leading Cross-Culturally: Covenant Relationships for Effective Christian Leadership.* Grand Rapids, MI: Baker Academic, 2008.

McIntosh, Gary L. *One Church, Four Generations: Understanding and Reaching All Ages in Your Church.* Grand Rapids, MI: Baker, 2002.

Moreau, A Scott. *Effective Intercultural Communication: A Christian Perspective.* Grand Rapids, MI: Baker Academic, 2014.

Plueddemann, James. *Leading Across Cultures: Effective Ministry and Mission in The Global Church.* Downers Grove, IL: InterVarsity, 2009.

Pollock, David, and Ruth Van Reken. *Third Culture Kids: Growing up Among Worlds.* Boston, MA: Nicholas Brealey, 2009.

Rah, Soong-Chan. Many Colors: *Cultural Intelligence for a Changing Church.* Chicago, IL: Moody, 2010.

Rendle, Gilbert R. *The Multigenerational Congregation: Meeting the Leadership Challenge.* Bethesda, MD: Alban Institute, 2001.

*Sydney Park, Soong-Chan Rah, and Al Tizon. *Honouring the Generations: Learning with Asian North American Congregations.* Valley Forge, PA: Judson, 2012.

Trompenaars, Fons, and Ed Voerman. *Servant Leadership across Cultures: Harnessing the Strength of the World's Most Powerful Leadership Philosophy.* New York, NY: McGraw-Hill, 2010.

Tucker, Frank. *Intercultural Communication for Christian Ministry.* Adelaide, SA: Frank Tucker, 2013.

*Wright, Walter. *Relational Leadership: A Biblical Model for Leadership Service.* Carlisle UK: Paternoster, 2000.

Appendix E
SUGGESTED REFLECTION QUESTIONS

For a personal retreat designed to enhance pastors' cultural awareness and intercultural competence

The conviction of using reflection questions arises from my interviews with the pastors. In the interviews, participating pastors showed that they did not reflect regularly. They also showed that they did not know *how* and *what* to reflect on. Therefore, I compile these questions for pastors' reflection in personal retreat.

Most of the questions in this section are not my own work. The questions are taken and slightly revised from the book *Leading Multicultural Teams*.[1] I have found these questions to have potential use in my ongoing work with Chinese pastors. As these questions are mainly for the pastors in Chinese churches, I have adapted them to the setting of Chinese churches' pastoral teams.

The purpose of these questions is for pastors to improve self-knowledge and self-awareness of their cultural constructs. New pastors may take time to reflect on these questions in their first two years. The questions are particularly valuable for new pastors joining an intercultural team, although pastors with longer service will also find them beneficial.

The list of questions is compiled for pastors' reflection in a personal retreat. If time is limited, pastors do not need to reflect

---

1   Hibbert and Hibbert, *Leading Multicultural Teams*, 213–25.

on all the questions in one sitting. Pastors can choose to reflect on some questions and leave others for subsequent retreats.

Questions on leadership

1. Leadership status and influence
a) Who are the most influential leaders in your pastoral team? Who is the wise man? Who is the powerbroker? Who the king-maker? Who is the whistle-blower? Who has the final authority? What sort of cultural values do you notice?
b) How many different ranks of status are recognised (for example, senior pastor, associate senior pastor, pastor, assistant pastor, pastoral workers)? What are the criteria for putting them in different ranks? Which of these criteria are culturally determined?

1. Leadership
a) How do people become leaders? Is there any kind of election or choosing for leadership? Is it by appointment? What are the criteria for choosing or appointing? To what extent is leadership appointment determined by cultural values?
b) Can women become leaders? In what areas? Does the wife of a leader have any role and any authority? Is such an arrangement for doctrinal, or cultural, reasons?

1. Decision making
a) How does the church make decisions? Is there any discussion before a decision? Do you notice any cultural values in the process of decision making?
b) Is there any ranking in the right to speak? Who has the final say? Why does the person have the final say? How does the church settle quarrels or disputes?

APPENDICES

Questions on assumptions and expectations

Note: Assumptions and expectations greatly determine the effectiveness of our communication. They affect our interpretation and understanding of underlying messages using verbal and non-verbal language. Assumptions are taken for granted and unrealistic expectations always bring dangerous confusion in relating to one another, particularly in cross-cultural settings. Therefore, pastors are encouraged to reflect on and identify personal assumptions and expectations.

1. Your personal life
   a) What are you expecting in terms of your living situation (house and neighbourhood)? What will the demands of daily living be?
   b) How will you relax, and what will you do for recreation? How will you spend your day off? What do other pastors do for relaxation and recreation?
   c) To what extent is your personal life shaped or determined by your team members' lifestyle? Do you notice any cultural values of your team members?

1. Language and cultural learning
   a) Apart from your first language, is there any other language(s) you will have to learn? Why will you have to learn that language? How fluent will you need to be in the language(s)? In what setting will that language be used?
   b) How much time will you have available on a daily or weekly basis for language learning? How long will you take to reach your ultimate goal in learning the language?
   c) Do you have any fears or struggles about things that you may find difficult to cope with in the culture?

d) How do you expect others to help you with this? Do you prefer personal learning or team learning? Why?

1. The way the team will function
a) How often will you meet as a whole team? For what purposes? What will be the main issues of discussion? Who will decide the issues of discussion?
b) How will your team leader lead (leadership style)? How much authority will he or she have?
c) What will your team leader expect from you? What will your team members expect from you? Are those expectations similar or different? If different, why? Do you notice any cultural values underlying expectations?
d) What level of friendships will you develop in your team? How much time will you spend together?
e) What degree, and what nature, of interpersonal tensions and conflict do you expect you will experience? What is your ability to deal with and resolve interpersonal problems?
f) What role do you play on the team?
g) How will you keep yourselves accountable to one another? Does someone keep them accountable to you?

1. Your personal ministry
a) What do you expect will be your role and primary responsibility?
b) What supervision and pastoral support do you expect from your team leader?
c) What will be your major personal and team accomplishments by the end of the first three months? First six months? First year?

1. Final reflection

APPENDICES

a) In which areas are the expectations of all team members similar? In which areas do your expectations differ?

b) What will you do about the areas in which you have differing expectations?

c) Reflect on these questions with reference to your cultural identity (Chinese, Australian, hybrid) and cultural values (power distance, high-low context, collectivism-individualism).

d) What biblical principles can be utilised in your reflection?

It is suggested that, after reflection, there should be a subsequent discussion with other team members.

Appendix F

SUGGESTED OUTLINE FOR POST-TRIP DEBRIEFING

Questions

According to Kolb's experiential learning theory,[1] pastors are likely to experience much cross-cultural exposure by joining short-term mission trips. Subsequent debriefing reflection will always deepen and enhance cross-cultural learning and competence. Debriefing reflection will also help participants gain perspective on short-term mission trips. Asking the right questions in debriefing can bring forth solid reflection on and intercultural insight into the trip experience.

Most of the questions in this section are not my own work. The questions are taken from two sources. The first one is from the Pioneers of Australia.[2] The second one is from a personal copy passed to me by Calvin Ma, the former national director of OMF Australia.[3] Most of the questions are slightly revised, specifically for the pastors of Chinese churches.

The questions listed below are best discussed in a group with a facilitator. Debriefing should be conducted as soon as the short-term mission trip is over. Every group member should be given a chance to share their observations and express their feelings.

As the discussion and sharing proceed, individual members can jot down some points for further reflection and journal writing.

---

1   Kolb, *Experiential Learning*.
2   Pioneers of Australia, *Guidelines*.
3   Ma, *Serve Asia Workers*.

APPENDICES

Post-trip debriefing questions with special attention to cultural experience

1. What expectations did you have for your trip? Were they realistic? Were they fulfilled? How so or why not?
2. How much do you know about your cultural identity, cultural values, and cross-cultural capability?
a) In what ways have you identified with the host culture? (language, values, beliefs, dress, food)
b) In what ways are your host culture and home culture dissimilar? (climatically, geographically, language, religion, standard of living, politically, customs)
3. Did you experience culture shock? In what ways?
a) What aspects of living in another culture did you find stressful?
b) Were you individualistic? Were you uncomfortable in group life?
c) Were you culturally sensitive? Did you offend other people easily and unintentionally?
d) Were you critical? Were you unable to participate and enjoy certain parts of the trip?
e) Were you calculating? Were you unable to gain acceptance by others?
f) Were you efficiency-oriented? Were you unable to enjoy and appreciate people?
g) How did the cultural and language adjustment affect your self-concept?
4. What were some ways that you found helpful in dealing with culture shock? Rest? Being away from people? Talking to people? Using your own language?

5. During this trip, what did you learn about yourself and your cultural self?
6. What did you learn about yourself and others? How well do you work in a team? What annoys you about other people? What attracts you to other people? Do you cope well with living in a community?
7. What did you learn about God? What did you notice about his way of blessing people from other cultures (his faithfulness, provision, his love for the lost, his love for you, his priorities)?
8. Have you changed culturally? In what ways?
9. How will your experience on this mission trip change your prayer life, your attitude towards possessions, your involvement in your church? What would you pray for to improve your intercultural competence?
10. What would have been good to know before you went on this trip? Knowledge of the other culture? Certain intercultural skills? Some language?

Appendix G
BIBLE STUDY SCHEDULE

On raising intercultural awareness and mobilising intercultural practice for a pastoral team

In the interviews with the pastors, some of them indicated that their pastoral teams could sometimes be reduced to business discussion and become primarily task-oriented. They expected more from the team, such as more mutual enrichment and learning. A pastoral team should be and could be a platform for mutual learning. As every pastor is of unique background and cultural exposure, a pastoral team can be converted into a learning organisation. As suggested by Senge, every organisation should be a learning organisation.[1]

Therefore, the Bible study is organised to enhance the ongoing development and enrichment of the pastors and pastoral teams in Chinese churches. The purpose of the Bible study schedule is for the pastoral team to have monthly Bible study on the topics of intercultural awareness and intercultural leadership. The study of suggested Bible passages is compiled in order that pastors can grasp the biblical and theological understandings of cultural issues and cultural values.

It is suggested that a certain period of time be set aside from the regular pastoral team meetings. It can be a once-a-month half-day learning session or once-six-month 'equip day'.

---

1   Senge, *Fifth Discipline*.

By default, the senior pastor can be the leader of the Bible study. Or sometimes individual pastors can be assigned to facilitate the Bible study, discussion and sharing.

If the Bible studies are done well, the results of studies can be converted into preaching programs. In turn, the whole church can benefit from the pastors' learning.

Month	Topic and learning outcome	Passage
January	Church: A people of redeemed sinners	Eph 2:12–22
February	Priority of relationship	1 Cor 3
March	Unity is Godlike	John 17
April	Same mind as Christ	Phil 2:5–11
May	Barnabas: A man of partnership	Acts 11:22–26; 13:1–3
June	Principles of intercultural communication	1 Cor 9:19–23
July	An example of high-context communication	Gen 23:1–15
August	A case study of personal conflicts	Acts 15:36–41
September	A case study of resolving personal conflict	1 Sam 24
October	A case study of resolving communal conflict	Josh 22
November	Acceptance in disputable matters	Rom 14
December	Daniel: A cross-cultural leader	Dan 1–2

Appendix H
ONE-DAY WORKSHOP DESIGN

In the interviews with pastors, they requested training and consultations on intercultural communication and developing a multicultural team. This one-day workshop is designed to provide such training and consultation for pastors in Chinese churches. The primary purpose of the workshop is to enhance team building across cultures by helping them experience and understand the cultural values of one another.

The ethos of the workshop is largely experiential in nature. It uses exercises and games. The participants go through certain experiences. Post-exercise debriefing and discussion are essential, to explore the cultural issues and cultural dimensions of interaction.

Some of the exercises and games are my own works. Other exercises and games are taken and slightly revised from various sources.[1] Some other works also inspired me in designing certain exercises.[2]

The optimum workshop size can be up to twenty. The participants of the workshop can be just pastors. If the number of pastors is not large enough, you may ask key lay leaders (elders, presbyters or deacons) to join.

If a one-day workshop is too intensive for some members, the workshop can be spread into half-day workshops over two weekends.

For the best result, some pre-reading and post-reading on CQ or cultural values is recommended.

---

[1] Kohls and Knight, *Developing Intercultural Awareness*; Berardo and Deardorff, *Building Cultural Competence*.
[2] Hill, 'Lifting the Fog'; Lustig and Koester, *Intercultural Competence*; Moreau, *Effective Intercultural Communication*.

As a variation, it is suggested that the workshop facilitator be invited to sit in and observe a pastoral team meeting. The facilitator may note the process and dynamics of the discussion, or even videotape the process. If possible, use a one-sided mirror room, so as to minimise disturbance and be less threatening during the recording. The observation may help the facilitator to have a deeper understanding of the team, so he or she can effectively facilitate the discussion in the workshop.

If the team of pastors is interested, some other training workshops can be organised, such as workshops on intercultural listening or non-verbal communication.

Suggested schedule for the day

Time	Activity
9:00–9:15	Welcome, introduction, ground rules for interaction
9:15–9:45	Exercise A: Ice-breaking—Push/Pull
9:45–10:00	Brief talk on intercultural leadership and CQ
10:00–10:40	Exercise B: What is in a name?
10:40–11:15	Morning tea
11:15–12:00	Exercise C: Discovering our cultural values
12:00–12:15	Brief talk on intercultural leadership and cultural values
12:15–13:15	Lunch
13:15–14:15	Exercise D: Case study—Maintaining harmony, saving face
14:15–15:15	Exercise E: Three chairs—Communication style
15:15–15:45	Afternoon tea
15:45–16:30	Exercise F: Personal reflection on intercultural friendships
16:30–17:00	Conclusion: Group sharing of learning and closing encouragement

APPENDICES

Exercise A: Ice-breaking—Push/Pull[3]

Goals: To develop an awareness of the importance of physical sensitivity and to help establish group cohesiveness

Materials: Audio device to play music of three to four minutes in length, such as the theme song from Chariots of Fire.

1. Instruct participants to walk around the room as the music plays. Tell them to form pairs and to stand face-to-face with arms up, bent at the elbow, hands open, palms out, with figures pointing up (typical 'hands-up' pose). Then, instruct them to push against their partner's palms and try to find a 'balance' in their pushing so that they are supported, and neither one is overpowered by the other. They can try different levels by stretching, bending their knees, or leaning from side to side.
2. Second, when you call 'Break and Pull,' both partners should stop pushing, hold hands (left hand to partner's right and right to partner's left), and begin to pull away from each other, again trying to find a balance.
3. Third, instruct them to form groups of three (or whatever number will allow all people to be in a group), and to repeat the push/pull sequence they just did in pairs. It may be more difficult to achieve a balance since more than two people are involved.
4. **Debriefing and discussion:** Begin the discussion by asking how the exercise relates to the workshop. By brainstorming this first question, issues related to space, touching, and other culture-based differences in nonverbal communication

---

3   This exercise is taken from Kohls and Knight, *Developing Intercultural Awareness*, 11.

can be introduced. The relationships between physical sensitivity and cultural sensitivity may also be fruitfully explored with questions related to personal and cultural reactions to the exercise. 'Were participants able to develop a balance in the push/pull, or was one person more or less active or forceful in the exercise?' You can also point out that this exercise may test the participants' tolerance for ambiguity.

Exercise B: What is in a name?

Goal: To highlight the cultural differences of every individual participant

Material: Pen and paper

1. Ask participants to write down their names, all of the names across their whole life. For example, official name, full name, maiden name, nickname, false/assumed name, Christian name, name known by family of origin, name known by school friends, name known by close friends, name in other languages, pseudonym, and names no longer used.

2. Have the participants read their names aloud, one by one.
3. Ask a few of them to share. Which of their names show their cultural identity? How do those names carry cultural traditions and cultural values?
4. If they were to give themselves a new name, what name would they give? And why?

Exercise C: Discover our cultural values[4]

Goal: To discover our cultural values by analysing heroes we admire

Groups size: Variable

1. Ask individuals to form small groups of four or five and then to compile a list of favourite heroes or heroines, ascertaining their most prominent characteristics and the values they imply. For example:
   a) Martin Luther King—action, optimism, future orientation, courage
   b) Nelson Mandela—peacemaking, inner strength, perseverance, endurance
   c) Michael Jackson—creative, musical, artistic
   d) Margaret Thatcher—uncompromising, leadership, assertive, determined
   e) Nicole Kidman—charming
   f) John Wayne—rugged individualism, self-help
2. Ask groups to share their analyses and compile a common list of cultural values.

---

[4] The exercise is taken, slightly revised, from Kohls and Knight, *Developing Intercultural Awareness*, 55.

3. Ask individuals to share their favourite hero and why.

Exercise D: Case study—Maintaining harmony, saving face[5]

The case: Jim Ellis, vice president of a North Carolina knitwear manufacturer, was sent to observe firsthand how operations were proceeding in its Korean plant and to help institute some new managerial procedures. Before any changes could be made, Jim wanted to learn as much as possible about the problems that existed at the plant. During his first weeks, he was met with bows, polite smiles and the continual denial of any significant problems. But Jim was enough of a realist to know that no manufacturing operation is without its problems. So after some creative research, he uncovered a number of problems that the local manager and staff were not acknowledging. None of the problems was particularly unusual or difficult to solve. But Jim was frustrated that no one would admit that any problem existed. 'If you don't acknowledge the problem, how do you expect to be able to solve them?' To further exasperate him, when a problem was finally brought to his attention, it was not mentioned until the end of the workday, when there was no time left to solve it.

1. What happened? Answer from the perspective of as many of the parties involved as possible.

---

5   The case and the discussion questions are taken, slightly revised, from Kohls and Knight, *Developing Intercultural Awareness*, 104.

APPENDICES

2. What is the situation or problem? Again, answer from the perspective of the people involved. How does it involve values, language, nonverbal?
3. How are the individuals in the case study related? Peers, guest-host?
4. How can the situation be resolved? Consider as many courses of action as possible.
5. What are the probable results (or repercussions) of each solution? Are the solutions at one extreme or the other, or is a compromise possible? Is a solution even possible? If there is no solution, how do Westerners, who generally feel that problems must have solutions, deal with it?
6. Is additional information needed to make a decision?
7. Can we change to fit the new situation instead of always expecting others to adapt to us?

Exercise E: Three chairs—Communication styles[6]

Goal: Practise and experience different communication styles

1. Have participants form groups of three and set up three chairs, with one chair facing the front of the room and the two other chairs on each side, facing the middle chair.
2. Tell the group the chair on the left is the position of the expert, the middle chair is the listener's place, and the right chair is the real story.
3. Assign a relevant topic, such as 'life in Australia' or 'life in Chinese family'.
4. Tell the group that the expert and the real story person will talk to the listener simultaneously, while the listener tries to listen and respond to both as best as possible. The two talkers are intentionally competing (realistically) for the listener's attention, and the goal is to see which talker holds the listener's attention more. The expert talks as if he or she were a specialist and may cite statistics and give factual information. The real story person talks like someone you would meet on the street this participant can tell a true story from his or her life or even make up a story related to the topic, but the story should be personal.

---

6 This exercised is adapted from Berardo and Deardorff, *Building Cultural Competence*, 238–40.

APPENDICES

5. After two minutes, call time and then have the participants change chairs and repeat the procedure with each person in a different role.
6. After two more minutes, have the participants change chairs one more time and repeat the activity.
7. This activity helps people understand the importance of resolving cultural differences together. Ask the following questions as debriefing.
8. How did you feel in this activity? Which role did you find most comfortable? Most uncomfortable?
9. Which roles did you find yourself listening and responding to more attentively—the person in the real story chair or the expert chair? Why?
10. How can different styles be used to increase effectiveness with people from different cultural backgrounds?
11. How does one's own communication style affect the way one receives information? Gives information?
12. What are some lessons learned, or what can you take away with you from this activity?
13. This activity illustrates different communication styles. For example, two people talking at once can be an example from a polychronic culture. Factual versus personal information is indicative of another style of communicating in different cultures.
14. The styles of communication can affect us as much or more than the words.
15. Communication styles are not right or wrong, just different, and it's very important to be aware of those different styles and how those styles ultimately have an impact on the content being conveyed.

16. Communication styles are culturally conditioned, and we often tend to resonate more with styles that are similar to the ways we have been culturally conditioned.

Exercise F: Personal reflection on intercultural friendship

Introduction: It is important to develop intercultural friendship. This exercise is to help us consider the essential dimensions of intercultural friendship.

1. Five changes that take place in friendship across cultures:[7]
   a) Friends interact more frequently, longer periods of time, more various settings
   b) More interactions mean more knowledge and shared experiences
   c) Increased knowledge of motives and behaviours means an increased ability to predict a friend's reaction and reduce uncertainty
   d) The sense of 'we-ness' increases among friends, interdependence and affection increase
   e) Characterised by a sense of caring, commitment, trust, and emotional attachment
2. Reflection questions:
   a) What are the risks in each of the changes in a cross-cultural setting?
   b) How might awareness of these areas of change impact the way you disciple someone in a cross-cultural setting?
3. Seven realities of cross-cultural friendship:[8]

---
7 Lustig and Koester, *Intercultural Competence*, 246.
8 Hill, 'Lifting the Fog', 266–68.

APPENDICES

a) Cross-cultural friendship must be intentional.
b) Cross-cultural friendship requires proximity.
c) Cross-cultural friendship must appreciate differences and similarities.
d) Cross-cultural friendship will cross economic classes.
e) Cross-cultural friendship involves vulnerability.
f) Cross-cultural friendship must be selective.
g) Cross-cultural friendship must be flexible

4. Reflection questions:

a) Identify which of the above items you would consider an area of strength. Do you think it would still be a strength in an intercultural setting? Why or why not?
b) Choose one of the items you find most difficult and explain what it might take for you personally to grow in this area.

5. Reflect on the following proverbs:[9]
a) Words are easy, but real friendship is difficult.
b) Friendships are like mushrooms: they cannot be forced (when getting them out of the ground).
c) Friendship is like fat; you eat it while it is still hot.
d) Friendship is like the body; you do not scratch where it does not itch.
e) I am because we are; we are because I am.
6. Reflection questions:
a) Discuss what you think is the meaning behind each proverb.
b) All these proverbs come from Uganda. What do they value in friendship?
c) How do their values differ from your own culture? How are they the same? Which one is most relevant to your present culture? And why?

---

[9] Moreau, *Effective Intercultural Communication*, 245.

BIBLIOGRAPHY

Adair, Wendi L., Ivona Hideg, and Jeffrey R. Spence. 'The Culturally Intelligent Team: The Impact of Team Cultural Intelligence And Cultural Heterogeneity on Team Shared Values.' *Journal of Cross-Cultural Psychology* 44, no. 6 (2013): 941–62.

Adida, Claire L. 'Too Close for Comfort? Immigrant Exclusion in Africa.' *Comparative Political Studies* 44, no. 10 (2011): 1370–96.

Adler, Peter S. 'Beyond Cultural Identity: Reflections on Cultural and Multicultural Man.' In *Intercultural Communication: A Reader*, edited by L. Samovar and R. Porter, 389–408. Belmont, CA: Wadsworth, 1998.

AFES. 'Evangelical Union Sydney University > Sydney.' AFES, 2016. Accessed 14 November 2016. https://www.afes.org.au/campus/evangelical-union-sydney-university-sydney.

AFES. 'FOCUS University of New South Wales > Kensington.' AFES, 2016. Accessed 14 November 2016. https://www.afes.org.au/campus/focus-university-new-south-wales-kensington.

Åkerlund, Truls. 'Son, Sent, and Servant: Johannine Perspectives on Servant Leadership Theory.' *Scandinavian Journal for Leadership and Theology*, no. 2 (2015). Accessed 2 December 2016. http://sjlt-journal.com/no2/son-sent-and-servant/.

Allen, Holly Catterton, and Christine Lawton Ross. *Intergenerational Christian Formation: Bringing the Whole Church Together in Ministry, Community and Worship.* Downers Grove, IL: InterVarsity, 2012.

Allender, Dan B. *Leading with A Limp: Take Full Advantage of Your Most Powerful Weakness*. Colorado Springs, CO: WaterBrook Press, 2011.

Alperson, Myra. *Dim Sum, Bagels, and Grits: A Sourcebook for Multicultural Families*. New York, NY: Farrar, Straus and Giroux, 2001.

Alves, Jose C. 'A Multilevel Analysis of the Association Among Individual Capabilities, Team Leadership Behaviours, and Performance in China.' Unpublished diss., Isenberg School of Management, University of Massachusetts, 2008.

Amidei, Kathie, Jim Merhaut, and John Roberto. *Generations Together: Caring, Praying, Learning, Celebrating and Serving Faithfully*. Naugatuck, CT: Lifelong Faith Associates, 2014.

Ancona, Deborah, Thomas W. Malone, and Wanda J. Orlikowski et al. 'In Praise of The Incomplete Leader.' *Harvard Business Review* 85, no. 2 (2007): 92–100.

Anderson-Umana, Lisa. 'Differences in Power Distances May Make Harmony on A Multicultural Team More Challenging.' *Common Ground Journal* 8, no. 1 (2010): 21–31.

Ang, Ien. 'Can One Say No to Chineseness? Pushing the Limits of The Diasporic Paradigm.' *Boundary 2* 25, no. 3 (1998): 223–42.

———. 'Together-in-Difference: Beyond Diaspora, Into Hybridity.' *Asian Studies Review* 27, no. 2 (2003): 141–54.

Ang, Ien, Lisa Law, Sharon Chalmers, and Mandy Thomas. *Alter/Asians: Asian-Australian Identities in Art, Media and Popular Culture*. Annandale, NSW: Pluto Press, 2000.

Ang, Soon, and A.C. Inkpen. 'Cultural Intelligence and Offshore Outsourcing Success: A Framework of Firm-level Intercultural Capability.' *Decision Sciences* 39, no. 3 (2008): 337–58.

BIBLIOGRAPHY

Ang, Soon, and Linn Van Dyne. 'Conceptualization of Cultural Intelligence: Definition, Distinctiveness and Nomological Network.' In *Handbook of Cultural Intelligence: Theory, Measurement, and Applications*, edited by Soon Ang and Linn Van Dyne, 3–15. Milton Park, UK: Routledge, 2015.

———. *Handbook of Cultural Intelligence*. Milton Park, Oxon, UK: Routledge, 2015.

Ang, Soon, Linn Van Dyne, and Christine Koh. 'Personality Correlates of the Four-Factor Model of Cultural Intelligence.' *Group & Organization Management* 31, no. 1 (2006): 100–123.

Ang, Soon, Linn Van Dyne, and Christine Koh et al. 'Cultural Intelligence: Its Measurement and Effects on Cultural Judgment and Decision Making, Cultural Adaptation and Task Performance.' *Management and Organization Review* 3, no. 3 (2007): 335–71.

Apitzsch, Ursula, and Irini Siouti. 'Biographical Analysis as an Interdisciplinary Research Perspective in the Field of Migration Studies.' *Research Integration* (2007):1–30.

Asante, Molefi Kete, and Alice Davis. 'Encounters in the Interracial and Intercultural Workplace.' In *Handbook of International and Intercultural Relations*, 374–91. Newbury Park, CA: Sage Publications, 1989.

Atkinson, Donald R., and Ruth H. Gim. 'Asian-American Cultural Identity and Attitudes toward Mental Health Services.' *Journal of Counseling Psychology* 36, no. 2 (1989): 209–12.

Atwater, Leanne E., and David Andrew Waldman. *Leadership, Feedback, and the Open Communication Gap*. New York, NY: Lawrence Erlbaum Associates, 2008.

Augsburger, David W. *Pastoral Counseling across Cultures.* Philadephia, PA: Westminster John Knox Press, 1986.

Augsburger, David W. *Conflict Mediation across Cultures: Pathways and Patterns.* Louisville, KY: Westminster John Knox Press, 1992.

Austin, Zubin, Paul A. M. Gregory, and Stephanie Chiu. 'Use of Reflection-in-Action and Self-Assessment to Promote Critical Thinking Among Pharmacy Students.' *American Journal of Pharmaceutical Education* 72, no. 3 (2008): 48.

Australian Bureau of Statistics. 'Table 72. Population, Sex and Country of Birth, States and Territories, 1901 Census.' Australian Bureau of Statistics, 2008. Accessed 7 September 2016. http://www.abs.gov.au/AUSSTATS/abs@.nsf/DetailsPage/3105.0.65.0012006?OpenDocument.

Australian Bureau of Statistics. 'The Chinese in Australia.' Australian Bureau of Statistics, 2012. Accessed 7 September 2016. http://www.abs.gov.au/ausstats/abs@.nsf/e/4A6A63F3D85F7770CA2569DE00200137?OpenDocument.

Australian College of Theology. 'Graduates.' Australian College of Theology, 2016. Accessed 10 October 2016. http://www.actheology.edu.au/graduates.php.

Australian Multicultural Advisory Council. 'The People of Australia: Australia's Multicultural Policy'. In *Australian Multicultural Advisory Council.* Greenway, ACT: Australian Government, Department of Social Services, 2014.

Bandura, Albert. 'Social Cognitive Theory in Cultural Context.' *Applied Psychology* 51, no. 2 (2002): 269–290.

Banks, Robert J., Bernice M. Ledbetter, and Max Pree. *Reviewing Leadership: A Christian Evaluation of Current Approaches.* Grand Rapids, MI: Baker Academic, 2004.

BIBLIOGRAPHY

Barna, Laray M. 'Stumbling Blocks in Intercultural Communication.' In *Basic Concepts of Intercultural Communication*, edited by Milton Bennett, 345–53. Yarmouth, ME: Intercultural Press, 1996.

Bass, Bernard M., and Ruth Bass. *The Bass Handbook of Leadership: Theory, Research, and Managerial Applications*. New York, NY: Free Press, 2008.

Bates, Gerald E. 'Missions and Cross-Cultural Conflict.' *Missiology: An International Review* 8, no. 1 (1980): 93–98.

Baumeister, Roy F., Jeremy P. Shapiro, and Dianne M. Tice. 'Two Kinds of Identity Crisis.' *Journal of Personality* 53, no. 3 (1985): 407–24.

Bean, Frank D., Susan K. Brown, and Mark A. Leach. 'Unauthorized Mexican Migration and the Socioeconomic Integration of Mexican Americans.' In *Diversity and Disparities: America Enters a New Century*, edited by John R. Logan, 341–74. New York, NY: Russell Sage Foundation, 2014.

Bean, Frank D., and Gillian Stevens. *America's Newcomers and the Dynamics of Diversity*. New York, NY: Russell Sage Foundation, 2003.

Beaudoin, Tom. *Virtual Faith: The Irreverent Spiritual Quest of Generation X*. San Francisco, CA: Jossey-Bass Publishers, 1998.

Benet-Martínez, Verónica, and Jana Haritatos. 'Bicultural Identity Integration (BII): Components and Psychosocial Antecedents.' *Journal of Personality* 73, no. 4 (2005): 1015–50.

Berardo, Kate, and Darla K. Deardorff. *Building Cultural Competence: Innovative Activities and Models*. Sterling, VA: Stylus, 2012.

Bird, Allan, Mark Mendenhall, and Michael J. Stevens et al. 'Defining the Content Domain of Intercultural Competence for Global Leaders.' *Journal of Managerial Psychology* 25, no. 8 (2010): 810–28.

Bloom, Allan. *Closing of the American Mind*. New York, NY: Simon and Schuster, 1987.

Bordas, Juana. *Salsa, Soul, and Spirit: Leadership for a Multicultural Age*. San Francisco, CA: Berrett-Koehler, 2012.

Boswell, Christina, and Peter R. Mueser. 'Introduction: Economics and Interdisciplinary Approaches in Migration Research.' *Journal of Ethnic and Migration Studies* 34, no. 4 (2008): 519–29.

Bottomley, Gillian. *From Another Place: Migration and the Politics of Culture*. Cambridge, UK: Cambridge University Press, 1992.

Branson, Mark Lau, and Juan F. Martinez. *Churches, Cultures and Leadership: A Practical Theology of Congregations and Ethnicities*. Downers Grove, IL: InterVarsity, 2011.

Braswell, George W. *Understanding World Religions: Hinduism, Buddhism, Taoism, Confucianism, Judaism, Islam*. Nashville, TN: Broadman & Holman Publishers, 1994.

Brettell, Caroline B., and James F. Hollifield. *Migration Theory: Talking across Disciplines*. New York, NY: Routledge, 2014.

Brewster, E. Thomas, and Elizabeth S. Brewster. 'Language Learning "Is" Communication "Is" Ministry!' *International Bulletin of Missionary Research* 6, no. 4 (1982): 160–64.

Briley, Donnel A., Michael W. Morris, and Itamar Simonson. 'Cultural Chameleons: Biculturals, Conformity Motives,

BIBLIOGRAPHY

and Decision Making.' *Journal of Consumer Psychology* 15, no. 4 (2005): 351–62.

Brookfield, Stephen. *Understanding and Facilitating Adult Learning: A Comprehensive Analysis of Principles and Effective Practices*. Buckingham, UK: Open University Press, 1986.

Brownell, Judi. 'Creating Strong Listening Environments: A Key Hospitality Management Task.' *International Journal of Contemporary Hospitality Management* 6, no. 3 (1994): 3–10.

Bryman, Alan. *Social Research Methods*. Oxford, UK: Oxford University Press, 2016.

Bücker, Joost, Olivier Furrer, and Yanyan Lin. 'Measuring Cultural Intelligence (CQ) A New Test of the CQ Scale.' *International Journal of Cross Cultural Management* 15, no. 3 (2015): 259–84.

Bücker, Joost, Olivier Furrer, and Erik Poutsma et al. 'The Impact of Cultural Intelligence on Communication Effectiveness, Job Satisfaction and Anxiety for Chinese Host Country Managers Working for Foreign Multinationals.' *The International Journal of Human Resource Management* 25, no. 14 (2014): 2068–87.

Burnley, Ian Harry. *The Impact of Immigration on Australia: A Demographic Approach*. South Melbourne, VIC: Oxford University Press, 2001.

Cahalan, K. A., and G. S. Mikoski. *Opening the Field of Practical Theology: An Introduction*. Plymouth, UK: Rowman and Littlefield, 2014.

Callaghan, Greg. 'Remembering Tiananmen.' *The Australian*, 2009. Accessed 2 September 2016. http://www.

theaustralian.com.au/news/remembering-tiananmen/story-e6frg6n6-1225712617852.

Calori, Roland, Michael Lubatkin, and Philippe Very. 'Control Mechanisms in Cross-border Acquisitions: An International Comparison.' *Organization Studies* 15, no. 3 (1994): 361–79.

Carroll, Jackson W., and Wade Clark Roof. *Bridging Divided Worlds: Generational Cultures in Congregations*. San Francisco, CA: Jossey-Bass, 2002.

Casey, Anthony. 'How Shall They Hear? The Interface of Urbanization and Orality in North American Ethnic Church Planting.' Unpublished diss., Southern Baptist Theological Seminary, 2013.

Casiño, Tereso C. 'Why People Move: A Prolegomenon to Diaspora Missiology.' *Torch Trinity Journal* 13, no. 1 (2010): 19–44.

Cha, Peter, S. Steve Kang, and Helen Lee. *Growing Healthy Asian American Churches: Ministry Insights from Groundbreaking Congregations*. Downers Grove, IL: InterVarsity, 2006.

Cha, Peter T. 'Building a Healthy Congregational Culture in Today's Postmodern World.' *Common Ground Journal* 6, no. 1 (2008): 21–30.

Chan, Simon, and Wai-ming Mak. 'The Impact of Servant Leadership and Subordinates' Organizational Tenure on Trust in Leader and Attitudes.' *Personnel Review* 43, no. 2 (2014): 272–87.

Chan, W. L. 陳韻琳. '網絡世代對教會的挑戰 (The Challenge of the Global Age).' *Pastoral Sharing* 9 (2000): 18–20.

Chan, Wing-Tsit. 'On Translating Certain Chinese Philosophical Terms.' In *Reflections on Things at Hand: The Neo-Confucian Anthology*, edited by Chu Hsi, Lü Tsu-Ch'ien and Wing-

BIBLIOGRAPHY

Tsit Chan, 359–69. New York, NY: Columbia University Press, 1967.

Chang, Hui-Ching, and G. Richard Holt. 'More Than Relationship: Chinese Interaction and the Principle of Kuan-Hsi.' *Communication Quarterly* 39, no. 3 (1991): 251–71.

Chechowich, Faye E. 'Intergenerational Ministry: A Review of Selected Publications since 2001.' *Christian Education Journal* 9, no. 1 (2012): 182–93.

Chen, Guo-Ming, Kristen Ryan, and Chaichin Chen. 'The Determinants of Conflict Management among Chinese and Americans.' *Intercultural Communication Studies* 9, no. 2 (2000): 163–78.

Chen, Stephen, Ronald Geluykens, and Chong Ju Choi. 'The Importance of Language in Global Teams: A Linguistic Perspective.' *Management International Review* 46, no. 6 (2006): 679–96.

Chen, Sylvia Xiaohua. 'Two Languages, Two Personalities? Examining Language Effects on Personality in the Bilingual Context.' Unpublished diss., Chinese University of Hong Kong, 2007.

Cheng, Bor-Shiuan et al. 'Paternalistic Leadership in Four East Asian Societies: Generalizability and Cultural Differences of the Triad Model.' *Journal of Cross-Cultural Psychology* 20, no. 10 (2014): 1–9.

Cheng, Clara. 'Spirituality in Cross-Cultural Conflict Management.' *William Carey International Development Journal* 1, no. 3 (2012): 1–12.

Chinese Christian Church. *Moving Forward: CCC Milsons Point 50 Anniversary Publication*. Sydney, NSW: Chinese Christian Church, 2015.

Chinese Christian Fellowship of Australia. 'Report of The Executive Committee.' Edited by the Chinese Christian Fellowship of Australia. Sydney, NSW: Sydney Chinese Christian Churches Association, 1965.

Chinese Christian Mission Australia. 'Church Index—New South Wales.' Chinese Christian Mission Australia, 2016. Accessed 7 September 2016. http://www.ccma.org.au/index.php?option=com_content&view=article&id=110&Itemid=71&lang=zh.

Chinese Coordination Centre of World Evangelism. 'General Secretary.' Chinese Coorindation Centre of World Evangelism, 2016. Accessed 14 November 2016. http://www.cccowe.org/content.php?id=about_general_secretary.

The Chinese Culture Connection. 'Chinese Values and the Search for Culture-Free Dimensions of Culture.' *Journal of Cross-Cultural Psychology* 18, no. 2 (1987): 143–64.

Chinese Presbyterian Church. *Chinese Presbyterian Church: Centenary Magazine 1893–1993*. Sydney, NSW: Chinese Presbyterian Church, 1994.

Chinese Theological College Australia. 'The Birth of the Vision.' Chinese Theological College Australia, 2008. Accessed 8 September 2016. http://www.ctca.org.au/en/the-birth-of-the-vision/.

Choi, Ching-yan. *Chinese Migration and Settlement in Australia*. Sydney, NSW: Sydney University Press, 1975.

BIBLIOGRAPHY

———. 'Chinese Migration and Settlement in Australia, with Special Reference to the Chinese in Melbourne.' PhD diss., Australian National University, 1971.

Choi, Sungho. 'Identity Crisis for the Diaspora Community.' In *Korean Diaspora and Christian Mission*, edited by S. Hun Kim and Wongsuk Ma, 25–34. Oxford, UK: Regnum, 2011.

Chua, Elizabeth G., and William B. Gudykunst. 'Conflict Resolution Styles in Low- and High-Context Cultures.' *Communication Research Reports* 4, no. 1 (1987): 32–37.

Chun, Do Myung. 'Kingdom-Centred Identity: The Case of Bicultural Korean-Brazilians.' In *Korean Diaspora and Christian Mission*, edited by S. Hun Kim and Wonsuk Ma, 242–59. Oxford, UK: Regnum, 2011.

Chung, Mei Ling. 'Chinese Young People and Spirituality: An Australian Study.' Unpublished diss., Australian Catholic University, 2006.

Citrin, Jack, David O. Sears, Christopher Muste, and Cara Wong. 'Multiculturalism in American public opinion.' *British Journal of Political Science* 31, no. 2 (2001): 247–75.

Cladis, George. *Leading the Team-Based Church: How Pastors and Church Staffs Can Grow Together into a Powerful Fellowship of Leaders*. San Francisco, CA: Jossey-Bass, 1999.

Clinton, J. Robert. 'Cross-Cultural Use of Leadership Concepts.' In *The Word among Us: Contextualizing Theology for Mission Today*, edited by Dean Gilliland, 183–98. Eugene, OR: Wipf & Stock, 2002.

Clyne, M. G. 'Language Policy and Community Languages.' In *The Australian people: An Encyclopedia of the Nation, Its People and Their Origins*, edited by James Jupp. North Ryde, NSW: Angus & Robertson, 1988.

Cohen, Robin. *The Cambridge Survey of World Migration*. Cambridge, UK: Cambridge University Press, 1995.

Collins-Mayo, Sylvia, Bob Mayo, and Sally Nash et al. *The Faith of Generation Y*. London, UK: Church House, 2010.

Collins, Jim. 'Level 5 Leadership. The Triumph of Humility and Fierce Resolve.' *Harvard Business Review* 79, no. 1 (2001): 66–76.

Conde-Frazier, Elizabeth, and Andrew Y. Lee. 'Intergenerational and Intercultural Issues.' *Common Ground Journal* 12, no. 1 (2015): 67–74.

Cosgrove, Charles H., Herold Weiss, and Khiok-Khng Yeo. *Cross-Cultural Paul: Journeys to Others, Journeys to Ourselves*. Grand Rapids, MI: Eerdmans, 2005.

Coughlan, James E., and Deborah J. McNamara. *Asians in Australia: Patterns of Migration and Settlement*. South Melbourne, VIC: Macmillan Education, 1997.

Covin, Teresa Joyce, Thomas A. Kolenko, and Kevin W. Sightler et al. 'Leadership Style and Post-Merger Satisfaction.' *Journal of Management Development* 16, no. 1 (1997): 22–33.

Cox, David R. *Migration and Welfare: An Australian Perspective*. Parramatta, NSW: Prentice Hall, 1987.

Cresciani, Gianfranco. 2003. *The Italians in Australia*. Cambridge UK: Cambridge University Press.

Creswell, John W. *Research Design: Qualitative, Quantitative, and Mixed Methods Approaches*. Thousand Oaks, CA: Sage, 2009.

BIBLIOGRAPHY

Crowder, George. *Theories of Multiculturalism: An Introduction.* Cambridge, UK: Polity, 2013.

Crowne, Kerri Anne, and Robert L. Engle. 'Antecedents of Cross-Cultural Adaptation Stress in Short-Term International Assignments.' *Organization Management Journal* 13, no. 1 (2016): 32–47.

Damarin, Suzanne. 'Schooling and Situated Knowledge: Travel or Tourism.' *Educational Technology* 33, no. 10 (1993): 27–32.

De Bary, William Theodore. *Neo-Confucian Orthodoxy and the Learning of the Mind-and-Heart.* New York, NY: Columbia University Press, 1981.

De Dreu, Carsten K. W., and Laurie R. Weingart. 'Task Versus Relationship Conflict, Team Performance, and Team Member Satisfaction: A Meta-Analysis.' *Journal of Applied Psychology* 88, no. 4 (2003): 741–49.

De Haan, Arjan, Karen Brock, and Ngolo Coulibaly. 'Migration, Livelihoods and Institutions: Contrasting Patterns of Migration in Mali.' *Journal of Development Studies* 38, no. 5 (2002): 37–58.

De Pree, Max. *Leading without Power: Finding Hope in Serving Community.* Holland, MI: Shepherd Foundation, 1997.

de Waal, André, and Mirna Sivro. 'The Relation between Servant Leadership, Organizational Performance, and the High-Performance Organization Framework.' *Journal of Leadership & Organizational Studies* 19, no. 2 (2012): 173–90.

Dean, Marcus. 'The Missionary as Cultural Pilgrim.' *Evangelical Missions Quarterly* 48, no. 1 (2012): 10–14.

Deci, E. L., and R. M. Ryan. *Intrinsic Motivation and Self-Determination in Human Behaviour*. New York, NY: Plenum, 1985.

Deng, Ling, and Paul Gibson. 'A Qualitative Evaluation on the Role of Cultural Intelligence in Cross-Cultural Leadership Effectiveness.' *International Journal of Leadership Studies* 3, no. 2 (2008): 181–97.

Department of Immigration and Citizenship. 'Fact Sheet 6—Australia's Multicultural Policy.' Australian Government, Department of Immigration and Citizenship, 2011. Accessed 14 November 2016. http://www.immi.gov.au/media/fact-sheets/06australias-multicultural-policy.htm.

Dodd, Carley H. *Dynamics of Intercultural Communication*. Dubuque, IA: William C. Brown, 1995.

Dodge, Bruce. 'Empowerment and the Evolution of Learning.' *Education+Training* 35, no. 5 (1993): 3–10.

Du-Babcock, Bertha. 'Topic Management and Turn Taking in Professional Communication: First- versus Second-Language Strategies.' *Management Communication Quarterly* 12, no. 4 (1999): 544–74.

Du-Babcock, Bertha, and Richard D Babcock. 'Patterns of Expatriate-Local Personnel Communication in Multinational Corporations.' *The Journal of Business Communication (1973)* 33, no. 2 (1996): 141–64.

Dustmann, Christian, and Ian P. Preston. 'Racial and Economic Factors in Attitudes to Immigration.' *The B.E. Journal of Economic Analysis & Policy* 7, no. 1 (2007): 1–39.

BIBLIOGRAPHY

Earley, P. Christopher, and Soon Ang. *Cultural Intelligence: Individual Interactions Across Cultures.* Palo Alto, CA: Stanford University Press, 2003.

Earley, P. Christopher, Soon Ang, and Joo-Seng Tan. *CQ: Developing Cultural Intelligence at Work.* Palo Alto, CA: Stanford University Press, 2006.

Earley, P. Christopher, and Elaine Mosakowski. 'Cultural Intelligence.' *Harvard Business Review* 82, no. 10 (2004): 139–46.

Eccles, Jacquelynne S., and Allan Wigfield. 'Motivational Beliefs, Values, and Goals.' *Annual Review of Psychology* 53, no. 1 (2002): 109–32.

Eckersley, Richard. 'Progress, Sustainability and Human Well-Being: Is a New Worldview Emerging?' *International Journal of Innovation and Sustainable Development* 1, no. 4 (2006): 304–17.

Elmer, Duane. *Cross-Cultural Conflict: Building Relationships for Effective Ministry.* Downers Grove, IL: InterVarsity, 1993.

Engebretson, Kath. 'Expressions of Religiosity and Spirituality among Australian 14 Year Olds.' *International Journal of Children's Spirituality* 7, no. 1 (2002): 57–72.

Englander, Magnus. 'The Interview: Data Collection in Descriptive Phenomenological Human Scientific Research.' *Journal of Phenomenological Psychology* 43, no. 1 (2012): 13–35.

Erikson, Erik H. *Identity: Youth and Crisis.* New York, NY: WW Norton & Co., 1968.

Fanning, Ruth M., and David M. Gaba. 'The Role of Debriefing in Simulation-Based Learning.' *Simulation in Healthcare:*

Journal of the Society for Simulation in Healthcare 2, no. 2 (2007): 115–25.

Fargues, Philippe. 'Immigration without Inclusion: Non-Nationals in Nation-Building in the Gulf States.' *Asian and Pacific Migration Journal* 20, nos 3–4, (2011): 273–92.

Filbeck, David. *Social Context and Proclamation: A Socio-Cognitive Study in Proclaiming the Gospel Cross-Culturally*. Pasadena, CA: William Carey Library, 1985.

First Light Care Association. 'History of FLC.' First Light Care Association, 2016. Accessed 14 November 2016. http://www.firstlightcare.org.au/aboutus#history.

Ford, Kevin Graham, and Jim Denney. *Jesus for a New Generation: Putting the Gospel in the Language of Xers*. Downers Grove, IL: InterVarsity, 1995.

Foster, Charles R. *Embracing Diversity: Leadership in Multicultural Congregations*. Herndon, VA: Alban Institute, 1997.

Foster, Charles R. *From Generation to Generation: The Adaptive Challenge of Mainline Protestant Education in Forming Faith*. Eugene, OR: Wipf & Stock, 2012.

Friedman, Edwin. *Generation to Generation: Family Process in Church and Synagogue*. New York, NY: Guilford, 2011.

Fu, P. P., T. K. Peng, Jeffrey C. Kennedy, and Gary Yukl. 'Examining the Preferences of Influence Tactics in Chinese Societies: A Comparison of Chinese Managers in Hong Kong, Taiwan and Mainland China.' *Organizational Dynamics* 33, no. 1 (2004): 32–46.

Fuligni, Andrew J., Vivian Tseng, and May Lam. 'Attitudes toward Family Obligations among American Adolescents with

BIBLIOGRAPHY

Asian, Latin American, and European Backgrounds.' *Child Development* 70 no. 4 (1999):1030–44.

Fulton, Brent. *China's Urban Christians: A Light that Cannot be Hidden*. Eugene, OR: Wipf & Stock, 2015.

Fung, Joseph. *UCEC Report on CIM (OMF) Centenary Thanksgiving Worship Service*. Sydney, NSW: United Chinese Evangelism Committee, 1990.

———. *Chairman's Report of the First Combined Chinese Youth Summer Conference (CCYSC) 1991*. Sydney, NSW: United Chinese Evangelism Committee. 1992.

———. 'SCCCA—History.' Sydney Chinese Christian Churches Association, 2016. Accessed 14 November 2016. http://sccca.org.au/history.

———. *United Chinese Evangelism Committee (Brief History)*. Sydney, NSW: n.d.

Gardner, Howard. *Frames of Mind: The Theory of Multiple Intelligences*. New York, NY: Basic, 1983.

Geertz, Clifford. *Works and Lives: The Anthropologist as Author*. Cambridge, UK: Polity, 1988.

George, Bill. *True North: Discover Your Authentic Leadership*. San Francisco, CA: John Wiley & Sons, 2010.

George, Bill, Peter Sims, and Andrew N. McLean et al. 'Discovering Your Authentic Leadership.' *Harvard Business Review* 85, no. 2 (2007): 129–38.

George, Sam. *Understanding the Coconut Generation: Ministry to the Americanized Asian Indians*. Niles, IL: Mall, 2006.

Gibbons, Dave. *The Monkey and the Fish: Liquid Leadership for a Third-Culture Church*. Grand Rapids, MI: HarperCollins Christian, 2009.

Gibbons, T. C. 'Revisiting the Question of Born Vs Made: Toward a Theory of Development of Transformational Leaders.' Unpublished diss., Fielding Institute, 1986.

Gilchrist, Roy, and Ailsa Thompson. *A Brief History of Central Baptist Church*. Sydney, NSW: Central Baptist Church, 2001.

Glazer, Sharon, Nina Hamedani, Kristina Kayton, and Amy Weinberg. 'Culture Research Landscape Throughout the United States Department of Defense.' *Toward Sustainable Development through Nurturing Diversity* (2014): 213.

Goffee, Rob, and Gareth Jones. 'Managing Authenticity.' *Harvard Business Review* 83, no. 12 (2005): 87–94.

Goldin, Ian, Geoffrey Cameron, and Meera Balarajan. *Exceptional People: How Migration Shaped Our World and Will Define Our Future*. Princeton, NJ: Princeton University Press, 2012.

Goplin, Vicky, Jeffrey Nelson, Mark Gardner, and Eileen Zahn. *Across the Generations: Incorporating All Ages in Ministry: The Why and How*. Minneapolis, MN: Augsburg Fortress, 2001.

Gough, Deborah. 'Thinking about Thinking.' *Research Roundup* 7, no. 2 (1991): 3–6.

Grbich, Carol. *Qualitative Data Analysis: An Introduction*. Thousand Oaks, CA: Sage, 2012.

Greenleaf, Robert K. *Servant Leadership*. New York, NY: Paulist, 1977.

BIBLIOGRAPHY

Greenleaf, Robert K., and Larry C. Spears. *The Power of Servant-Leadership*. San Francisco, CA: Berrett-Koehler, 1998.

Groody, Daniel G. 'Crossing the Divide: Foundations of a Theology of Migration and Refugees.' *Theological studies* 70, no. 3 (2009): 638–67.

———. 'A Theology of Migration.' *America* 204, no. 3 (2011): 18–20.

Groody, Daniel G, and Gioacchino Campese. *A Promised Land, A Perilous Journey: Theological Perspectives on Migration*. Notre Dame, IN: University of Notre Dame Press, 2008.

Guerra, Carmel, and Robert Douglas White. *Ethnic Minority Youth in Australia: Challenges and Myths*. Hobart, TAS: National Clearing House for Youth Studies, 1995.

Hagberg, Janet. *Real Power: The Stages of Personal Power in Organizations*. Minneapolis, MN: Winston, 1984.

Hagen-Zanker, Jessica. 'Why do People Migrate? A Review of the Theoretical Literature.' Maastricht University, Maastricht Graduate School of Governance, 2008. Accessed 6 December 2016. https://mpra.ub.uni-http://mpra.ub.uni-muenchen.de/28197/.

Hall, Edward T. *Beyond Culture*. Garden City, NY: Anchor, 1976.

———. *The Silent Language*. New York, NY: Doubleday, 1959.

Hall, Stuart. 'Cultural Identity and Diaspora.' *Framework* 37 (1990): 222–37.

———. 'The Question of Cultural Identity.' In *Modernity and Its Futures*, 274–316. Cambridge, UK: Polity, 1992.

———. 'The Question of Cultural Identity.' In *Modernity: An Introduction to Modern Societies*, edited by Stuart Hall,

David Held, and Don Hubert Hubert, 596–623. Malden, MA: Blackwell, 1996.

Hammer, Mitchell R. 'Clarifying Inaccurate Statements Characterizing the Intercultural Development Inventory in Matsumoto and Hwang (2013) JCCP Article1.' 2015. *idiinventory.com website*.

———. 'The Intercultural Conflict Style Inventory: A Conceptual Framework and Measure of Intercultural Conflict Resolution Approaches.' *International Journal of Intercultural Relations* 29, no. 6 (2005): 675–95.

Hammerton, A. James, and Eric Richards. *Speaking to Immigrants: Oral Testimony and the History of Australian Migration*. Canberra, ACT: Centre for Immigration and Multicultural Studies, Research School of Social Sciences, Australian National University, 2002.

Harris, John R., and Michael P. Todaro. 'Migration, Unemployment and Development: A Two-Sector Analysis.' *The American Economic Review* 60, no. 1 (1970): 126–42.

Harzig, Christiane, and Dirk Hoerder. *What is Migration History*. Cambridge UK: Polity, 2009.

Haug, Sonja. 'Migration Networks and Migration Decision-Making.' *Journal of Ethnic and Migration Studies* 34, no. 4 (2008): 585–605.

Hawley, Dale. 'Research on Missionary Kids and Families: A Critical Review.' Missions Resource Network, 2004. Accessed 2 December 2016. https://www.mrnet.org/research-on-missionary-kids-and-families-critical-review-adobe-pdf.

Heidegger, Martin. *Being and Time*. Translated by John Macquarrie and Edward Robinson. New York, NY: Harper & Row, 1962.

BIBLIOGRAPHY

Heifetz, Ronald Abadian, and Donald L. Laurie. 'The Work of Leadership.' *Harvard Business Review* 75, no. 1 (1997): 124–34.

Hermans, Hubert J. M., and Harry J. G. Kempen. 'Moving Cultures: The Perilous Problems of Cultural Dichotomies in a Globalizing Society.' *American Psychologist* 53, no. 10 (1998): 1111–20.

Hesselgrave, David J., and Edward Rommen. 'A Contextualization of the New Birth Message: An Evangelistic Tract for Chinese People.' In *Contextualization: Meanings, Methods, and Models*, edited by David J. Hesselgrave and Edward Rommen. Leicester, UK: Apollos, 1989.

Hibbert, Evelyn, and Richard Hibbert. *Leading Multicultural Teams*. Pasadena, CA: William Carey Library, 2014.

Hibbert, Richard Y. 'Enhancing WEC Church Planting Teams: A Study of Factors Influencing Their Effectiveness.' Unpublished diss., Columbia International University, 2002.

Hiebert, Paul G. *Cultural Anthropology*. Grand Rapids, MI: Baker, 1976.

———. *Transforming Worldviews: An Anthropological Understanding of How People Change*. Grand Rapids, MI: Baker Academic, 2008.

Hilborn, David, and Matt Bird. *God and the Generations: Youth, Age and the Church Today*. Carlisle, UK: Paternoster, 2002.

Hill, Harriet. 'Lifting the Fog on Incarnational Ministry.' *Evangelical Missions Quarterly* 29, no. 3 (1993): 262–69.

Ho, C. H., and James E. Coughlan. 'The Chinese in Australia: Immigrants from the People's Republic of China, Malaysia, Singapore, Taiwan, Hong Kong and Macau.' In *Asians in*

Australia: Patterns of Migration and Settlement, edited by James E. Coughlan and Deborah J. McNamara, 120–70. South Melbourne, VIC: Macmillan Education, 1997.

Hofstede, Geert. *Cultures and Organizations: Software of the Mind*. New York, NY: McGraw-Hill, 1991.

Hofstede, Geert, Gert Jan Hofstede, and Michael Minkov. *Cultures and Organizations: Software of the Mind*. New York, NY: McGraw-Hill, 2010.

Hong, Ying-yi, Grace Ip, and Chi-yue Chiu et al. 'Cultural Identity and Dynamic Construction of the Self: Collective Duties and Individual Rights in Chinese and American Cultures.' *Social Cognition* 19, no. 3, special issue (2001): 251–68.

Horton, Sarah. 'A Mother's Heart is Weighed Down with Stones: A Phenomenological Approach to the Experience of Transnational Motherhood.' *Culture, Medicine, and Psychiatry* 33, no. 1 (2009): 21–40.

House, Robert J. et al. *Culture, Leadership, and Organizations: The GLOBE Study of 62 Societies*. Thousand Oaks, CA: Sage, 2004.

Hughes, Philip J. *The Baptists in Australia*. Nunawading, VIC: Christian Research Association, 1996.

Hughes, Richard L. *Leadership: Enhancing the Lessons of Experience*. New York, NY: McGraw-Hill, 2015.

Huntington, Samuel P. *The Clash of Civilizations and the Remaking of World Order*. New York, NY: Simon & Schuster, 1996.

Huynh, Que-Lam, Angela-Minh, Tu D. Nguyen, and Verónica Benet-Martínez. 'Bicultural Identity Integration.' In *Handbook of Identity Theory and Research*, 827–42. New York, NY: Springer, 2011.

BIBLIOGRAPHY

Hynie, Michaela, Richard N. Lalonde, and Nam S. Lee. 2006. 'Parent-Child Value Transmission among Chinese Immigrants to North America: The Case of Traditional Mate Preferences.' *Cultural Diversity and Ethnic Minority Psychology* 12 (2): 230–244.

Ibrahim, Farah A., and Jianna R. Heuer. *Cultural and Social Justice Counseling.* Switzerland: Springer International, 2016.

Isaacs, Mareasa R., and Marva P. Benjamin. *Towards a Culturally Competent System of Care. Volume II: Programs Which Utilize Culturally Competent Principles.* Washington, DC: CASSP Technical Assistance Center, 1991.

Islam, Gazi. 'Social Identity Theory.' In *Encyclopedia of Critical Psychology*, edited by Thomas Teo, 1781-3. New York, NY: Springer New York, 2014.

Ivison, Duncan. *The Ashgate Research Companion to Multiculturalism.* Surrey, UK: Ashgate, 2010.

Jackson, Darrell, and Alessia Passarelli. *Mapping Migration, Mapping Churches' Responses in Europe: Belonging, Community and Integration: The Witness and Service of Churches in Europe.* Geneva, CH: Churches' Commission for Migrants in Europe and the World Council of Churches, 2016.

Jackson, Michael. 'The Shock of the New: On Migrant Imaginaries and Critical Transitions.' *Ethnos* 73, no. 1 (2008): 57–72.

Jacobsen, Eric O. *The Three Tasks of Leadership: Worldly Wisdom for Pastoral Leaders.* Grand Rapids, MI: Eerdmans, 2009.

Jandt, Fred E. *An Introduction to Intercultural Communication: Identities in a Global Community.* Thousand Oaks, CA: Sage, 2015.

Jensen, Lene Arnett, Jeffrey Jensen Arnett, and Jessica McKenzie. 'Globalization and Cultural Identity.' In *Handbook of Identity Theory and Research*, 285–301. New York, NY: Springer, 2011.

Johnson, R. Burke, Anthony J. Onwuegbuzie, and Lisa A. Turner. 'Toward a Definition of Mixed Methods Research.' *Journal of Mixed Methods Research* 1, no. 2 (2007): 112–33.

Jones, Susan R., and Marylu K. McEwen. 'A Conceptual Model of Multiple Dimensions of Identity.' *Journal of College Student Development* 41, no. 4 (2000): 405–14.

Jupp, James. *Australian People: An Encyclopedia of the Nation, Its People and Their Origins*. North Ryde, NSW: Angus & Robertson, 1988.

———. *From White Australia to Woomera: The Story of Australian Immigration*. Cambridge UK: Cambridge University Press, 2002.

Jupp, James. 'Politics, Public Policy and Multiculturalism.' In *Multiculturalism and Integration: A Harmonious Relationship*, edited by Michael Clyne and James Jupp, 41–52. Canberra, ACT: ANU Press, 2013.

Kamp, Alanna. 'Chinese Australian Women in White Australia: Utilising Available Sources to Overcome the Challenge of "Invisibility".' *Chinese Southern Diaspora Studies* 6 (2013): 75–101.

Kasper, Wolfgang. *Sustainable Immigration and Cultural Integration*. St Leonards, NSW: Centre for Independent Studies, 2002.

Kim, Bryan S. K., Donald R. Atkinson, and Peggy H. Yang. 'The Asian Values Scale: Development, Factor Analysis, Validation,

BIBLIOGRAPHY

And Reliability.' *Journal of Counseling Psychology* 46, no. 3 (1999): 342–52.

Kim, Jung Ha. *Bridge-Makers and Cross-Bearers: Korean-American Women and the Church.* Atlanta, GA: Scholars Press, 1997.

Kim, Young Yun. *Becoming Intercultural: An Integrative Theory of Communication and Cross-Cultural Adaptation.* Thousand Oaks, CA: Sage, 2001.

Kluckhohn, Florence R., and Fred L. Strodtbeck. *Variations in Value Orientations.* Evanston, IL: Row, Peterson, 1961.

Kochman, Thomas. *Black and White Styles in Conflict.* Chicago, IL: University of Chicago Press, 1981.

Koh, Christine, Damien Joseph, and Soon Ang. 'Cultural Intelligence and the Global Information Technology Workforce.' In *Handbook of Technology Management*, edited by Hossein Bidgoli, 828–44. Chichester, UK: John Wiley & Sons, 2009.

Kohls, L. *Survival Kit for Overseas Living: For Americans Planning to Live and Work Abroad.* Chicago, IL: Nicholas Brealey, 1976.

Kohls, L. Robert, and John Mark Knight. *Developing Intercultural Awareness: A Cross-Cultural Training Handbook.* Yarmouth, ME: Intercultural, 1994.

Kolb, David A. *Experiential Learning: Experience as the Source of Learning and Development.* Upper Saddle River, NJ: Prentice Hall, 1984.

Kraft, Charles H. *Anthropology for Christian Witness.* Maryknoll, NY: Orbis, 1996.

Kraidy, Marwan M. 'Hybridity in Cultural Globalization.' *Communication Theory* 12, no. 3 (2002): 316–39.

Kühnen, Ulrich, et al. 'Challenge Me! Communicating in Multicultural Classrooms.' *Social Psychology of Education* 15, no. 1 (2012): 59–76.

Kymlicka, Will. 'Liberal Theories of Multiculturalism.' In *Rights, Culture and the Law: Themes from the Legal and Political Philosophy of Joseph Raz*, edited by Lukas H. Meyer, Stanley L. Paulson and Thomas W. Pogge, 229–52. Oxford, UK: Oxford University Press, 2003.

Lalonde, Richard N., and Benjamin Giguère. 'When Might the Two Cultural Worlds of Second Generation Biculturals Collide.' *Canadian Diversity* 6 (2008): 58–62.

Lane, Patty. *A Beginner's Guide to Crossing Cultures: Making Friends in A Multicultural World*. Downers Grove, IL: InterVarsity Press, 2009.

Laniak, Timothy. *Shepherds after My Own Heart: Pastoral Traditions and Leadership in the Bible*. Downers Grove, IL: InterVarsity, 2006.

Law, Frankie. *Annual Report 2016: Sydney Chinese Christian Churches Association*. Sydney, NSW: Sydney Chinese Christian Churches Association, 2016.

Law, Gail. 'A Model for the American Ethnic Chinese Churches.' *Theology News and Notes* December (1984): 21–26.

Law, T. L. '澳洲華人教會的文化轉變 (The Cultural Change of the Chinese Churches in Australia).' *Great Commission Quarterly* 26 (2000): 10–11.

Lawrence, James. *Engaging Gen Y: Leading Well across the Generations*. Nottingham, UK: Grove, 2012.

BIBLIOGRAPHY

Lessard-Clouston, Michael. 'Seven Biblical Themes for Language Learning.' *Evangelical Missions Quarterly* 48, no. 2 (2012): 172–79.

Leung, Kwok. 'Beliefs in Chinese Culture.' In *The Oxford Handbook of Chinese Psychology*, edited by Michael Harris Bond, 221–40. New York, NY: Oxford University Press, 2010.

———. 'Some Determinants of Conflict Avoidance.' *Journal of Cross-Cultural Psychology* 19 (1988): 125–36.

Leung, Kwok, Soon Ang, and Mei Ling Tan. 'Intercultural Competence.' *Annual Review of Organizational Psychology and Organizational Behavior* 1, no. 1 (2014): 489–519.

Lewins, F. 'Assimilation and Integration.' In *The Australian People: An Encyclopedia of the Nation, Its People and Their Origins*, edited by James Jupp. North Ryde, NSW: Angus & Robertson, 1988.

Lewis, Richard. *When Teams Collide: Managing the International Team Successfully*. London, UK: Nicholas Brealey, 2012.

Liden, Robert C., Sandy J. Wayne, and Chenwei Liao et al. 'Servant Leadership and Serving Culture: Influence on Individual and Unit Performance.' *Academy of Management Journal* 57, no. 5 (2014): 1434–52.

Liden, Robert C., Sandy J. Wayne, and Hao Zhao et al. 'Servant Leadership: Development of a Multidimensional Measure and Multi-Level Assessment.' *The Leadership Quarterly* 19, no. 2 (2008): 161–77.

Lievens, Filip, Michael M. Harris, and Etienne Van Keer et al. 'Predicting Cross-Cultural Training Performance: The Validity of Personality, Cognitive Ability, and Dimensions Measured by an Assessment Center and a Behavior

Description Interview.' *Journal of Applied Psychology* 88, no. 3 (2003): 476–89.

Ling, Samuel, and Clarence Cheuk. *The 'Chinese' Way of Doing Things: Perspectives on American-Born Chinese and the Chinese Church in North America*. Pasadena, CA: China Horizon, 1999.

Lingenfelter, Sherwood G. *Transforming Culture: A Challenge for Christian Mission*. Grand Rapids, MI: Baker Academic, 1998.

Lingenfelter, Sherwood G. *Leading Cross-Culturally: Covenant Relationships for Effective Christian Leadership*. Grand Rapids, MI: Baker Academic, 2008.

Little, David. 'Learner Autonomy and Second/Foreign Language Learning.' Subject Centre for Languages, Linguistics and Area Studies, 2003. Accessed 16 December 2016. https://www.llas.ac.uk//resources/gpg/1409.

Liu, Shuang. 'Searching for a Sense of Place: Identity Negotiation of Chinese Immigrants.' *International Journal of Intercultural Relations* 46 (2015): 26–35.

Livermore, David. *Cultural Intelligence: Improving Your CQ to Engage Our Multicultural World*. Grand Rapids, MI: Baker Academic, 2009.

Livermore, David. *Leading with Cultural Intelligence: The Real Secret to Success*. NY: American Management Association, 2015.

———. *Serving with Eyes Wide Open: Doing Short-Term Missions with Cultural Intelligence*. Grand Rapids, MI: Baker, 2012.

Lustig, Myrone W., and Jolene Koester. *Intercultural Competence: Interpersonal Communication Across Cultures*. Boston, MA: Allyn & Bacon, 2003.

BIBLIOGRAPHY

Ma, Calvin. *Serve Asia Workers Debriefing Form.* Sydney, NSW: OMF Australia, n.d.

———. 'Questionnaire on Mission Involvement among Chinese Churches in Sydney.' Chinese Churches for Mission, 2004. Accessed 14 November 2016. file:///C:/Users/Michael/Documents/Outreaching/OMF/CCFM/Questionnaire%20of%20mission%20involvement%20in%20Chinese%20churches.htm.

Manley, Ken R. *In the Heart of Sydney: Central Baptist Church, 1836–1986.* Sydney, NSW: Central Baptist Church, 1987.

Manning, Patrick, and Tiffany Trimmer. *Migration in World History.* Milton Park, UK: Routledge, 2013.

Mar, Wendy Lu. *So Great a Cloud of Witnesses: A History of the Chinese Presbyterian Church, Sydney 1893–1993.* Sydney, NSW: Chinese Presbyterian Church, Sydney, 1993.

Markus, Andrew. 'White Australia.' In *The Oxford Companion to Australian History*, edited by Graeme Davison, John Bradley Hirst and Stuart Macintyre, 686–88. South Melbourne, VIC: Oxford University Press, 2001.

Markus, Hazel R., and Shinobu Kitayama. 'Culture and the Self: Implications for Cognition, Emotion, and Motivation.' *Psychological Review* 98, no. 2 (1991): 224–53.

Marriage & Family For Christ. 'About Marriage & Family For Christ.' Marriage & Family For Christ, 2016. Accessed 14 November 2016. http://www.mffc.org.au/en/about/mffcau/.

Marschan-Piekkari, Rebecca, Denice Welch, and Lawrence Welch. 'In the Shadow: The Impact of Language on Structure, Power and Communication in the Multinational.' *International Business Review* 8, no. 4 (1999): 421–40.

Martins, Susanne. 'Intercultural Communication and Cultural Intelligence in the Workplace.' PhD diss., Murdoch University, 2013.

Massey, Douglas S., Joaquin Arango, and Graeme Hugo. 'Theories of International Migration: A Review and Appraisal.' *Population & Development Review* 19, no. 3 (1993): 431–66.

Matsumoto, David, and Hyisung C. Hwang. 'Assessing Cross-Cultural Competence: A Review of Available Tests.' *Journal of Cross-Cultural Psychology* 44 (2013): 849–73.

Matthews, Barbara Marshall. 'The Chinese Value Survey: An Interpretation of Value Scales and Consideration of Some Preliminary Results.' *International Education Journal* 1, no. 2 (2000): 117–26.

Matveev, Alexei V., and Miwa Yamazaki Merz. 'Intercultural Competence Assessment: What are its Key Dimensions across Assessment Tools?' In *Toward Sustainable Development Through Nurturing Diversity: Selected Papers from the Twenty-First Congress of the International Associate for Cross-Cultural Psychology*, edited by L. T. B. Jackson, D. Meiring, F. J. R. Van de Vijver, E. S. Idemoudia, & W. K. Gabrenya Jr. 2014. Accessed 2 December 2016. https://scholarworks.gvsu.edu/iaccp_papers/128/.

McCrindle, Mark. 'Generations Defined.' In *The ABC of XYZ: Understanding the Global Generations*. Sydney, NSW: University of New South Wales, 2009.

McDowell, Christopher, and Arjan De Haan. *Migration and Sustainable Livelihoods: A Critical Review of the Literature*. Brighton, UK: Institute of Development Studies, 1997.

BIBLIOGRAPHY

McGowan, Barry. 'Transnational Lives: Colonial Immigration Restrictions and the White Australia Policy in the Riverina District of New South Wales, 1860–1960.' *Chinese Southern Diaspora Studies* 6 (2013): 45–63.

McIntosh, Gary L. *One Church, Four Generations: Understanding and Reaching All Ages in Your Church.* Grand Rapids, MI: Baker, 2002.

McLaren, Peter. 'White Terror and Oppositional Agency: Towards a Critical Multiculturalism.' In *Multiculturalism: A Crtical Reader*, edited by David Theo Goldberg, 45–74. Oxford, UK: Blackwell, 1994.

McLuhan, Marshall, 'The Medium is the Message.' In *In Understanding Media: The Extensions of Man*, 23–35. New York, NY: Signet, 1964.

McNeal, Reggie. *A Work of Heart: Understanding How God Shapes Spiritual Leaders.* San Francisco, CA: Jossey-Bass, 2011.

Megarrity, Lyndon. 'Under the Shadow of the White Australia Policy: Commonwealth Policies on Private Overseas Students 1945–1972.' *Change: Transformations in Education* 8, no. 2 (2005): 31–51.

Melchar, David E., and Susan M. Bosco. 'Achieving High Organization Performance through Servant Leadership.' *The Journal of Business Inquiry* 9, no. 1 (2010): 74–88.

Mendenhall, Mark E., and Joyce Osland. *Global Leadership: Research, Practice, and Development.* Milton Park, UK: Routledge, 2008.

Mendenhall, Mark, and Gary Oddou. 'The Dimensions of Expatriate Acculturation: A Review.' *Academy of Management Review* 10, no. 1 (1985): 39–47.

Merritt, Carol Howard. *Tribal Church: Ministering to the Missing Generation.* Herndon, VA: Alban Institute.

Messer, Michi, Renee Schroeder, and Ruth Wodak. *Migrations: Interdisciplinary Perspectives.* New York, NY: Springer, 2012.

Mohammad, Robina. '"Insiders" and/or "Outsiders": Positionality, Theory and Praxis.' In *Qualitative Methodologies for Geographers: Issues And Debates*, edited by Claire Dwyer Melanie Limb, 101–17. London, UK: Arnold, 2001.

Mok, Aurelia. 'Cultural Identity Integration and Frame Switching: Evidence for a Nonconscious Motivated Process.' Unpublished diss., Columbia University, 2010.

Mok, Man Soo. *Anthropology from Asian Missiological Insights.* New York, NY: Peter Lang, 2013.

Moreau, A. Scott. *Effective Intercultural Communication: A Christian Perspective.* Grand Rapids, MI: Baker Academic, 2014.

Morr, Christy. 'The Role of Friendship in Spiritual Formation.' *Christian Education Journal* 4, no. 2 (2000): 45–62.

Morreale, S. P., B. H. Spitzberg, and J. K. Barge. *Human Communication: Motivation, Knowledge & Skills.* Belmont, CA: Wadsworth/Thomas Learning, 2001.

Morris, Michael W., Aurelia Mok, and Shira Mor. 'Cultural Identity Threat: The Role of Cultural Identifications in Moderating Closure Responses to Foreign Cultural Inflow.' *Journal of Social Issues* 67, no. 4 (2011): 760–73.

Morse, John J., and Francis R. Wagner. 'Measuring the Process of Managerial Effectiveness.' *Academy of Management Journal* 21, no. 1 (1978): 23–35.

BIBLIOGRAPHY

Moustakas, Clark. *Phenomenological Research Methods*. Thousand Oaks, CA: Sage, 1994.

Mowry, Bill J. 'A Contextualized/Transactional Model for Leadership Development.' *Christian Education Journal* 13, no. 1 (1992): 61–69.

Multicultural NSW China. 'Birthplace—China (excl. SARs and Taiwan), Year of Arrival.' NSW Government, 2011. Accessed 30 July 2015. http://multiculturalnsw. id.com.au/multiculturalnsw/birthplace-by-year-of-arrival?COIID=5038.

Multicultural NSW Hong Kong. 'Birthplace—Hong Kong (SAR of China), Year of Arrival.' NSW Government, 2011. Accessed 30 July 2015. http://multiculturalnsw. id.com.au/multiculturalnsw/birthplace-by-year-of-arrival?COIID=5039.

Neuliep, James W. *Intercultural Communication: A Contextual Approach*. Thousand Oaks, CA: Sage, 2014.

Newman, Jerry, Bhal Bhatt, and Thomas Gutteridge. 'Determinants of Expatriate Effectiveness: A Theoretical and Empirical Vacuum.' *Academy of Management Review* 3, no. 3 (1978): 655–61.

Newman, Karen L., and Stanley D. Nollen. 'Culture and Congruence: The Fit between Management Practices and National Culture.' *Journal of International Business Studies* 27, no. 4 (1996): 753–79.

Ng, Kok-Yee, and P. Christopher Earley. 'Culture + Intelligence: Old Constructs, New Frontiers.' *Group & Organization Management* 31, no. 1 (2006): 4–19.

Ng, Kok-Yee, Linn Van Dyne, and Soon Ang. 'Beyond International Experience: the Strategic Role of Cultural Intelligence for Executive Selection in IHRM.' In *Handbook of International Human Resource Management: Integrating People, Process, and Context*, edited by P. R. Sparrow, 97–113. West Sussex, UK: John Wiley & Sons, 2009.

———. 'Developing Global Leaders: The Role of International Experience and Cultural Intelligence.' In *Advances in Global Leadership*, edited by W.H. Mobley, Y. Wang and M. Li, 225–250. Bingley, UK: Emerald Group, 2009.

———. 'From Experience to Experiential Learning: Cultural Intelligence as a Learning Capability for Global Leader Development.' *Academy of Management Learning & Education* 8, no. 4 (2009): 511–26.

Ngan, Lucille Lok-Sun, and Chan Kwok-Bun. *The Chinese Face in Australia: Multi-generational Ethnicity among Australian-Born Chinese*. New York, NY: Springer, 2012.

Norheim, Bard-Eirik Hallesby. 'The Global Youth Culture: Targeting and Involving Youth in Global Mission.' In *The Church Going Glocal: Mission and Globalisation*, edited by Tormod Engelsviken, Erling Lundeby, and Dagfinn Solheim, 168–75. Oxford, UK: Regnum, 2011.

Nowicka, Magdalena. 'Mobile Locations: Construction of Home in a Group of Mobile Transnational Professionals.' *Global Networks* 7, no. 1 (2007): 69–86.

NSW Migration Heritage Centre. '1901 Immigration Restriction Act.' NSW Migration Heritage Centre, 2007. Accessed 7 September 2016. http://www.migrationheritage.nsw.gov.au/exhibition/objectsthroughtime/immigration-restriction-act/.

BIBLIOGRAPHY

NSW Migration Heritage Centre. 'Objects Through Time: Australian Migration History Timeline, 1945–1965.' NSW Migration Heritage Centre, 2010. accessed 7 September 2016. http://www.migrationheritage.nsw.gov.au/exhibition/objectsthroughtime-history/1945-1965/.

NSW State Records. 'Immigration from Many Lands.' NSW Government State Records, n. d. Accessed 10 August 2015. http://www.records.nsw.gov.au/state-archives/research-topics/immigration/immigration-from-many-lands.

Nunan, David. 'Learner Strategy Training in the Classroom: An Action Research Study.' In *Methodology in Language Teaching: An Anthology of Current Practice*, edited by Jack C. Richards and Willy A. Renandya, 133–43. Cambridge, UK: Cambridge University Press, 2002.

Oddou, G., and C. Derr. 'European MNC Strategies for Internationalizing Managers: Current and Future Trends.' *Research in Personnel and Human Resources Management* 3 (1993): 157–70.

Osland, Asbjorn. 'The Role of Leadership and Cultural Contingencies in Total Quality Management in Cwentral America.' *Journal of Business and Management* 3 (1996): 64–80.

Osmer, Richard R. *Practical Theology: An Introduction.* Grand Rapids, MI: Eerdmans, 2008.

Oyserman, Daphna, and Izumi Sakamoto. 'Being Asian American: Identity, Cultural Constructs, and Stereotype Perception.' *The Journal of Applied Behavioral Science* 33, no. 4 (1997): 435–53.

Padilla, Elaine, and P. Phan. *Contemporary Issues of Migration and Theology.* New York NY: Palgrave Macmillan, 2013.

Palmer, Alison. *'Issues Facing Returning Missionaries and How Spiritual Direction Can Help.'* Unpublished diss., Spiritual Growth Ministries, 1999.

Park, M. Sydney, Soong-Chan Rah and Al Tizon. *Honoring the Generations: Learning with Asian North American Congregations.* Valley Forge, PA: Judson, 2012.

Pasa, Selda Fikret, Hayat Kabasakal, and Muzaffer Bodur. 'Society, Organisations and Leadership in Turkey.' *Applied Psychology* 50, no. 4 (2001): 559–89.

Pascoe, Robin. *Raising Global Nomads: Parenting Abroad in an On-Demand World.* Vancouver, BC: Expatriate, 2006.

Patterson, Kathleen A. 'Servant Leadership: A Theoretical Model.' Unpublished diss., Graduate School of Business, Regent University, 2003.

Pattison, Stephen. *Saving Face: Enfacement, Shame, Theology.* Farnham, UK: Ashgate, 2016.

Paulhus, Delroy L., and Simine Vazire. 'The Self-Report Method.' In *Handbook of Research Methods in Personality Psychology*, 224–39. New York, NY: Guilford, 2007.

Peltokorpi, Vesa. 'Intercultural Communication in Foreign Subsidiaries: The Influence of Expatriates' Language and Cultural Competencies.' *Scandinavian Journal of Management* 26, no. 2 (2010): 176–88.

Peterson, Eugene H. *The Contemplative Pastor: Returning to the Art of Spiritual Direction.* Grand Rapids, MI: Eerdmans, 1993.

Phinney, Jean S. 'When We Talk about American Ethnic Groups, What Do We Mean?' *American Psychologist* 51, no. 9 (1996): 918–27.

BIBLIOGRAPHY

Phinney, Jean S., Anthony Ong and Tanya Madden. 'Cultural Values and Intergenerational Value Discrepancies in Immigrant and Non-Immigrant Families.' *Child Development* 71, no. 2 (2000): 528–39.

Pieterse, Jan Nederveen. 'Globalization as Hybridization.' *ISS Working Paper Series/General Series* 152 (1993): 1–18.

Pioneers of Australia. *Guidelines for a Pioneers Debrief.* Sydney, NSW: Pioneers of Australia, 2006.

Plato. *Plato's Meno*. Newburyport, MA: Focus, 2004.

Plueddemann, James. *Leading across Cultures: Effective Ministry and Mission in the Global Church*. Downers Grove, IL: InterVarsity Academic, 2009.

Pollock, David, and Ruth Van Reken. *Third Culture Kids: Growing up among Worlds*. Boston, MA: Nicholas Brealey, 2009.

Powell, Ruth. 'Australian Church Health and Generational Differences.' In *NCLS Occasional Paper*. Sydney, NSW: NCLS Research, 2008.

Powell, Ruth, and Kathy Jacka. 'Generations Approach Church Differently.' In *NCLS Occasional Paper*: NCLS Research, 2008.

Presbitero, Alfred. 'Cultural Intelligence (CQ) in Virtual, Cross-Cultural Interactions: Generalizability of Measure and Links to Personality Dimensions and Task Performance.' *International Journal of Intercultural Relations* 50 (2016): 29–38.

Prior, Alan C. *Some Fell on Good Ground: A History of the Beginnings and Development of the Baptist Church in New South Wales, Australia 1831–1965*. Sydney, NSW: Baptist Union of New South Wales, 1966.

Pung, Alice. *Growing up Asian in Australia*. Melbourne, VIC: Black Inc., 2008.

Putranto, Nur Arief Rahmatsyah, and Achmad Ghazali. 'The Effect of Cultural Intelligence to Knowledge Sharing Behaviour in University Students.' Conference paper. Bali, Indonesia: International DSI and Asia Pacific DSI Conference, 2013.

Quaife, Geoffrey Robert. *Gold and Colonial Society, 1851–1870*. Stanmore, NSW: Cassell Australia, 1975.

Rah, Soong-Chan. *Many Colors: Cultural Intelligence for a Changing Church*. Chicago, IL: Moody, 2010.

Rainer, Thom S.. *The Bridger Generation*. Nashville, TN: B&H, 2006.

Rambo, Lewis R., and Lawrence A. Reh. 'The Phenomenology of Conversion.' In *Handbook of Religious Conversion*, edited by H.N. Malony and S. Southard, 229–58. Birmingham, AL: Religous Education Press, 1992.

Ramirez, Andrea Reyes. 'Impact of Cultural Intelligence Level on Conflict Resolution Ability: A Conceptual Model and Research Proposal.' *Emerging Leadership Journeys* 3, no. 1 (2010): 42–56.

Rendle, Gilbert R. *The Multigenerational Congregation: Meeting the Leadership Challenge*. Bethesda, MD: Alban Institute, 2001.

Richards, Jack Croft. *Teaching Listening and Speaking*. New York, NY: Cambridge University Press, 2008.

Richardson, Ronald W. *Creating a Healthier Church: Family Systems Theory, Leadership, and Congregational Life*. Minneapolis, MN: Augsburg, Fortress, 1996.

BIBLIOGRAPHY

Robert, Dana L. 'Cross-Cultural Friendship in the Creation of Twentieth-Century World Christianity.' *International Bulletin of Missionary Research* 35, no. 2 (2011): 100–107.

Robert, Dana L. 'Global Friendship as Incarnational Missional Practice.' *International Bulletin of Missionary Research* 39, no. 4 (2015): 180–4.

Roberts, Gary. *Christian Scripture and Human Resource Management: Building a Path to Servant Leadership Through Faith*. New York, NY: Palgrave MacMillan, 2015.

Roberts, Gary. *Developing Christian Servant Leadership: Faith-Based Character Growth at Work*. New York, NY: Palgrave MacMillan, 2015.

Rockstuhl, Thomas, and Kok-Yee Ng. 'The Effects of Cultural Intelligence on Interpersonal Trust in Multicultural Teams.' In *Handbook of Cultural Intelligence: Theory, Measurement, and Applications*, edited by S. Ang and L. Van Dyne, 206–20. Milton Park, UK: Routledge, 2015.

Rodrigues, C. A. 'The Situation and National Culture as Contingencies for Leadership Behavior: Two Conceptual Models.' *Advances in International Comparative Management: A Research Annual* 5 (1990): 51–68.

Roembke, Lianne. *Building Credible Multicultural Teams*. Pasadena, CA: William Carey Library, 2000.

Rouse, Ruth, and Stephen Neill. *A History of the Ecumenical Movement*. London, UK: S.P.C.K., 1954.

Roxburgh, Alan J. *Reaching a New Generation: Strategies for Tomorrow's Church*. Downers Grove, IL: InterVarsity, 1993.

Russell, Robert F., and Gregory A. Stone. 'A Review of Servant Leadership Attributes: Developing a Practical Model.'

Leadership & Organization Development Journal 23, no. 3 (2002): 145–57.

Ryan, Erin, et al. 'When Socrates Meets Confucius: Teaching Creative and Critical Thinking across Cultures through Multilevel Socratic Method.' *Nebraska Law Review* 92, no. 2 (2013): 289–348.

Samovar, Larry A., Richard E. Porter, and Edwin R. McDaniel. *Communication Between Cultures*. Boston, MA: Wadsworth, Cengage Learning, 2007.

Sarantakos, Sotirios. *Social Research*. Houndmills, UK: Palgrave Macmillan, 2013.

Schiavon, Jorge A. 'Migration Studies in Mexico: Interdisciplinary Studies for a Multi-Tiered Phenomenon.' *Migration Studies* 4, no. 3 (2016): 455–7.

Schlägel, Christopher, and Marko Sarstedt. 'Assessing the Measurement Invariance of the Four-Dimensional Cultural Intelligence Scale across Countries: A Composite Model Approach.' *European Management Journal* 34, no. 6 (2016): 633–49.

Schmidt, Richard W. 'The Role of Consciousness in Second Language Learning.' *Applied Linguistics* 11, no. 2 (1990): 129–58.

Schwartz, Seth J., Koen Luyckx, and Vivian L. Vignoles. *Handbook of Identity Theory and Research*. New York, NY: Springer, 2011.

Schwartz, Seth J., Byron L. Zamboanga, and Liliana Rodriguez et al. 'The Structure of Cultural Identity in an Ethnically Diverse Sample of Emerging Adults.' *Basic and Applied Social Psychology* 29, no. 2 (2007): 159–73.

BIBLIOGRAPHY

Schwartz, Shalom H. 'Beyond Individualism/Collectivism: New Cultural Dimensions of Values.' In *Individualism and Collectivism: Theory, Method, and Application*, edited by U. Kim, H. C. Triandis and C. Kagitcibasi. Thousand Oaks, CA: Sage Publications, 1994.

———. 'Individualism-Collectivism Critique and Proposed Refinements.' *Journal of Cross-Cultural Psychology* 21, no. 2 (1990): 139–57.

———. 'A Theory of Cultural Values and Some Implications for Work.' *Applied Psychology* 48, no. 1 (1999): 23–47.

Schwenk, Charles R. 1990. 'Effects of Devil's Advocacy and Dialectical Inquiry on Decision Making: A Meta-Analysis.' *Organizational Behavior and Human Decision Processes* 47 (1): 161–76.

Sendjaya, Sen, James C. Sarros, and Joseph C. Santora. 'Defining and Measuring Servant Leadership Behaviour in Organizations.' *Journal of Management Studies* 45, no. 2 (2008): 402–24.

Senge, Peter M. *The Fifth Discipline: The Art and Practice of the Learning Organization*. London, UK: Random House, 2006.

Shannon, Lu M., and Thomas M. Begley. 'Antecedents of Four-Factor Model of Cultural Intelligence.' In *Handbook of Cultural Intelligence*, edited by Soon Ang and Linn Van Dyne. Milton Park, UK: Routledge, 2015.

Shen, Yuan Fang. *Dragon Seed in the Antipodes: Chinese Australian Autobiographies*. Calton South, VIC: Melbourne University Press, 2001.

Shokef, Efrat, and Miriam Erez. 'Cultural Intelligence and Global Identity in Multicultural Teams.' In *Handbook of Cultural*

Intelligence: Theory, Measurement and Applications, edited by S. Ang and L. Van Dyne, 177–91. Milton Park, UK: Routledge, 2015.

Shuster, Marguerite. *Power, Pathology, Paradox: The Dynamics of Evil and Good*. Grand Rapids, MI: Zondervan, 2012.

Smith, David Howard. *Confucius*. London, UK: Temple Smith, 1973.

Smith, Donald K. *Creating Understanding: A Handbook for Christian Communication across Cultural Landscapes*. Grand Rapids, MI: Zondervan, 1992.

Smith, Lindsay. 'Hidden Dragons: The Archaeology of Mid to Late Nineteenth-Century Chinese Communities in Southeastern New South Wales.' Unpublished diss., Canberra, ACT, The Australian National University, 2006.

Smolicz, J. J. 'Cultural Diversity.' In *The Australian People: An Encyclopedia of the Nation, its People and their Origins*, edited by James Jupp. North Ryde, NSW: Angus & Robertson, 1988.

Spears, Larry C. 'Character and Servant Leadership: Ten Characteristics of Effective, Caring Leaders.' *The Journal of Virtues & Leadership* 1, no. 1 (2010): 25–30.

Stead, Valerie. 'Mentoring: A Model for Leadership Development?' *International Journal of Training and Development* 9, no. 3 (2005): 170–84.

Sternberg, Robert J., and Douglas K. Detterman. *What is Intelligence?: Contemporary Viewpoints on Its Nature and Definition*. Norwood, N.J.: Ablex, 1986.

Stewart, Edward, and Milton Bennett. *American Cultural Patterns: A Cross-Cultural Perspective*. Yarmouth, ME: Intercultural, 1991.

BIBLIOGRAPHY

Stone, Deborah. 'The Second Generation.' *The Sunday Age*, 21 January 1996.

Stroink, Mirella L., and Richard N. Lalonde. 'Bicultural Identity Conflict in Second-Generation Asian Canadians.' *The Journal of Social Psychology* 149, no. 1 (2009): 44–65.

Stubbings, Jo-Ann. 'We're All Aussies Now.' *The Age*, 10 September 1995.

Sun, Wai Kwong. '論海外華人的下一代 (On the Next Generation of Overseas Chinese).' *Great Commission Bi-monthly* 82 (2009): 7–9.

Sussman, Nan M. 'The Dynamic Nature of Cultural Identity Throughout Cultural Transitions: Why Home Is Not So Sweet.' *Personality and Social Psychology Review* 4, no. 4 (2000): 355–73.

Swinton, John, and Harriet Mowat. *Practical Theology and Qualitative Research*. London, UK: SCM, 2006.

Sydney Chinese Christian Churches Association. 'About SCCCA.' Sydney Chinese Christian Churches Association, 2016. Accessed 14 November 2016. http://sccca.org.au/about.

Tan, Betty O. S. 'The Contextualization of the Chinese New Year Festival.' *Asia Journal of Theology* 15, no. 1 (2001): 115–32.

Tan, Carole. '"The Tyranny of Appearance": Chinese Australian Identities and the Politics of Difference.' *Journal of Intercultural Studies* 27, nos. 1–2 (2006): 65–82.

Tan, Shaun. *The Arrival*. New York, NY: Arthur Levine, 2006.

Tanu, Danau. 'Global Nomads: Towards a Study of "Asian" Third Culture Kids.' In *Proceedings of the 17th Biennial Conference of the Asian Studies Association of Australia*, edited by Marika Vicziany. Melbourne, VIC: The Asian Studies Association of Australia, 2008.

Tharapos, Meredith Ann. 'Cultural Intelligence in the Transnational Education Classroom: The Case of Australian Accounting Academics.' Unpublished PhD diss., RMIT University, 2015.

Thomas, David C., and Elizabeth C. Ravlin. 'Responses of Employees to Cultural Adaptation by a Foreign Manager.' *Journal of Applied Psychology* 80, no. 1 (1995): 133–46.

Ting-Toomey, Stella. 'Intercultural Conflict Style: A Face-Negotiation Theory.' In *Theories in Intercultural Communication*, edited by Y. Y. Kim and W. B. Gudykunst, 213–35. Newsbury Park, CA: Sage, 1988.

———. 'Intercultural Conflict Training: Theory-Practice Approaches and Research Challenges.' *Journal of Intercultural Communication Research* 36, no. 3 (2007): 255–71.

Tjosvold, Dean. *Working Together to Get Things Done: Managing for Organizational Productivity*. Lexington, MA: Lexington Books, 1988.

Todd, Terry L. 'Incarnational Learners: Overcoming Language and Culture Barriers Involves Repudiating One's Privileges.' *Evangelical Missions Quarterly* 35, no. 4 (1999): 446–52.

Tong, Daniel. *A Biblical Approach to Chinese Traditions and Beliefs*. Singapore: Genesis, 2003.

Travaglia, Joanne, Karen Herne, and Elizabeth Weiss. *Who Do You Think You Are?: Second Generation Immigrant Women in Australia*. Broadway, NSW: Women's Redress, 1993.

Triandis, Harry C. *Individualism and Collectivism: New Directions in Social Psychology*. Boulder, CO: Westview, 1995.

BIBLIOGRAPHY

Trompenaars, Fons, and Charles Hampden-Turner. *Riding the Waves of Culture: Understanding Diversity in Global Business*. Boston, MA: Nicholas Brealey, 2012.

Trompenaars, Fons, and Ed Voerman. *Servant Leadership across Cultures: Harnessing the Strength of the World's Most Powerful Leadership Philosophy*. New York, NY: McGraw-Hill, 2010.

Tsui, Anne S, Hui Wang, and Katherine Xin et al. '"Let a Thousand Flowers Bloom": Variation of Leadership Styles Among Chinese CEOs.' *Organizational Dynamics* 33, no. 1 (2004): 5–20.

Tu, Wei-Ming. 'Cultural China: The Periphery as the Center.' *Daedalus* 134, no. 4 (2005):145–67.

———. 'Probing the "Three Bonds" and "Five Relationships" in Confucian Humanism.' In *Confucianism and the Family: A Study of Indo-Tibetan Scholasticism*, edited by Walter H. Slote and George A. De Vos, 121–36. Albany, NY: University of New York Press, 1998.

Tucker, Frank. *Intercultural Communication for Christian Ministry*. Adelaide, SA: Frank Tucker, 2013.

Tung, May Pao-May. *Chinese Americans and Their Immigrant Parents: Conflict, Identity, and Values*. New York, NY: The Haworth Clinical Practice Press, 2000.

Tung, Rosalie L. 'U.S. Multinationals: A Study of Their Selection and Training Procedures for Overseas Assignments.' *Academy of Management Proceedings* 1979, no. 1 (1979): 298–301.

Tweed, Roger G., and Darrin R. Lehman. 'Learning Considered within a Cultural Context: Confucian and Socratic Approaches.' *American Psychologist* 57, no. 2 (2002): 89–99.

Ueda, Keiko. 'Sixteen Ways to Avoid Saying "No" in Japan.' In *Intercultural Encounters with Japan: Communication-Contact and Conflict; Perspectives from the International Conference on Commnication across Cultures*, edited by John Condon and Mitsuko Saito, 185–92. Tokyo, Japan: Simul, 1974.

Umaña-Taylor, Adriana J. 'Ethnic Identity.' In *Handbook of Identity Theory and Research*, 791–809. New York, NY: Springer, 2011.

UN-Department of Economic and Social Affairs. 'World Migration in Figures.' In *United Nations High-Level Dialogue on Migration and Development*. 2013.

UN Web Services Section, Department of Public Information, United Nations. '244 Million International Migrants Living Abroad Worldwide, New UN Statistics Reveal.' UN Web Services Section, Department of Public Information, United Nations, 2016. Accessed 17 June 2016. http://www.un.org/sustainabledevelopment/blog/2016/01/244-million-international-migrants-living-abroad-worldwide-new-un-statistics-reveal/.

United Nations Population Division. 'Trends in International Migration, 2015.' United Nations, Department of Economic and Social Affairs, 2015. Accessed 21 June 16. http://www.un.org/en/development/desa/population/migration/publications/wallchart/index.shtml.

Useem, R. H., and R. D. Downie. 'Third-Culture Kids.' *Today's Education* 65, no. 3 (1976):103–5.

Van Driel, Marinus, and William K. Gabreya Jr. 'Cross-Level Measurement of Cross-Cultural Competence: Using the Cultural Intelligence Scale as an Example.' In *7th*

BIBLIOGRAPHY

Biennial Equal Opportunity, Diversity, & Culture Research Symposium, 311–17. Patrick Air Force Base, FL: Defense Equal Opportunity Management Institute, 2009.

Van Dyne, Linn. 'The 20-item, Four Factor Cultural Intelligence Scale (CQS).' Cultural Intelligence Center, 2005. Accessed 6 October 2015. http://www.linnvandyne.com/shortmeasure.html.

Van Dyne, Linn, Soon Ang, and Christine Koh. 'Development and Validation of the CQS: The Cultural Intelligence Scale.' In *Handbook on Cultural Intelligence: Theory, Measurement and Applications*, edited by S. Ang and L. Van Dyne, 16–40. Milton Park, UK: Routledge, 2015.

Van Dyne, Linn, Soon Ang, and Kok Yee Ng et al. 'Sub-Dimensions of the Four Factor Model of Cultural Intelligence: Expanding the Conceptualization and Measurement of Cultural Intelligence.' *Social and Personality Psychology Compass* 6, no. 4 (2012): 295–313.

Van Manen, Max, and C. A. Adams. 'Phenomenology'. In *International Encyclopedia of Education*, edited by Brian K. Petersen, Eva Baker and Barry McGaw. Oxford, UK: Elsevier, 2010.

Vanderwell, Howard A. *The Church of All Ages: Generations Worshiping Together*. Herndon, VA: Alban Institute, 2008.

Vargas-Silva, Carlos. *Handbook of Research Methods in Migration*. Cheltenham, UK: Elgar, 2012.

Viviani, Nancy. *The Long Journey: Vietnamese Migration and Settlement in Australia*. Carlton, VIC: Melbourne University Press, 1984.

Vogelgesang, Gretchen, Rachel Clapp-Smith, and Noel Palmer. 'The Role of Authentic Leadership and Cultural Intelligence in Cross-Cultural Contexts: An Objectivist Perspective.' *International Journal of Leadership Studies* 5, no. 2 (2009): 102–17.

Wallenberg-Lerner, Helena, and Waynne B. James. 'Important Components Needed in Today's Global Society From a Cross-Cultural Perspective.' *Journal of International and Global Studies* 6, no. 1 (2014): 14–29.

Walton, R. E. 'Interorganizational Decision Making and Identity Conflict.' In *Interorganizational Decision Making*, edited by Matthew Tuite, Roger K. Chisholm and Michael Radnor. Chicago, IL: Aldine, 1972.

Wan, Enoch. 'Rethinking Missiology in the Context of the 21st Century: Global Demographic Trends and Diaspora Missiology.' *Great Commission Research Journal* 2, no. 1 (2010): 7–20.

Wan, Enoch, and Sadiri Joy Tira. 'Diaspora Missiology and Missions in the Context of the Twenty-First Century.' *Torch Trinity Journal* 13, no. 1 (2010): 45–56.

Wang, G. 'Power, Rights and Duties in Chinese History.' In *The Chineseness of China*, edited by G. Wang, 165–86. Hong Kong, China: Oxford University Press, 1991.

Wang, Kenneth T., Puncky Paul Heppner, Lei Wang, and Fengkan Zhu. 'Cultural Intelligence Trajectories in New International Students: Implications for the Development of Cross-Cultural Competence.' *International Perspectives in Psychology: Research, Practice, Consultation* 4, no. 1 (2015): 51–65.

BIBLIOGRAPHY

Webb, Allan. *The Heart of Godly Leadership*. Ormond, VIC: OMF International, Hudson, 2002.

Weber, M. *The Religion of China*. New York, NY: The Free Press, 1951.

Weems, Lovett Hayes, and Ann A. Michel. *The Crisis of Younger Clergy*. Nashville, TN: Abingdon, 2008.

White, Naomi Rosh, and Peter B. White. *Immigrants and the Media: Case Studies in Newspaper Reporting*. Melbourne, VIC: Longman Cheshire, 1983.

Whorf, Benjamin Lee. *Language, Thought, and Reality: Selected Writings of Benjamin Lee Whorf*. Edited by John B. Carroll. New York, NY: John Wiley, 2012.

Willis, Mark. 'Learning to Speak All over Again.' *Evangelical Missions Quarterly* 32, no. 4 (1996): 435–36.

Winston, Bruce E. *Be a Leader for God's Sake: From Values to Behaviors*. Virginia Beach, VA: Regent University, School of Leadership Studies, 2002.

Wong, Chi-Sum, and Kenneth S. Law. 'The Effects of Leader and Follower Emotional Intelligence on Performance and Attitude: An Exploratory Study.' *The Leadership Quarterly* 13, no. 3 (2002): 243–74.

Wong, Hoover. *Lecture Notes from 'Multiculturalism'*. Hong Kong: China Graduate School of Theology, 1992.

Wright, Walter. *Relational Leadership: A Biblical Model for Leadership Service*. Carlisle UK: Paternoster, 2000.

Yang, Fenggang. *Chinese Christians in America: Conversion, Assimilation, and Adhesive Identities*. University Park, PA: The Pennsylvania State University Press, 1999.

Yang, K. S. '"Yuan" and Its Functions in Contemporary Life.' *Chinese Cultural Renaissance* 15 (1982): 19–42.

Yarwood, A. T. 'The White Australia Policy.' In *The Australian People: An Encyclopedia of the Nation, Its People, and Their Origins*, edited by James Jupp, 77–83. North Ryde, NSW: Angus & Robertson, 1988.

Yazdiha, Haj. 'Conceptualizing Hybridity: Deconstructing Boundaries through The Hybrid.' *Formations* 1, no. 1 (2010): 31–38.

Yep, Jeanette, Peter Cha, and Van Riesen. *Following Jesus without Dishonoring Your Parents*. Downers Grove, IL: InterVarsity, 2009.

Yong, Amos. 'Review Essay Asian American Religions.' *Nova Religio: The Journal of Alternative and Emergent Religions* 9 (2006): 92–107.

York, Barry. 'White Australia Policy—The Beginning of the End 50 Years Ago.' Museum of Australian Democracy at Old Parliament House, 2016. Accessed 7 September 2016. http://moadoph.gov.au/blog/white-australia-policy-the-beginning-of-the-end-50-years-ago/.

Yu, Chi-Ping. 'Filial Piety and Chinese Pastoral Care.' *Asia Journal of Theology* 4 (1990): 316–28.

Yukl, Gary. 'How Leaders Influence Organizational Effectiveness.' *The Leadership Quarterly* 19, no. 6 (2008): 708–22.

———. 'Leading Organizational Learning: Reflections on Theory and Research.' *The Leadership Quarterly* 20, no. 1 (2009): 49–53.

———. *Leadership in Organizations*. Upper Saddle River, NJ: Pearson Prentice Hall, 2006.

BIBLIOGRAPHY

Yukl, Gary A., and Wendy S. Becker. 'Effective Empowerment in Organizations.' *Organization Management Journal* 3, no. 3 (2006): 210–31.

Yum, June Ock. 'The Impact of Confucianism on Interpersonal Relationships and Communication Patterns in East Asia.' *Communication Monographs* 55, no. 4 (1988): 374–88.

Zhang, David. '回應社會的變遷—雪梨華人教會發展的反思(Reflection on Development of Sydney Chinese Churches).' *Global Missiology* 2, no. 9 (2013).

Zhou, Min. 'Segmented Assimilation: Issues, Controversies, and Recent Research on the New Second Generation.' *International Migration Review* 31, no. 4 (1997): 975–1008.

Zinzius, Birgit. *Chinese America: Stereotype and Reality: History, Present, and Future of the Chinese Americans*. New York, NY: Peter Lang, 2005.

Zubrzycki, J. 'Multicultural Australia.' In *The Australian People: An Encyclopedia of the Nation, its People and their Origins*, edited by James Jupp. North Ryde, NSW: Angus & Robertson, 1988.

www.ingramcontent.com/pod-product-compliance
Lightning Source LLC
Chambersburg PA
CBHW070418010526
44118CB00014B/1802